BLACK
IDENTITY
A THEMATIC
READER

BLACK IDENTITY

A THEMATIC READER

FRANCIS E. KEARNS
HERBERT H. LEHMAN COLLEGE

HOLT, RINEHART and WINSTON

*New York   Chicago   San Francisco
Atlanta   Dallas*

Library of Congress Catalog Card Number: 77-107439
SBN: 03-082792-2
Printed in the United States of America

9 8 7 6 5 4 3 2 1

Preface

Black Identity: A Thematic Reader is a collection of short stories, poems, a short play, and personal essays written by both blacks and whites, on the themes of Negro experience and identity in America. Intended as a *literary* approach to a *social* topic, the book also presents essays of social analysis and commentary, but these pieces have only a secondary role to play.

Black Identity is not an anthology of exclusively Afro-American writing. Though most of the writers brought together here are black, the collection also includes several important white writers, since I feel that the question of black identity has been one of the major questions to which American writers have had to respond, whether with anger, rationalization, or disdain. James Baldwin put this thought more succinctly, though, when he wrote: "If you don't know my name, you don't know your own."

An underlying assumption in the book's design is that a text intended chiefly for use in the English class ought to have a literary rather than a social purpose; it ought to place its emphasis on individual works of sufficient artistic quality to merit close critical study. Granted that it is impossible to make a complete separation between *literary* and *social* concerns in a book of this nature, even should the editor wish to do so,

I believe that the social end fulfilled when a student arrives at an intelligent understanding of a Ralph Ellison story might be far more important than that fulfilled when he comes to perceive the sociological and economic factors which underlie our racial dilemma.

Whatever social purpose the book achieves—and I think it may accomplish a significant one—will be achieved unobtrusively. The book will not engage in well-intentioned but unconsciously condescending attempts at black ego boosting nor will it engage in editorial generalizations about white racism. Rather, it assumes that there is no necessity for arguing the points that there are and have been major black writers in America, that the "American Dilemma" of racism has had a profound effect on the imagination of both black and white writers, and that an examination of works in this area is particularly appropriate today.

The book employs a format and apparatus that make it immediately relevant to such typical concerns of the English class as analysis of irony and point of view, evaluation of descriptive detail, and examination of argumentative technique. It also presents selections written, for the most part, by major or familiar writers, though a number of unfamiliar authors and works have been included in the hope that they may lend the book a certain piquancy.

An attempt has been made to avoid the type of elaborate critical apparatus which might usurp the teacher's function. Thus, while the first half of the reader employs questions on individual selections and suggests topics for general discussion, the second half is free of such apparatus. Of the book's two parts, the first consists of five chapters in each of which selections are grouped around a specific theme. Each selection is followed by a few specific questions designed to encourage the student to read the work closely. At the end of each chapter there are some broad comments and questions which involve comparison and contrast of ideas, attitudes, and artistic devices found in the particular works making up the chapter. One purpose of these more general questions is to suggest topics for classroom discussion and written reports. Part Two, which covers roughly half the book's length, presents in chronological order a number of selections still dealing with Afro-American identity and experience but centered around no particular theme. No apparatus is employed here and the teacher is free either to treat the works independently or to relate them to topics discussed in Part One.

The five chapters of Part One are: (1) "Heritage," which presents works dealing with the lot of the slave and the institution of slavery; (2) "We Wear the Mask," which is concerned with the various roles played and masks worn by Negroes in America; (3) "Brutality," which centers around descriptions of violent racial incidents and variety of authorial response; (4) "If We Must Die," which focuses on black militancy; and (5) "The Barrier," which presents works involving cross-racial sexual attitudes. In choosing works for these five chapters I have tried to keep in mind the usual aims of literary discussion in basic English courses. Thus Chapter One could be approached from the points of view of argumentation or analysis of detail. One piece offers a pre-Civil War Southern rationale of slavery while the others focus on its horror. Chapter Two, dealing with masks and images, offers several interesting problems in persona, point of view, and irony. In Chapter Three the authors have paid a great deal of attention to descriptive detail and nuance of vocabulary in order to bring home the horror of the racial incidents described. At the same time this chapter affords interesting contrasts in point of view: the adult and the Negro view of brutality in the McKay, Hughes, and Brooks poems versus the child's and the white man's view in the Tate poem; the bitter indignation of McKay versus the attempt at compassion even toward white racists in Brooks. Chapter Four centers around militancy, a topic sufficiently controversial and contemporary to provide the basis for lively argumentative writing. Chapter Five offers interesting illustrations of irony, since several works look with amused detachment on the hypocrisy involved in cross-racial sexual attitudes, whereas one selection treats the same topic with poignancy and another approaches it with indignation.

F.E.K.

New York City
January 1970

Contents
Part One

CHAPTER ONE: HERITAGE   **3**

RICHARD WRIGHT: OUR STRANGE BIRTH   5

ROBERT HAYDEN: MIDDLE PASSAGE   15

WILLIAM JOHN GRAYSON: from THE HIRELING AND THE SLAVE   23

PAUL LAURENCE DUNBAR: CHRISMUS ON THE PLANTATION   35

KATHERINE ANN PORTER: THE WITNESS   39

EDWARD BRATHWAITE: PRELUDE   43

PERSPECTIVE: CHARLES HAMILTON
OUR NAT TURNER AND WILLIAM STYRON'S CREATION   47

CHAPTER TWO: WE WEAR THE MASK   53

C. W. CHESNUTT: THE GOOPHERED GRAPEVINE   55

PAUL LAURENCE DUNBAR: WE WEAR THE MASK   69

COUNTEE CULLEN: FOR PAUL LAURENCE DUNBAR   71

STEPHEN CRANE: THE KNIFE   73

GWENDOLYN BROOKS: THE WHITE TROOPS HAD THEIR ORDERS
BUT THE NEGROES LOOKED LIKE MEN   85

JAMES BALDWIN: EQUAL IN PARIS   87

LANGSTON HUGHES: DINNER GUEST: ME   103

PERSPECTIVE: ELDRIDGE CLEAVER: from SOUL ON ICE
THE MUHAMMAD ALI—PATTERSON FIGHT   105

CHAPTER THREE: BRUTALITY   111

CLAUDE MCKAY: THE LYNCHING   113

LANGSTON HUGHES: SILHOUETTE   115

ALLEN TATE: THE SWIMMERS   117

GWENDOLYN BROOKS: THE CHICAGO **DEFENDER** SENDS A MAN
TO LITTLE ROCK, FALL, 1957   121

PERSPECTIVE: MALCOLM X: from NIGHTMARE
in the AUTOBIOGRAPHY OF MALCOLM X   125

CHAPTER FOUR: IF WE MUST DIE   131

CLAUDE MCKAY: IF WE MUST DIE   133

LEROI JONES: A CONTRACT (FOR THE DESTRUCTION AND
REBUILDING OF PATERSON)   135

BEN CALDWELL: THE JOB   137

GWENDOLYN BROOKS: MALCOLM X   145

LANGSTON HUGHES: BLACK PANTHER   147

FLANNERY O'CONNOR: EVERYTHING THAT RISES MUST CONVERGE   149

PERSPECTIVE: FRANTZ FANON: from CONCERNING VIOLENCE
in THE WRETCHED OF THE EARTH   165

CHAPTER FIVE: THE BARRIER   171

COUNTEE CULLEN: SONG OF PRAISE   173

CLAUDE MCKAY: THE BARRIER   175

LANGSTON HUGHES: MELLOW   177

C. W. CHESNUTT: A MATTER OF PRINCIPLE   179

JOHN A. WILLIAMS: SON IN THE AFTERNOON   197

PERSPECTIVE: JOHN HOWARD GRIFFIN: from BLACK LIKE ME   205

Part Two

NAT TURNER: THE CONFESSIONS (AS REPORTED
BY THOMAS R. GRAY) 213

W. E. B. DUBOIS: OF MR. BOOKER T. WASHINGTON AND OTHERS
from THE SOULS OF BLACK FOLK 227

JAMES WELDON JOHNSON: O BLACK AND UNKNOWN BARDS 239

COUNTEE CULLEN: YET DO I MARVEL, SIMON
THE CYRENIAN SPEAKS, and MOOD 241

ARNA BONTEMPS: A BLACK MAN TALKS OF REAPING 245

RICHARD WRIGHT: THE ETHICS OF LIVING JIM CROW 247

EUDORA WELTY: POWERHOUSE 259

MARGARET WALKER: FOR MY PEOPLE 271

M. B. TOLSON: DARK SYMPHONY 273

RALPH ELLISON: FLYING HOME 277

DUDLEY RANDALL: BOOKER T. AND W.E.B. 295

LANGSTON HUGHES: NAME IN PRINT 297

NORMAN MAILER: THE WHITE NEGRO: SUPERFICIAL REFLECTIONS
ON THE HIPSTER 301

ELLEN DOUGLAS: JESSE   321

NORMAN PODHORETZ: MY NEGRO PROBLEM—AND OURS   337

WILLIAM MELVIN KELLEY: THE ONLY MAN ON LIBERTY STREET   351

BLACK IDENTITY

Part One

CHAPTER ONE: HERITAGE

CHAPTER TWO: WE WEAR THE MASK

CHAPTER THREE: BRUTALITY

CHAPTER FOUR: IF WE MUST DIE

CHAPTER FIVE: THE BARRIER

Part One

Chapter One
Heritage

OUR STRANGE BIRTH

MIDDLE PASSAGE

FROM THE HIRELING AND THE SLAVE

CHRISMUS ON THE PLANTATION

THE WITNESS

PRELUDE

OUR NAT TURNER AND WILLIAM STYRON'S CREATION

Richard Wright
Our Strange Birth

Each day when you see us black folk upon the dusty land of the farms or upon the hard pavement of the city streets, you usually take us for granted and think you know us, but our history is far stranger than you suspect, and we are not what we seem.

Our outward guise still carries the old familiar aspect which three hundred years of oppression in America have given us, but beneath the garb of the black laborer, the black cook, and the black elevator operator lies an uneasily tied knot of pain and hope whose snarled strands converge from many points of time and space.

We millions of black folk who live in this land were born into Western civilization of a weird and paradoxical birth. The lean, tall, blond men of England, Holland, and Denmark, the dark, short, nervous men of France, Spain, and Portugal, men whose blue and gray and brown eyes glinted with the light of the future, denied our human personalities, tore us from our native soil, weighted our legs with chains, stacked us like cord-wood in the foul holes of clipper ships, dragged us across thousands of miles of ocean, and hurled us into another land, strange and hostile, where for a second time we felt the slow, painful process of a new birth amid conditions harsh and raw.

The immemorial stars must have gazed down in amazement at the lowly of England and Europe, who, with hearts full of hope, pushed out to sea to urge rebellion against tyranny and then straightway became engaged in the slave trade, in the buying and selling of our human bodies. And those same stars must have smiled when, following the War of Independence, the Lords of the Land in the South relaxed their rigid slave code ever so little to square their guilty conscience with the lofty ideals of the rights of man for which they had fought and died; but never did they relax their code so much as to jeopardize their claim of ownership of us.

Our captors were hard men, brutal men; yet they held locked somewhere within their hearts the fertile seeds that were to sprout into a new world culture, that were to blossom into a higher human consciousness. Escaping from the fetid medieval dens, angrily doffing the burial sheets of feudal religion, and flushed with a new and noble concept of life, of its inherent dignity, of its unlimited possibilities, of its natural worth, these men leaped upon the road of progress; and their leap was the windfall of our tragedy. Their excessive love of life wove a deadly web of slavery that snared our naked feet. Their sense of the possibility of building a more humane world brought devastation and despair to our pointed huts on the long, tan shores of Africa. We were an unlucky people; the very contours and harbors of our native land conspired against our freedom. The coastline of our Africa was long and flat and easy to invade; we had no mountains to serve as natural forts from behind which we could fight and stave off the slave traders.

We had our own civilization in Africa before we were captured and carried off to this land. You may smile when we call the way of life we lived in Africa "civilization," but in numerous respects the culture of many of our tribes was equal to that of the lands from which the slave captors came. We smelted iron, danced, made music, and recited folk poems; we sculptured, worked in glass, spun cotton and wool, wove baskets and cloth; we invented a medium of exchange, mined silver and gold, made pottery and cutlery; we fashioned tools and utensils of brass, bronze, ivory, quartz, and granite; we had our own literature, our own systems of law, religion, medicine, science, and education; we painted in color upon rocks; we raise cattle, sheep, and goats; we planted and harvested grain—in short, centuries before the Romans ruled, we lived as men.

Our humanity, however, did not save us; the New England Puritans and the imperialists of Europe erected the traffic in our bodies into the "big business" of the eighteenth century, and but few industries the world has ever known have yielded higher profits. There were "tricks of the trade" then as now; the slave traders, operators of fleets of stench-ridden sailing vessels, were comparable to our contemporary "captains of industry" and "tycoons of finance," and the Union Jack and the Stars and Stripes fluttered from the masts of men-of-war as the ensign of protection for "free trade" in our bodies. It was mainly the kings of vast rum distilleries who owned the ships that scoured the seven seas in search of our bodies. Jew as well as Gentile took part in these voyages of plunder. Nation waged war against nation for the right to buy and sell us, just as today they fight for "markets and raw materials." To Africa the traders brought rum and swapped it to corrupt chiefs for our bodies; we were then taken to the colonies, the West Indies, Cuba, and Brazil and used as currency to buy molasses; the molasses in turn was taken to the distilleries of New England and bartered for rum, which formed the basis for another slave voyage.

The slave ships, equipped for long voyages, were floating brothels for the slave traders of the seventeenth and eighteenth centuries. Bound by heavy chains, we gazed impassively upon the lecherous crew members as they vented the pent-up bestiality of their starved sex lives upon our sisters and wives. This was a peculiar practice which, as the years flowed past, grew into a clandestine but well-established institution which the owners of cotton and tobacco plantations upheld, and which today, in large measure, accounts for the widespread mulatto population in the United States. Indeed, there were slave-breeding farms. Slaves were valuable; cotton meant cash and each able-bodied slave could be depended upon to produce at least 5000 pounds of cotton each year.

The *Mayflower*'s nameless sister ship, presumably a Dutch vessel, which stole into the harbor of Jamestown in 1619 and unloaded her human cargo of 20 of us, was but the first such ship to touch the shores of this New World, and her arrival signalized what was to be our trial for centuries to come. More than 14,000,000 of us were brought to America alone. For every 100 of us who survived the terrible journey across the Atlantic, the so-called "middle passage" of these voyages, 400 of us perished. During three hundred years—the seventeenth, eighteenth, and nineteenth centuries—more than 100,000,000 of us were torn from our African homes. Until the dawn of the nineteenth century, slavery was legal the world over.

Laid out spoon-fashion on the narrow decks of sailing ships, we were transported to this New World so closely packed that the back of the head of one of us nestled between the legs of another. Sometimes 720 of us were jammed into a space 20 feet wide, 120 feet long, and 5 feet high. Week after week we would lie there, tortured and gasping, as the ship heaved and tossed over the waves. In the summer, down in the suffocating depths of those ships, on an eight- or ten-week voyage, we would go crazed for lack of air and water, and in the morning the crew of the ship would discover many of us dead, clutching in rigor mortis at the throats of our friends, wives, or children.

During the seventeenth century, to protect themselves against the overwhelming influx of us, some governments launched numerous men-of-war to track down and seize the slave ships. We captives did not know whether to feel dread or joy when a man-of-war was sighted, for the captain would command that a few of us be pitched alive into the sea as moral bait to compel the captain of the pursuing ship to desist from his duty. Every mile or so one of us would be bound fast to a cask or spar and tossed overboard with the hope that the sight of our forlorn struggle against the sea would stir such compassion in the heart of the captain of the man-of-war that he would abandon pursuit, thereby enabling the slave ships to escape.

At other times, when we were sick, we were thrown alive into the sea and the captain, pilgrim of progress, would studiously enter into the ship's log two words that would balance all earthly accounts: "jettisoned cargo."

At still other times we went on hunger strikes; but the time allotted us to starve to death was often too short, and the ship would arrive in port before we had outwitted the slave traders. The more ambitious slavers possessed instruments with which to pry our teeth apart and feed us forcibly. Whenever we could we leaped into the sea.

To quench all desire for mutiny in us, they would sometimes decapitate a few of us and impale our black heads upon the tips of the spars, just as years later they impaled our heads upon the tips of pine trees for miles along the dusty highways of Dixie to frighten us into obedience.

Captivity under Christendom blasted our lives, disrupted our families, reached down into the personalities of each one of us and destroyed the very images and symbols which had guided our minds and feelings in the effort to live. Our folkways and folk tales, which had once given meaning and sanction to our actions, faded from consciousness. Our gods were dead and answered us no more. The trauma of leaving our African home, the suffering of the long middle passage, the thirst, the hunger, the horrors of the slave ship—all these hollowed us out, numbed us, stripped us, and left only physiological urges, the feelings of fear and fatigue.

Against the feudal background of denials of love and happiness, the trade in our bodies bred god-like men who exalted honor, enthroned impulse, glorified aspiration, celebrated individuality, and fortified the human heart to strive against the tyrannical forms of nature and to bend obstreperous materials closer to a mold that would slake human desire. As time elapsed, these new men seized upon the unfolding discoveries of science and invention, and figuratively, their fingers became hot as fire and hard as steel. Literature, art, music, and philosophy set their souls aflame with a desire for the new mode of living that had come into the world. Exploration opened wide the entire surface of the earth as a domain of adventure.

Window glass, drugs to dull pain, printing presses, larger ships, bigger and more powerful guns—these and a thousand other commodities began to spread across the area of man's living and give it a new quality. Never before had human life on earth felt more confident; human feelings grew sensitive and complex, and human sentiment, pouring from the newly released human organism, wrapped itself about the whole world, each man and object in it, creating an all-powerful atmosphere of ambition and passion in which we black slaves were the main objects of exploitation.

Sustained by an incredible hope such as the world had never felt before, the slavers continued to snatch us by the millions from our native African soil to be used as tools to till the tobacco, rice, sugar-cane, and cotton plantations; they built powerful empires, replete with authority and comfort, and, as a protecting superstructure, they spun tight ideological webs of their right to domination. Daily these eager men slashed off the rotting trappings of feudal life, a life which for centuries had endowed man with a metaphysical worth, rank, use, and order; and, in its stead, they launched the foundations of a new dispensation to prove that man could step beyond the boundaries of ignorance and superstition and live by reason. And they shackled millions of us to labor for them, to give them the instrumentalities.

But as we blacks toiled, millions of poor free whites, against whom our slave labor was pitted, were rendered indigent and helpless. The gold of slave-grown cotton concentrated the political power of the Old South in the hands of a few Lords of the Land, and the poor whites decreased in number as we blacks increased. To protect their delicately balanced edifice of political power, the Lords of the Land proceeded to neutralize the strength of us blacks and the growing restlessness of the poor whites by dividing and ruling us, by inciting us against one another. But, complementing this desire for safety, there was the growth of the hunger for more wealth, and the Lords of the Land increased their importations of us, and in turn we blacks continued to squeeze the poor whites to lower levels of living. Fear became the handmaid of cotton culture, spreading and deepening; but the slave ships sailed on, bringing thousands of us yearly to the New World.

The beginning of the eighteenth century marked the rise of a fully developed anti-slavery sentiment in the North. Tardily, the French Revolution captured to some degree the imagination of the New England Puritans, and again there sounded a passionate, humanitarian belief in the rights of man; and, overlapping this, there came the religious exhortations of the Quakers, with their mystical belief in the Golden Rule. And we black tools responded as fervently as did the rest of mankind to the call of Liberty, Equality, and Fraternity, to the expressed conviction that all men were equal in the sight of God. Fury swept the hearts of the Lords of the Land who heard spilling from the thick, black lips of their tools the first broken syllables of freedom, the first stammered assertions of manhood. The foundations of their world trembled and they turned their eyes to God, seized whips, knives, or guns, and rushed forth, bellowing to set aright the order of the universe.

In the latter part of the eighteenth century, however, the conduct of most of the Lords of the Land began to alter toward us. To evade the prevailing Christian injunction that all baptized men are free, and to check our growing record of revolt, they culled from the Bible a thousand quotable verses admonishing us slaves to be true to our masters. Thereupon they felt that they had squared conscience with practice, and they extended Christian salvation to us without granting the boon of freedom. This dual attitude, compounded of a love of gold and God, was the beginning of America's paternalistic code toward her black maid, her black industrial worker, her black stevedore, her black dancer, her black waiter, her black share-cropper; it was a code of casual cruelty, of brutal kindness, of genial despotism, a code which has survived, grown, spread, and congealed into a national tradition that dominates, in small or large measure, all black and white relations throughout the nation until this day.

How did this paradoxical amalgam of love and cruelty come to be? Well, men are many and each has his work to do. A division of labor among men, splitting them up into groups and classes, enables whole segments of populations to be so influenced by their material surroundings that they see but a little phase of the complex process of their lives and the whole is obscured from them, thereby affording them the unfortunate opportunity to move and work at cross-purposes with one another, even though in their hearts they may feel that they are engaged in a crusade of common hope.

So our bent backs continued to give design and order to the fertile plantations. Stately governmental structures and vast palatial homes were reared by our black hands to reflect the genteel glory of the new age. And the Lords of the Land created and administered laws in the belief that *their* God ruled in Heaven, that He sanctioned this new day. After they had amassed mountains of wealth, they compared the wretchedness of our lives with the calm gentility of theirs and felt that they were truly the favored of God. The lyrical mantle of prayer and hymn, accordingly, justified and abetted our slavery; and whenever we murmured against the degradation of the plantation, the Lords of the Land acted against us with whips and hate to protect their God-sanctioned civilization.

Our black bodies were good tools that had to be kept efficient for toil. Therefore, when schools were built, it was decreed that we must not partake of the teaching in them. When praises were sung to God, it was decided that we must not lift our voices in common hymn. Time and again we rose and struck angrily for freedom; sometimes we revolted in two's and three's; at other times we rose by the thousands, trying to break through the white wall that hemmed us in.

Convinced now at last of peril, the Lords of the Land began to drape their possessions in the protective hues of rationalism, to write and preach of their humanity and justice, but they found that the lash and the mob were needed to keep their positions of power, and soon these twin serpents of terror were organically entwined about the columns of legal government.

The eyes of the Lords of the Land grew challenging; but, blinded by the glittering prize they sought to keep, they could not detect the stealthy forces at work in the world, forces which were destined to wreck their empire and disperse us black men like whirling atoms upon the face of the earth.

The hope which had lured millions of restless men into the New World still lived precariously in many hearts, untouched by the fever of possession and the seduction of power. From English and Yankee brains there came in quick succession the spinning jenny, the spinning mule, and the application of steam power. There began to crawl across the landscape lumbering machines that magically threatened to turn millions of our black fingers idle. And the generous earth, once so green and so new, began to rot the seed and stunt the plant, forcing the Lords of the Land, in their search for new soil, to migrate westward, where they clashed with free men to whom the slave ethic was useless and obnoxious.

Eastern industry, which had begun to flood the nation with commodities, was owned by men who wielded a new type of authority. Free white labor of the North and West built thousands upon thousands of buildings—dwellings, shops, factories, mills, and foundries—and the Bosses of the Buildings, the bankers foresaw that the day was coming when we slaves would not be worth the food we ate. These men grew alarmed over the fate of their nation and over their own ultimate racial identity in face of the black tide of us who were being poured out of the clipper ships.

The opinion of the nation divided into two opposing constellations: a world of machines and a world of slaves. Two groups of leaders sprang up: the Bosses of the Buildings and the Lords of the Land. As the full consequences of the two divergent ways of life became manifest, millions began an impassioned questioning of the basis of the ideas which they had sought to make operative in the New World. A small minority, both north and south, felt outraged at a system of human bondage that nullified all they had so ardently striven to build, and many sensitive men grew violent against *all* government and went up and down the land propounding the principles of passive resistance and civil disobedience.

In an atmosphere of such tension, the whites began to distrust each other. Therefore, when the Bosses of the Buildings suggested that we blacks be deported and colonized, the Lords of the Land rose and threatened to resort to a wholesale breeding of slaves in order not to be deprived of our living bodies. And, on the other hand, when the Lords of the Land, afraid of our growing numbers and increasing rebelliousness, suggested that the entire nation be taxed to raise money to deport us, the Bosses of the Buildings declared that such a course would destroy the capital of the nation, stifle productivity, and crush the poor whites, who were already being smothered in the slave atmosphere. But as we blacks continued to multiply and spread, the Lords of the Land sought to distribute us on the plantations so that our population would never exceed that of the whites or grow so great in any one area as to constitute an insurrectionary danger.

To enjoy a spell more of time in their cool mansions, the majority of the Lords of the Land disciplined the animal panic in their hearts and decided to hang on; they declared their independence, and war was waged for new lands to expand in, for the right to import more of us to raise cotton. And the Bosses of the Buildings, eager to manufacture and sell their commodities, stood against them in four years of battle to protect themselves, their future, and their hope of an industrial civilization.

We were freed because of a gnawing of some obscure sense of guilt, because of a cloudy premonition of impending disaster, because of a soil becoming rapidly impoverished, because of the hunger for fresh land, because of the new logic of life that came in the wake of clanking machines—it was all these things, and not the strength of moral ideals alone, that lessened the grip of the Lords of the Land upon us.

We black men and women in America today, as we look back upon scenes of rapine, sacrifice, and death, seem to be children of a devilish aberration, descendants of an interval of nightmare in history, fledglings of a period of amnesia on the part of men who once dreamed a great dream and forgot.

1941

Questions

1. At the opening of the essay, Wright refers to the reader's view of "us black folk." What audience does Wright assume and what preconceptions on the part of that audience does the essay suggest he has assumed?

2. One of the chief instruments used by Wright is paradox, a device defined by the **Standard College Dictionary** as "a statement seemingly absurd or contradictory, yet in fact true." One example of paradox is Wright's reference to the " 'free trade' in our bodies." What other examples of paradox do you find? What would seem to be the chief paradox in the history of America's involvement with slavery, according to this essay?

3. One of the most horrible aspects of slavery was the "middle passage," the transportation of slaves from Africa to America. What details does Wright cite to suggest the horror of the "middle passage"?

4. What does Wright say of the involvement of Christianity with slavery?

5. At the time Wright wrote this piece he was still a member of the Communist Party. What Marxist elements do you find in the essay? Where

does he touch on such topics as class struggle and capitalism? What are his characteristic terms of reference to capitalists?

6. In concluding the essay Wright offers a summary of the causes of Abolition. Does this seem a reasoned and historically valid view? What reasons for Abolition are usually cited in popular accounts of the Civil War?

cannot kill the deep immortal human wish,
the timeless will.

"But for the storm that flung up barriers   120
of wind and wave, *The Amistad*, señores,
would have reached the port of Príncipe in two,
three days at most; but for the storm we should
have been prepared for what befell.
Swift as the puma's leap it came. There was   125
that interval of moonless calm filled only
with the water's and the rigging's usual sounds,
then sudden movement, blows and snarling cries
and they had fallen on us with machete
and marlinspike. It was as though the very   130
air, the night itself were striking us.
Exhausted by the rigors of the storm,
we were no match for them. Our men went down
before the murderous Africans. Our loyal
Celestino ran from below with gun   135
and lantern and I saw, before the cane-
knife's wounding flash, Cinquez,
that surly brute who calls himself a prince,
directing, urging on the ghastly work.
He hacked the poor mulatto down, and then   140
he turned on me. The decks were slippery
when daylight finally came. It sickens me
to think of what I saw, of how these apes
threw overboard the butchered bodies of
our men, true Christians all, like so much jetsam.   145
Enough, enough. The rest is quickly told:
Cinquez was forced to spare the two of us
you see to steer the ship to Africa,
and we like phantoms doomed to rove the sea
voyaged east by day and west by night,   150
deceiving them, hoping for rescue,
prisoners on our own vessel, till
at length we drifted to the shores of this
your land, America, where we were freed
from our unspeakable misery. Now we   155
demand, good sirs, the extradition of
Cinquez and his accomplices to La

Havana. And it distresses us to know
there are so many here who seem inclined
to justify the mutiny of these blacks.   160
We find it paradoxical indeed
that you whose wealth, whose tree of liberty
are rooted in the labor of your slaves
should suffer the august John Quincy Adams
to speak with so much passion of the right   165
of chattel slaves to kill their lawful masters
and with his Roman rhetoric weave a hero's
garland for Cinquez. I tell you that
we are determined to return to Cuba
with our slaves and there see justice done.   170
       Cinquez—
or let us say 'the Prince'—Cinquez shall die."

The deep immortal human wish,
the timeless will:

    Cinquez its deathless primaveral image,   175
    life that transfigures many lives.

Voyage through death
                  to life upon these shores.

1966

Questions

1. To what does the opening line—"Jesús, Estrella, Esperanza, Mercy"—
    refer? What irony is implicit here?
2. What view of Christianity does the poem offer?
3. What is Hayden's purpose in referring in Section II to the "vanity and
    greed" of "nigger kings" (lines 75-76) who dealt in the slave trade?
4. The poem opens and closes with the lines: "voyage through death /
    to life upon these shores." Is the line ironic? (Note Hayden's reference
    to the shore at the opening of Section III.) Does the reference to a
    "voyage through death / to life upon these shores" carry a new con-
    notation when it is repeated at the poem's conclusion? Note that the
    repetition follows an account of the 1839 slave mutiny aboard the

Amistad, one of the most widely discussed slave rebellions in nineteenth-century America. Led by Cinquez, an African prince, the slaves seized control of the Spanish ship and landed at Montauk Point, New York. An elaborate legal and political battle followed in which the former slaves were defended by John Quincy Adams and others against extradition to Havana. Ultimately the U. S. Supreme Court recognized the right of black men to kill abductors and would-be masters while seeking freedom after having been carried off from their homes as slaves.

William John Grayson
from The Hireling
and the Slave

Part First

Oh, mortal man, that livest here by toil,
   Do not complain of this thy hard estate;
That, like an emmet, thou must ever moil,
   Is a sad sentence of an ancient date;
And, certes, there is for it reason great.
*   *   *   *   *
Withouten that would come a heavier bale,
Loose life, unruly passions, and diseases pale.
CASTLE OF INDOLENCE.

Fallen from primeval innocence and ease,
When thornless fields employed him but to please,[1]
The laborer toils; and from his dripping brow

---

[1] *"Cursed is the ground for thy sake; * * * thorns and thistles shall it bring forth to thee; * * * in the sweat of thy brow shalt thou eat bread."*—Genesis. (*Grayson's note.*)

23

Moistens the length'ning furrows of the plow;
In vain he scorns or spurns his altered state,   5
Tries each poor shift, and strives to cheat his fate;
In vain new-shapes his name to shun the ill—
Slave, hireling, help—the curse pursues him still;
Changeless the doom remains, the mincing phrase
May mock high Heaven, but not reverse its ways.   10
How small the choice, from cradle to the grave,
Between the lot of hireling, help, or slave!
To each alike applies the stern decree
That man shall labor; whether bond or free,
For all that toil, the recompense we claim—   15
Food, fire, a home and clothing—is the same.
   The manumitted serfs of Europe find
Unchanged this sad estate of all mankind;
What blessing to the churl has freedom proved,
What want supplied, what task or toil removed?   20
Hard work and scanty wages still their lot,
In youth o'erlabored, and in age forgot,
The mocking boon of freedom they deplore,
In wants and labors never known before.[2]
   Free but in name—the slaves of endless toil,   25
In Britain still they turn the stubborn soil,
Spread on each sea her sails for every mart,
Ply in her cities every useful art;
But vainly may the peasant toil and groan
To speed the plow in furrows not his own;   30
In vain the art is plied, the sail is spread,
The day's work offered for the daily bread;
With hopeless eye, the pauper hireling sees
The homeward sail swell proudly to the breeze,
Rich fabrics wrought by his unequaled hand,   35
Borne by each breeze to every distant land;
For him, no boon successful commerce yields,
For him no harvest crowns the joyous fields,
The streams of wealth that foster pomp and pride,
No food nor shelter for his wants provide;   40
He fails to win, by toil intensely hard,
The bare subsistence—labor's least reward.

[2] *Pauperism began with the abolition of serfage.*—Westminster Review. (*Grayson's note.*)

In squalid hut—a kennel for the poor,
Or noisome cellar, stretched upon the floor,
His clothing rags, of filthy straw his bed,   45
With offal from the gutter daily fed,
Thrust out from Nature's board, the hireling lies:
No place for him that common board supplies,
No neighbor helps, no charity attends,
No philanthropic sympathy befriends;   50
None heed the needy wretch's dying groan,
He starves unsuccor'd, perishes unknown.
    These are the miseries, such the wants, the cares,
The bliss that freedom for the serf prepares;
Vain is his skill in each familiar task,   55
Capricious Fashion shifts her Protean mask,
His ancient craft gives work and bread no more,
And Want and Death sit scowling at his door.

    Taught by the master's efforts, by his care
Fed, clothed, protected many a patient year,   60
From trivial numbers now to millions grown,
With all the white man's useful arts their own,
Industrious, docile, skilled in wood and field,
To guide the plow, the sturdy axe to wield,
The Negroes schooled by slavery embrace   65
The highest portion of the Negro race;
And none the savage native will compare,
Of barbarous Guinea, with its offspring here.
    If bound to daily labor while he lives,
His is the daily bread that labor gives;   70
Guarded from want, from beggary secure,
He never feels what hireling crowds endure,
Nor knows, like them, in hopeless want to crave,
For wife and child, the comforts of the slave,
Or the sad thought that, when about to die,   75
He leaves them to the cold world's charity,
And sees them slowly seek the poor-house door—
The last, vile, hated refuge of the poor.
    Still Europe's saints, that mark the motes alone
In other's eyes, yet never see their own,   80
Grieve that the slave is never taught to write,
And reads no better than the hireling white;

Do their own plowmen no instruction lack,
Have whiter clowns more knowledge than the black?
Has the French peasant, or the German boor,   85
Of learning's treasure any larger store;
Have Ireland's millions, flying from the rule
Of those who censure, ever known a school?
A thousand years and Europe's wealth impart
No means to mend the hireling's head or heart;   90
They build no schools to teach the pauper white,
Their toiling millions neither read nor write;
Whence, then, the idle clamor when they rave
Of schools and teachers for the distant slave?

   And why the soft regret, the coarse attack,   95
If Justice punish the offending black?
Are whites not punished? When Utopian times
Shall drive from earth all miseries and crimes,
And teach the world the art to do without
The cat, the gauntlet, and the brutal knout,   100
Banish the halter, galley, jails, and chains,
And strip the law of penalties and pains;
Here, too, offense and wrong they may prevent,
And slaves, with hirelings, need no punishment:
Till then, what lash of slavery will compare   105
With the dread scourge that British soldiers bear?
What gentle rule, in Britain's Isle, prevails,
How rare her use of gibbets, stocks, and jails!
How much humaner than a master's whip,
Her penal colony and convict ship!   110
Whose code of law can darker pages show,
Where blood for smaller misdemeanors flow?
The trifling theft or trespass, that demands
For slaves light penance from a master's hands,
Where Europe's milder punishments are known,   115
Incurs the penalty of death alone.
   And yet the master's lighter rule insures
More order than the sternest code secures;
No mobs of factious workmen gather here,
No strikes we dread, no lawless riots fear;   120
Nuns, from their convent driven, at midnight fly,
Churches, in flames, ask vengeance from the sky,
Seditious schemes in bloody tumults end,

Parsons incite, and senators defend,
But not where slaves their easy labors ply,   125
Safe from the snare, beneath a master's eye;
In useful tasks engaged, employed their time,
Untempted by the demagogue to crime,
Secure they toil, uncursed their peaceful life,
With labor's hungry broils and wasteful strife.[3]   130
No want to goad, no faction to deplore,
The slave escapes the perils of the poor.

Part Second

See yonder poor o'erlabored wight,
    So abject, mean, and vile,
Who begs a brother of the earth
    To give him leave to toil,
And see his lordly fellow-worm
    The poor petition spurn,
Unmindful though a weeping wife
    And helpless offspring mourn.—*Burns.*

Where hireling millions toil, in doubt and fear,
For food and clothing all the weary year,
Content and grateful if their masters give,   135
The boon they beg—to labor and to live;
While dreamers task their idle wits to find
A short-hand method to enrich mankind,
And Fourier's scheme or Owen's plans entice
Expectant thousands with some deep device   140
For raising wages, for abating toil,
And reaping crops from ill-attended soil:
If, while the anxious multitudes appear,
Now glad with hope, now yielding to despair,
A seraph form, descending from the skies,   145
In mercy sent, should meet their wond'ring eyes,
And, smiling, offer to each suppliant there
The promised good that fills the laborer's prayer—
Food, clothing, freedom from the wants, the cares,

[3] *The late Preston strike lost to the parties—masters and workmen—over two millions of dollars, and ended where it began. (Grayson's note.)*

The pauper hireling ever feels or fears;   150
And, at their death, these blessings to renew,
That wives and children may enjoy them too,
That, when disease or age their strength impairs,
Subsistence and a home should still be theirs—
What wonder would the gracious boon impart,   155
What grateful rapture swell the peasant's heart!
How freely would the hungry list'ners give
A life-long labor thus secure to live!
   And yet the life, so unassailed by care,
So blessed with moderate work, with ample fare,   160
With all the good the starving pauper needs,
The happier slave on each plantation leads;
Safe from harassing doubts and annual fears,
He dreads no famine in unfruitful years;
If harvests fail from inauspicious skies,   165
The master's providence his food supplies;
No paupers perish here for want of bread,
Or lingering live, by foreign bounty fed;
No exiled trains of homeless peasants go,
In distant climes, to tell their tales of woe: 170
Far other fortune, free from care and strife,
For work, or bread, attends the Negro's life,
And Christian slaves may challenge as their own,
The blessings claimed in fabled states alone—
The cabin home, not comfortless, though rude,   175
Light daily labor, and abundant food,
The sturdy health that temperate habits yield,
The cheerful song that rings in every field,
The long, loud laugh, that freemen seldom share,
Heaven's boon to bosoms unapproached by care,   180
And boisterous jest and humor unrefined,
That leave, though rough, no painful sting behind;
While, nestling near, to bless their humble lot,
Warm social joys surround the Negro's cot,
The evening dance its merriment imparts,   185
Love, with his rapture, fills their youthful hearts,
And placid age, the task of labor done,
Enjoys the summer shade, the winter sun,
And, as through life no pauper want he knows,
Laments no poor-house penance at its close.   190

Safe in Ambition's trumpet call to strife,
No conscript fears harass his quiet life,
While the crushed peasant bleeds—a worthless thing,
The broken toy of emperor or king;
Calm in his peaceful home, the slave prepares   195
His garden-spot, and plies his rustic cares;
The comb and honey that his bees afford,
The eggs in ample gourd compactly stored,
The pig, the poultry, with a chapman's art,
He sells or barters at the village mart,   200
Or, at the master's mansion, never fails
An ampler price to find and readier sales.
   There, when December's welcome frosts recall
The friends and inmates of the crowded hall,
To each glad nursling of the master's race   205
He brings his present, with a cheerful face
And offered hand—of warm, unfeigning heart,
In all his master's joys he claims a part,
And, true as clansman to the Highland chief,
Mourns every loss, and grieves in all his grief;   210
When Christmas now, with its abundant cheer
And thornless pleasure, speeds the parting year,
He shares the common joy—the early morn
Wakes hunter, clamorous hound, and echoing horn,
Quick steps are heard, the merry season named,   215
The loiterers caught, the wonted forfeit claimed,
In feasts maturing busy hands appear,
And jest and laugh assail the ready ear;
Whose voice, than his, more gayly greets the dawn,
Whose foot so lightly treads the frosty lawn,   220
Whose heart as merrily, where mirth prevails,
On every side the joyous season hails?
Around the slaughtered ox—a Christmas prize,
The slaves assembling stand with eager eyes,
Rouse, with their dogs, the porker's piercing cry,   225
Or drag its squealing tenant from the sty;
With smile and bow receive their winter dues,
The strong, warm clothing and substantial shoes,
Blankets adorned with stripes of border red,
And caps of wool that warm the woolier head;   230
Then clear the barn, the ample area fill,

In the gay jig display their vigorous skill;
No dainty steps, no mincing measures here—
Ellsler's trained graces—seem to float in air,
But hearts of joy and nerves of living steel,   235
On floors that spring beneath the bounding reel;
Proud on his chair, with magisterial glance
And stamping foot, the fiddler rules the dance;
Draws, if he nods, the still unwearied bow,
And gives a joy no bearded bands bestow;   240
The triple holiday, on angel wings,
With every fleeting hour a pleasure brings;
No ennui clouds, no coming cares annoy,
Nor wants nor sorrows check the Negro's joy.
   His, too, the Christian privilege to share   245
The weekly festival of praise and prayer;
For him the Sabbath shines with holier light,
The air grows balmier, and the sky more bright;
Winter's brief suns with warmer radiance glow,
With softer breath the gales of autumn blow,   250
Spring with new flowers more richly strews the ground,
And summer spreads a fresher verdure round;
The early shower is past; the joyous breeze
Shakes patt'ring rain-drops from the rustling trees,
And with the sun, the fragrant offerings rise   255
From Nature's censers to the bounteous skies;
With cheerful aspect, in his best array,
To the far forest church he takes his way;
With kind salute the passing neighbor meets,
With awkward grace the morning traveler greets,   260
And joined by crowds, that gather as he goes,
Seeks the calm joy the Sabbath morn bestows.
There no proud temples to devotion rise,
With marble domes that emulate the skies,
But bosomed deep in ancient trees, that spread   265
Their limbs o'er mouldering mansions of the dead,
Moss-cinctured oaks and solemn pines between,
Of modest wood, the house of God is seen,
By shaded springs, that from the sloping land
Bubble and sparkle through the silver sand,   270
Where high o'er arching laurel blossoms blow,
Where fragrant bays breathe kindred sweets below,

And elm and ash their blended arms entwine
With the bright foliage of the mantling vine:
In quiet chat, before the hour of prayer, 275
Masters and slaves in scattered groups appear;
Loosed from the carriage, in the shades around,
Impatient horses neigh and paw the ground;
No city discords break the silence here,
No sounds unmeet offend the listener's ear; 280
But rural melodies of flocks and birds,
The lowing, far and faint, of distant herds,
The mocking-bird, with minstrel pride elate,
The partridge whistling for its absent mate,
The thrush's solitary notes prolong, 285
Bold, merry blackbirds swell the general song;
The crested cardinal, of scarlet hue,
The jay, with restless wing of softer blue,
The cawing crow—upon the loftiest pine
Cautious and safe—their various voices join. 290
   When now the pastor lifts his earnest eyes,
And hands outstretched, a suppliant to the skies,
No rites of pomp or pride beguile the soul,
No organs peal, no clouds of incense roll,
But, line by line, untutored voices raise, 295
Like the wild birds, their simple notes of praise,
And hearts of love, with true devotion, bring
Incense more pure to Heaven's eternal King;
On glorious themes their humble thoughts employ,
And rise transported with no earthly joy; 300
The blessing said, the service o'er, again
Their swelling voices raise the sacred strain;
Lingering, they love to sing of Jordan's shore,
Where sorrows cease, and toil is known no more.
   Not toil alone the fortune of the slave— 305
He shares the sports and spoils of wood and wave;
Through the dense swamp, where wilder forests rise
In tangled masses, and shut out the skies,
Where the dark covert shuns the noontide blaze,
With agile step he threads the pathless maze; 310
The hollow gum with searching eye explores,
Traces the bee to its delicious stores,
The ringing axe with ceaseless vigor plies,

And from the hollow scoops the luscious prize.
   When Autumn's parting days grow cold and brief,   315
Light hoar-frost sparkles on the fallen leaf,
The breezeless pines, at rest, no longer sigh,
Bright, pearl-like clouds hang shining in the sky,
And on strong pinions, in the clear blue light,
Exulting falcons wheel their towering flight,   320
With short, shrill cry arrest the cheerful flow
Of song, and hush the frightened fields below.
When to the homestead flocks and herds incline,
Sonorous conchs recall the rambling swine,
And from the fleecy field the setting sun   325
Sends home the slave, his easy harvest done;
In field and wood he hunts the frequent hare,
The wild hog chases to the forest lair;
Entraps the gobbler; with persuasive smoke
Beguiles the 'possum from the hollow oak;   330
On the tall pine-trees' topmost bough espies
The crafty coon—a more important prize—
Detects the dodger's peering eyes, that glow
With fire reflected from the blaze below;
Hews down the branchless trunk with practiced hand,   335
And drives the climber from his nodding stand:
Downward at last he springs, with crashing sound,
Where Jet and Pincher seize him on the ground;
Yields to the hunter the contested spoil,
And pays, with feast and fur, the evening toil.   340
   If breezes sleep, and clouds obscure the light,
The boatman tries the fortune of the night,
Launches the swift canoe—on either side
Dips his light paddle in the sparkling tide;
By bank and marshy isle, with measured force   345
And noiseless stroke, directs his quiet course;
Still, at the bow, a watchful partner stands,
The leaded meshes ready in his hands,
Prepared and prompt to cast—the torch's beam
Gleams like a gliding meteor on the stream;   350
Along the shore the flick'ring firelight steals,
Shines through the deep, and all its wealth reveals;
The spotted trout its mottled side displays,
Swift shoals of mullet flash beneath the blaze;

He marks their rippling course; through cold and wet,   355
Lashes the flashing wave with dextrous net,
With poised harpoon the bass or drum assails,
And strikes the barb through silv'ry tinted scales.
   On sandy islets, when, in early June,
With lustrous glory looks the full-orbed moon,   360
And, spreading from the eye, her pearly light
Shines on the billows tremulously bright,
When swelling tides—the winds and waves at rest—
Tempt the shy turtle to her simple nest,
That, scooped in sand, and hid with curious art,   365
Waits the quick life that summer suns impart,
The Negro's watchful step the beach explores,
In the loose sand detects its secret stores,
Pursues the fugitive's slow, cumbrous flight,
And wins his crowning trophy from the night.   370
   No need has he the poacher's doom to fear,
Himself ensnared, while sedulous to snare;
To him no keeper closes field or wood,
Nor laws forbid the riches of the flood;
Shrimp, oyster, mullet, an Apician feast,   375
Fit for the taste of pampered prince or priest,
He freely takes, nor dreads the partial law
That seeks the boon of Nature to withdraw
From common use, for Fortune's sated son,
A pastime only for his rod or gun,   380
Kept for an idler's sport, preserved and fed,
While hungry thousands cry aloud for bread.
   Still braver sports are his when April showers
Give life and beauty to the joyous flowers,
When jasmines, through the wood, to early spring,   385
In golden cups, their dewy incense bring,
White dogwood blossoms sparkle through the trees,
The grape's wild fragrance scents the morning breeze,
And with the warmer sun and balmier air,
The finny myriads to their haunts repair: 390
Such sports are his—with ready jest and glee,
Where bold Port Royal spreads its mimic sea;
Far in the north—the length'ning bay and sky
Blent into one—its shining waters lie,
And southward, breaking on the shelving shore,   395

Meet the sea-wave, and swell its endless roar;
On either hand gay groups of islands show
Their charms reflected in the stream below:
No sunnier lands, no lovelier isles than these,
No happier homes the weary traveler sees!   400

1856

Questions

1. Written on the eve of the Civil War by a South Carolinian, "The Hireling and the Slave" was published in 1856 as an answer to "Uncle Tom's Cabin" and other anti-slavery works. In arguing for the superiority of the slave's lot to that of the hireling, to what misfortunes of the hireling does Grayson point? What advantages does the slave enjoy? To what examples of hypocrisy on the part of European critics of slavery does Grayson refer? Is Grayson's argument convincing? What are its fallacies?

2. What verse form does Grayson employ? Is this form appropriate for the expression of his social views?

3. Identify Fourier and Owen in line 139.

4. Throughout the second part of the poem the slave's daily life is seen in a context of pleasant associations, such as Christmas or the coming of spring flowers. What other pleasant or nostalgic associations does Grayson employ?

5. Grayson characteristically employs a benign vocabulary when dealing with the slave's lot. For example, he uses the term "cot" in referring to the slave's living quarters, while another writer might have used "hut" or "hovel." Identify other examples of the poet's use of a softened or benign vocabulary. Nevertheless, the poet occasionally utilizes animal imagery in referring to Negro slaves. Can you find examples of this latter usage?

6. Analyze the background details used to reflect the pleasantness of the slave's life. Do they fall into any noticeable patterns?

7. Though the poem is centered on a debate over the merits of the slave's life versus those of the hireling's, another debate, one made familiar by such eighteenth-century poems as Oliver Goldsmith's "The Deserted Village" and Robert Burns' "The Cotter's Saturday Night," plays an important part in Part Second. Discuss this latter debate.

Paul Laurence Dunbar
Chrismus on the Plantation

It was Chrismus Eve, I mind hit fu' a mighty gloomy day—
Bofe de weathah an' de people—not a one of us was gay;
Cose you'll t'ink dat's mighty funny 'twell I try to mek hit cleah,
Fu' a da'ky's allus happy when de holidays is neah.

But we wasn't, fu' dat mo'nin' Mastah'd tol' us we mus' go,   5
He'd been payin' us sence freedom, but he couldn't pay no mo';
He wa'n't nevah used to plannin' 'fo' he got so po' an' ol',
So he gwine to give up tryin', an' de homestead mus' be sol'.

I kin see him stan'in' now erpon de step ez cleah ez day,
Wid de win' a-kind o' fondlin' thoo his haih all thin an' gray;   10
An' I 'membah how he trimbled when he said, "It's ha'd fu' me,
Not to mek yo' Chrismus brightah, but I 'low it wa'n't to be."

All de women was a-cryin', an' de men, too, on de sly,
An' I noticed somep'n shinin' even in ol' Mastah's eye.
But we all stood still to listen ez ol' Ben come f'om de crowd   15

Reprinted by permission of Dodd, Mead & Company, Inc. from *The Complete Poems of Paul Laurence Dunbar.*

35

An' spoke up, a-try'n' to steady down his voice and mek it
    loud:—

"Look hyeah, Mastah, I's been servin' yo' fu' lo! dese many
    yeahs,
An' now, sence we's got freedom an' you's kind o' po', hit 'pears
Dat you want us all to leave you 'cause you don't t'ink you can
    pay.
Ef my membry hasn't fooled me, seem dat whut I hyead you say.   20

"Er in othah wo'ds, you wants us to fu'git dat you's been kin',
An' ez soon ez you is he'pless, we's to leave you hyeah behin'.
Well, ef dat's de way dis freedom ac's on people, white or black,
You kin jes' tell Mistah Lincum fu' to tek his freedom back.

"We gwine wo'k dis ol' plantation fu' whatevah we kin git,   25
Fu' I know hit did suppo't us, an' de place kin do it yit.
Now de land is yo's, de hands is ouahs, an' I reckon we'll be
    brave,
An' we'll bah ez much ez you do w'en we has to scrape an' save."

Ol' Mastah stood dah trimblin', but a-smilin' thoo his teahs,
An' den hit seemed jes' nachul-like, de place fah rung wid
    cheahs.   30
An' soon ez dey was quiet, some one sta'ted sof' an' low:
"Praise God," an' den we all jined in, "from whom all blessin's
    flow!"

Well, dey wasn't no use tryin', ouah min's was sot to stay,
An' po' ol' Mastah couldn't plead ner baig, ner drive us 'way,
An' all at once, hit seemed to us, de day was bright agin,   35
So evahone was gay dat night, an' watched de Chrismus in.

1899

Questions

1. Generally regarded as America's first major black poet, Dunbar
    achieved wide readership in the late nineteenth century, a period some-

times termed the "mauve decade" because of its predilection for sentimentality. Define sentimentality and discuss its operation in the poem.

2. What assumptions about the institution of slavery are implicit in the
    poem? Compare Dunbar's view with that of Grayson.

3. Read W. E. B. DuBois' essay on Booker T. Washington printed in part
    two of this reader and discuss the relation of Dunbar's poem to the
    "accommodationist" tradition in which DuBois places Washington.

4. Like Robert Burns, Dunbar wrote two types of poems, one in dialect and
    the other in "literary" English. What is the effect of Negro dialect in
    this poem? Would the effect be different if the poem were composed in
    "poetic" diction? Ironically, though Dunbar hoped to build his reputation
    on his works in "literary" English, he is best remembered today for his
    dialect poems. Contrast the diction of "Chrismus on the Plantation" with
    that of "We Wear the Mask" in Chapter Two. What effects are produced
    by the differing diction? Is Dunbar's use of "Negro dialect" demeaning?

Katherine Anne Porter
The Witness

Uncle Jimbilly was so old and had spent so many years bowed over things, putting them together and taking them apart, making them over and making them do, he was bent almost double. His hands were closed and stiff from gripping objects tightly, while he worked at them, and they could not open altogether even if a child took the thick black fingers and tried to turn them back. He hobbled on a stick; his purplish skull showed through patches in his wool, which had turned greenish gray and looked as if the moths had got at it.

He mended harness and put half soles on the other Negroes' shoes, he built fences and chicken coops and barn doors; he stretched wires and put in new window panes and fixed sagging hinges and patched up roofs; he repaired carriage tops and cranky plows. Also he had a gift for carving miniature tombstones out of blocks of wood; give him almost any kind of piece of wood and he could turn out a tombstone, shaped very like the real ones, with carving, and a name and date on it if they were needed. They were often needed, for some small beast or bird was always dying and having to be buried with proper ceremonies: the cart draped as a hearse, a shoe-box coffin with a pall over it, a profuse floral outlay, and, of course, a tombstone. As he worked, turning the long blade of his bowie knife deftly in circles to cut a flower, whittling and smoothing the back and sides, stopping now and then to hold it at arm's lengh and examine it with one eye closed, Uncle Jimbilly would talk in a low, broken, abstracted, murmur, as if to himself; but he was really saying something he meant one to hear. Sometimes it would be an incomprehensible ghost story; listen ever so carefully, at the end it was impossible to decide whether Uncle Jimbilly himself had seen the ghost, whether it was a real ghost at all, or only another man dressed like one; and he dwelt much on the horrors of slave times.

"Dey used to take 'em out and tie 'em down and whup 'em," he muttered, "wid gret big leather strops inch thick long as yo' ahm, wid round holes bored in 'em so's evey time dey hit 'em de hide and de meat done come off dey bones in little round chunks. And wen dey had whupped 'em wid de strop till dey backs was all raw and bloody, dey spread dry cawnshucks on dey backs and set 'em afire and pahched 'em, and den dey poured vinega all ovah 'em . . . Yassuh. And den, the ve'y nex day dey'd got to git back to work in the fiels or dey'd do the same thing right ovah agin. Yassah. Dat was it. If dey didn't git back to work dey got it all right ovah agin."

The children—three of them: a serious, prissy older girl of ten, a thoughtful sad looking boy of eight, and a quick flighty little girl of six—sat disposed around Uncle Jimbilly and listened with faint tinglings of embarrassment. They knew, of course, that once upon a time Negroes had been slaves; but they had all been freed long ago and were now only servants. It was hard to realize that Uncle Jimbilly had been born in slavery, as the Negroes were always saying. The children thought that Uncle Jimbilly had got over his slavery very well. Since they had known him, he had never done a single thing that anyone told him to do. He did his work just as he pleased and when he pleased. If you wanted a tombstone, you had to be very careful about the way you asked for it. Nothing could have been more impersonal and faraway than his tone and manner of talking about slavery, but they wriggled a little and felt guilty. Paul would have changed the subject, but Miranda, the little quick one, wanted to know the worst. "Did they act like that to you, Uncle Jimbilly?" she asked.

"No, *mam*," said Uncle Jimbilly. "Now whut name you want on dis one? Dey nevah did. Dey done 'em dat way in the rice swamps. I always worked right here close to the house or in town with Miss Sophia. Down in the swamps . . ."

"Didn't they ever die, Uncle Jimbilly?" asked Paul.

"Cose dey died," said Uncle Jimbilly, "cose dey died—dey died," he went on, pursing his mouth gloomily, "by de thousands and tens upon thousands."

"Can you carve 'Safe in Heaven' on that, Uncle Jimbilly?" asked Maria in her pleasant, mincing voice.

"To put over a tame jackrabbit, Missy?" asked Uncle Jimbilly indignantly. He was very religious. "A heathen like dat? No, *mam*. In de swamps dey used to stake 'em out all day and all night, and all day and all night and all day wid dey hans and feet tied so dey couldn't scretch and let de muskeeters eat 'em alive. De muskeeters 'ud bite 'em tell dey was all swole up like a balloon all over, and you could heah 'em howlin and prayin all ovah the swamp. Yassuh. Dat was it. And nary a drop of watah noh a moufful of braid . . . Yassuh, dat's it. Lawd, dey done it. Hosanna! Now take dis yere tombstone and don' bother me no more . . . or I'll . . ."

Uncle Jimbilly was apt to be suddenly annoyed and you never knew why. He was easily put out about things, but his threats were always so exorbitant that not even the most credulous child could be terrified by them. He was always going to do something quite horrible to somebody and then he was going to dispose of the remains in a revolting manner. He was going to skin somebody alive and nail the hide on the barn door, or he was just getting ready to cut off somebody's ears with a hatchet and pin them on Bongo, the crop-eared brindle dog. He was often all prepared in his mind to pull somebody's teeth and make a set of false teeth for Ole Man Ronk . . . Ole Man Ronk was a tramp who had been living all summer in the little cabin behind the smokehouse. He got his rations along with the Negroes and sat all day mumbling his naked gums. He had skimpy black whiskers which appeared to be set in wax, and angry red eyelids. He took morphine, it was said; but what morphine might be, or how he took it, or why, no one seemed to know . . . Nothing could have been more unpleasant than the notion that one's teeth might be given to Ole Man Ronk.

The reason why Uncle Jimbilly never did any of these things he threatened was, he said, because he never could get round to them. He always had so much other work on hand he never seemed to get caught up on it. But some day, somebody was going to get a mighty big surprise, and meanwhile everybody had better look out.

1935

Questions

1. Do you think Miss Porter intends that the reader take literally Uncle Jimbilly's descriptions of the cruel treatment of slaves?
2. What purpose is served by the several references to the miniature tombstones carved by Uncle Jimbilly?
3. Has Uncle Jimbilly "got over his slavery very well"? Describe the old man's characterization. Are there any antithetical elements in his character? Describe his relationship with the children in the story.

Edward Brathwaite
Prelude

Memories are smoke
lips we can't kiss
hands we can't hold
will never be
enough for us;   5
for we have learned
to live with sun
with sin
with soil
with rock   10
with iron
toil

no dreams
for us
no hopes   15
no scabs
to heal

in the hot
sun neither
no screams   20
no whip rope
lash

no sweat-
ing free-
ness either.   25
Just give us
what we earn
in bright bold
cash
before we   30
smash
and grab
it.

To hell
with Af-   35
rica
to hell
with Eu-
rope too,
just call my blue   40
black bloody spade
a spade and kiss
my ass. O-
kay? So
let's begin.   45

1967

Questions

1. How does Brathwaite differ from Wright and Hayden in his view of the
    Negro historical heritage?
2. What is the poem's view of past injustices suffered by Negroes? Does it
    demand compensation for such suffering? Does it forgive ancient wrongs?

3. To what does this poem's last statement—"So let's begin"—refer?

4. Is "Prelude" a "militant" poem?

5. Compare the view of money in this poem to that offered by Ben Caldwell's militant play "The Job."

Charles V. Hamilton
Our Nat Turner and William Styron's Creation

William Styron classifies his story as "a meditation on history." It is important for us, then, to view it in this sense and to see precisely what this means in terms of white America's ability or inability to come to terms with the black man in this country. This book is a best seller because it raises and treats all the problems of black people versus whites —the assertive black male, the white woman bugaboo, violence, freedom—and the ultimate treatment reinforces what white America wants to believe about black America. The treatment, in other words, turns out right for whites.

Black youth (and some not so youthful) today who are challenging the values and practices of this society, especially in regard to race, find Styron's book a prime example of the obstacles to overcome. Black youth on college campuses I visit across this country, who form black student associations and who insist on a redefinition of historical and educational legitimacy, can never and should never accept the portrayal (or is the word "betrayl"?) of Nat Turner as set forth by

Styron. Granted, Styron is entitled to his literary license, but black people today cannot afford the luxury of having their leaders manipulated and toyed with. Nat Turner struck a blow for freedom; Nat Turner was a revolutionary who did *not* fail, but rather one who furthered the idea and cause of freedom precisely because he chose to act for freedom. Black people today must not permit themselves to be divested of their historical revolutionary leaders. And it is incumbent upon blacks to make this clear to the Styrons and to all those who read his book and are soothed.

We will not permit Styron's "meditation" to leave unchallenged an image of Nat Turner as a fanatical black man who dreams of going to bed with white women, who holds nothing but contempt for his fellow blacks, and who understands, somewhat, the basic human desire to be free but still believes in the basic humanity of some slaveholders.

We will not permit Styron to picture unchallenged Nat Turner as a leader who did not understand that the military defeat should not be confused with the ideological victory: i.e., a blow for freedom. The rebellion of 1831, led by Nat Turner, is important today for blacks to understand and whites to accept precisely because its lesson is that there will be leaders who *will* rise up—against all odds—to strike blows for freedom against an oppressive, inhumane system. And there can be no refuge in the thought that Turner felt himself divinely inspired or waited for signs from heaven, etc. The important thing is that the desire for human freedom resides in the black breast as well as in any other. No amount of explicating about the harshness of slavery or the gentleness of slavery, about the docility of the masses of slaves, etc., can keep that desire from exploding. Man—black or white or yellow or red—moves to maximize his freedom: THAT is the lesson of Nat Turner that Styron did not deal with.

Styron's literary mind can wander about homosexuality and the like, and his vast readership can have their stereotypes strengthened by an image of a black preacher who is irrational and weak (unable to kill, excepting some white woman he loves) and uncertain. But black people should reject this; and white people should not delude themselves.

Let us see how Styron's "meditation on history" fits perfectly with traditional, widely acclaimed historical accounts of the event and the institution of slavery. And in doing this, we will see how his book feeds the distortions of white America. I will cite two major historical texts, sources used widely in colleges and high schools. First—simply to observe the uses of history—note how Professor Thomas A. Bailey in his *The American Pageant: A History of the Republic* describes the American revolution:

> The revolutionists were blessed with outstanding leadership. Washington was a giant among men; Benjamin Franklin was a master among diplomats. . . . The Americans, in addition, enjoyed the moral advantage that came from what they regarded as a just cause. . . . The brutal truth is that only a select minority of the American colonials attached themselves to the cause of independence with a spirit of selfless devotion. These were the dedicated souls who bore the burden of battle and the risks of defeat; these were the freedom-loving patriots who deserved the gratitude and approbation of generations yet unborn. Seldom have so few done so much for so many [pp. 100–103].

Now let us see how this same objective, white American scholar deals with Nat Turner:

> Fanatical Nat Turner, a semi-educated Negro preacher who had visions, organized a conspiracy which resulted in the butchering of about sixty white Virginians, mostly women and children. The outburst was speedily crushed, but an understandable wave of hysteria swept over the South [pp. 369–370].

(When I taught at a southern Negro college, a black history professor once told me: "Oh, I always use Bailey's *American Pageant*. It is simple and clear and my students like it and find it easy to read.") To my knowledge, Professor Bailey, then on the faculty at Stanford University, is not noted for racist or anti-black views.

One other source is useful, *The American Republic* (Vol. 1, to 1865) by Richard Hofstadter, William Miller, and Daniel Aaron. Note their treatment of slavery:

> The kindliest slaveholder, either as a buyer or seller, was sometimes forced to break up Negro families. In short, the slaveholder was frequently victimized by the system.
>
> But there is a brighter side of the picture. Even some of the antislavery men acknowledged that ordinarily the slaves were adequately housed, clothed, and fed. The slave's diet of pork, corn-meal, molasses, and greens was coarse and monotonous, and the slave quarters were unhygienic by modern standards. But many poor-white farmers lived

no better. Slaves worked no longer than many northern agricultural and industrial laborers and, in areas where the "task" system was employed, a slave might complete his assigned chores by early afternoon and spend the rest of the day as he chose. Progressive planters encouraged their slaves to cultivate truck gardens and keep pigs and chickens for their use or to sell. Incentive payments, holidays, and entertainments alleviated the drudgery on some plantations, and where the work became too exacting the slaves developed their own slow-down techniques. House-servants found life much easier than field hands, and some gifted slaves were rewarded with positions of trust and responsibility. It seems true enough that many white southerners treated their slaves affectionately and that many slaves responded to this treatment with loyalty and devotion [pp. 514–515].

Styron's novel is in this historical tradition. He does not assign to Nat Turner a basic revolutionary desire to overcome oppression. In fact, Styron clearly asserts that Turner and his followers needed specific traumatic acts to galvanize them into action: being whipped unmercifully, being sold by a "decent" owner to a tyrant, having one's wife and children taken. On the other hand, Styron joins that school of thought which believes that the kinder you treat the subjects, the more likely they are to rebel. This is related to the current notion of growing black militancy resulting from rising expectations. Some of us black Americans view human bondage as bad per se, and we believe that Nat Turner, with his basically revolutionary temperament had to strike out against that bondage. He was the real freedom-lover, the true freedom-fighter.

Styron dwells on the reason the slaves would kill those masters who were kinder to them—like Travis. This, indeed, should be a message. The focus is on the fact that they were "masters," not that they were kinder than other masters. And so the white liberal today tries to remove himself from the racism of the system, without understanding that he is part of the racist system, and those of us who are real live victims of that system cannot afford irrelevant distinctions. The white liberal feels that rhetoric and good intentions are sufficient to relieve him of responsibility. He is sadly mistaken. To him, the problem is abstract, academic. To us, it is real, tangible.

Styron imputes irony to the fact that "almost the only white man in the county who owned a truly illustrious reputation for cruelty to Negroes escaped the blade of our retribution." The implication being, of course, that all the violence still did not get the "right" ones, that the "good" whites suffered. And, thus, further evidence of failure. Nonsense! Then and now. The Nathaniel Francises in Styron's story exist precisely because of the support—covert or overt—of the "good white folk." No sensitive black man today confuses this point—whether Styron does or not.

It is perfectly clear why Styron's book would be a hit on the American market: it confirms white America's racist feelings. Here was an ungrateful slave, taught to read by his master, who repaid that "gift" by murder. (See what happens when you try to be a little kind to them.) Here was the fanatical black leader who held profound contempt for his own people and who led them into a senseless bloodbath destined to fail, all the while he dreamed of copulating with "Miss Anne." (They are really incapable of sticking together or of being leaders. All they really want is to have sexual intercourse with our women.) Here was the visionary who frequently doubted himself and his venture. (They are little children who really must be led and brought along slowly—for their own sake.) And, of course, here was the final act of nobility on the part of the Great White Father—Gray, the attorney—who extends the hand of forgiveness through the bars. (We must be patient and understanding with these little savages. We must show them that we are big enough to forgive.)

If this is Styron's (and white America's) "meditation on history," let the record show that this is meditation mired in misinterpretation, and that this is history many of us black people reject.

Nat Turner is our hero, unequivocally understood. He is a man who had profound respect and love for his fellow blacks and who respected black womanhood and held utter contempt for those white slavemasters who violated the purity and beauty of our black women. Nat Turner *was a success* because he perpetuated the *idea* of freedom—freedom at all cost. He will not be denied his place in the revolutionary annals of black people by white people who—through the guise of art or otherwise—feel a conscious or subconscious need to belittle him. If white America feels a need to relieve its conscience, to soften *its* confession, let it be clear that it will not be done, unchallenged, at the expense of our black brothers—past or present. That day is done. That deed is denounced.

1968

Topics for General Discussion and Written Reports on Chapter One

1. Analyze the brutal details of slavery presented in the preceding selections. What aspect of slavery seems most horrifying? Which selection seems most effective in capturing the awfulness of slavery? Why?
2. Discuss the case for the benignity of slavery offered by Grayson and Dunbar. How are their chief points countered by details in the other selections?
3. Discuss the relationship between Christianity and slavery as it appears in these selections.
4. Read Goldsmith's "The Deserted Village" and Burns' "The Cotter's Saturday Night" and discuss Grayson's indebtedness to these poems.
5. Charles V. Hamilton's essay, "Our Nat Turner and William Styron's Creation," quotes from the "traditional, widely acclaimed historical accounts of the event and the institution of slavery" found in two popular textbooks. To what extent do these history book passages affirm or contradict the attitudes found in the Chapter One selections from Wright, Hayden, Grayson, Dunbar, and Porter?

Chapter Two
We Wear the Mask

THE GOOPHERED GRAPEVINE

WE WEAR THE MASK

FOR PAUL LAURENCE DUNBAR

THE KNIFE

THE WHITE TROOPS HAD THEIR ORDERS
BUT THE NEGROES LOOKED LIKE MEN

EQUAL IN PARIS

DINNER GUEST: ME

THE MUHAMMAD ALI—PATTERSON FIGHT

Charles W. Chesnutt
The Goophered Grapevine

Some years ago my wife was in poor health, and our family doctor, in whose skill and honesty I had implicit confidence, advised a change of climate. I shared, from an unprofessional standpoint, his opinion that the raw winds, the chill rains, and the violent changes of temperature that characterized the winters in the region of the Great Lakes tended to aggravate my wife's difficulty, and would undoubtedly shorten her life if she remained exposed to them. The doctor's advice was that we seek, not a temporary place of sojourn, but a permanent residence, in a warmer and more equable climate. I was engaged at the time in grape-culture in northern Ohio, and, as I liked the business and had given it much study, I decided to look for some other locality suitable for carrying it on. I thought of sunny France, of sleepy Spain, of Southern California, but there were objections to them all. It occurred to me that I might find what I wanted in some one of our own Southern States. It was a sufficient time after the war for conditions in the South to have become somewhat settled; and I was enough of a pioneer to start a new industry, if I could not find a place where grape-culture had been tried. I wrote to a cousin who had gone into the turpentine business in central North Carolina. He assured me, in response to my inquiries, that no better place could be found in the South than the State and neighborhood where he lived; the climate was perfect for health, and, in conjunction with the soil, ideal for grape-culture; labor was cheap, and land could be bought for a mere song. He gave us a cordial invitation to come and visit him while we looked into the matter. We accepted the invitation, and after several days of leisurely travel, the last hundred miles of which were up a river on a sidewheel steamer, we reached our destination, a quaint old town, which I shall call Patesville, because, for one reason, that is not its name. There was a red brick market-house in the public square, with a tall tower, which held a four-faced clock that struck the hours, and from which there pealed out a curfew at nine o'clock. There were two or three hotels, a court-house, a jail, stores, offices, and all the appurtenances of a county seat and a commercial emporium; for while Patesville numbered only four or five thousand inhabitants, of all shades of complexion, it was one of the principal towns in North Carolina, and had a considerable trade in cotton and naval stores. This business activity was not immediately apparent to my unaccustomed eyes. Indeed, when I first saw the town, there brooded over it a calm that seemed almost sabbatic in its restfulness, though I learned later on that underneath its somnolent exterior the deeper currents of life—love and hatred, joy and despair, ambition and avarice, faith and friendship—flowed not less steadily than in livelier latitudes.

We found the weather delightful at that season, the end of summer, and were hospitably entertained. Our host was a man of means and evidently regarded our visit as a pleasure, and we were therefore correspondingly at our ease, and in a position to act with the coolness of judgment desirable in making so radical a change in our lives. My cousin placed a horse and buggy at our disposal, and himself acted as our guide until I became somewhat familiar with the country.

I found that grape-culture, while it had never been carried on to any great extent, was not entirely unknown in the neighborhood. Several planters thereabouts had attempted it on a commercial scale, in former years, with greater or less success; but like most Southern industries, it had felt the blight of war and had fallen into desuetude.

I went several times to look at a place that I thought might suit me. It was a plantation of considerable extent, that had formerly belonged to a wealthy man by the name of McAdoo. The estate had been for years involved in litigation between disputing heirs, during which period shiftless cultivation had well-nigh exhausted the soil. There had been a vineyard of some extent on the place, but it had not been attended to since the war, and had lapsed into utter neglect. The vines

—here partly supported by decayed and broken-down trellises, there twining themselves among the branches of the slender saplings which had sprung up among them—grew in wild and unpruned luxuriance, and the few scattered grapes they bore were the undisputed prey of the first comer. The site was admirably adapted to grape-raising; the soil, with a little attention, could not have been better; and with the native grape, the luscious scuppernong, as my main reliance in the beginning, I felt sure that I could introduce and cultivate successfully a number of other varieties.

One day I went over with my wife to show her the place. We drove out of the town over a long wooden bridge that spanned a spreading mill-pond, passed the long whitewashed fence surrounding the county fair-ground, and struck into a road so sandy that the horse's feet sank to the fetlocks. Our route lay partly up hill and partly down, for we were in the sand-hill county; we drove past cultivated farms, and then by abandoned fields grown up in scrub-oak and short-leaved pine, and once or twice through the solemn aisles of the virgin forest, where the tall pines, well-nigh meeting over the narrow road, shut out the sun, and wrapped us in cloistral solitude. Once, at a cross-roads, I was in doubt as to the turn to take, and we sat there waiting ten minutes—we had already caught some of the native infection of restfulness—for some human being to come along, who could direct us on our way. At length a little negro girl appeared, walking straight as an arrow, with a piggin full of water on her head. After a little patient investigation, necessary to overcome the child's shyness, we learned what we wished to know, and at the end of about five miles from the town reached our destination.

We drove between a pair of decayed gateposts—the gate itself had long since disappeared—and up a straight sandy lane, between two lines of rotting rail fence, partly concealed by jimson-weeds and briers, to the open space where a dwelling-house had once stood, evidently a spacious mansion, if we might judge from the ruined chimneys that were still standing, and the brick pillars on which the sills rested. The house itself, we had been informed, had fallen a victim to the fortunes of war.

We alighted from the buggy, walked about the yard for a while, and then wandered off into the adjoining vineyard. Upon Annie's complaining of weariness I led the way back to the yard, where a pine log, lying under a spreading elm, afforded a shady though somewhat hard seat. One end of the log was already occupied by a venerable-looking colored man. He held on his knees a hat full of grapes, over which he was smacking his lips with great gusto, and a pile of grapeskins near him indicated that the performance was no new thing. We approached him at an angle from the rear, and were close to him before he perceived us. He respectfully rose as we drew near, and was moving away, when I begged him to keep his seat.

"Don't let us disturb you," I said. "There is plenty of room for us all."

He resumed his seat with somewhat of embarrassment. While he had been standing, I had observed that he was a tall man, and, though slightly bowed by the weight of years, apparently quite vigorous. He was not entirely black, and this fact, together with the quality of his hair, which was about six inches long and very bushy, except on the top of his head, where he was quite bald, suggested a slight strain of other than negro blood. There was a shrewdness in his eyes, too, which was not altogether African, and which, as we afterwards learned from experience, was indicative of a corresponding shrewdness in his character. He went on eating the grapes, but did not seem to enjoy himself quite so well as he had apparently done before he became aware of our presence.

"Do you live around here?" I asked, anxious to put him at his ease.

"Yas, suh. I lives des ober yander, behine de nex' san'-hill, on de Lumberton plank-road."

"Do you know anything about the time when this vineyard was cultivated?"

"Lawd bless you, suh. I knows all about it. Dey ain' na'er a man in dis settlement w'at won' tell you ole Julius McAdoo 'uz bawn en raise' on dis yer same plantation. Is you de Norv'n gemman w'at's gwine ter buy de ole vimya'd?"

"I am looking at it," I replied; "but I don't know that I shall care to buy unless I can be reasonably sure of making something out of it."

"Well, suh, you is a stranger ter me, en I is a stranger ter you, en we is bofe strangers ter one anudder, but 'f I 'uz in yo' place, I wouldn' buy dis vimya'd."

"Why not?" I asked.

"Well, I dunno whe'r you b'lieves in cunj'in' er not,—some er de w'ite wolks don't, er says dey don't,—but de truf er de matter is dat dis yer ole vimya'd is goophered."

"Is what?" I asked, not grasping the meaning of this unfamiliar word.

"Is goophered,—cunju'd, bewitch'."

He imparted this information with such solemn earnestness, and with such an air of confidential mystery, that I felt somewhat interested, while Annie was evidently much impressed, and drew closer to me.

"How do you know it is bewitched?" I asked.

"I wouldn' spec' fer you ter b'lieve me 'less you know all 'bout de fac's. But ef you en young miss dere doan' min' lis'nin' ter a ole nigger run on a minute er two w'ile you er restin', I kin 'splain to you how it all happen'."

We assured him that we would be glad to hear how it all happened, and he began to tell us. At first the current of his memory—or imagination—seemed somewhat sluggish; but as his embarrassment wore off, his language flowed more freely, and the story acquired perspective and coherence. As he became more and more absorbed in the narrative, his eyes assumed a dreamy expression, and he seemed to lose sight of his auditors, and to be living over again in monologue his life on the old plantation.

"Ole Mars Dugal' McAdoo," he began, "bought dis place long many years befo' de wah, en I 'member well w'en he sot out all dis yer part er de plantation in scuppernon's. De vimes growed monst'us fas', en Mars Dugal' made a thousan' gallon er scuppernon' wine eve'y year.

"Now, ef dey's an'thing a nigger lub, nex' ter 'possum, en chick'n, en watermillyums, it's scuppernon's. Dey ain' nuffin dat kin stan' up side'n de scuppernon' fer sweetness; sugar ain't a suckumstance ter scuppernon'. W'en de season is nigh 'bout ober, en de grapes begin ter swivel up des a little wid de wrinkles er ole age,—w'en de skin git sof' en brown,—den de scuppernon' make you smack yo' lip en roll yo' eye en wush fer mo'; so I reckon it ain' very 'stonishin' dat niggers lub scuppernon'.

"Dey wuz a sight er niggers in de naberhood er de vimya'd. Dere wuz ole Mars Henry Brayboy's niggers, en ole Mars Jeems McLean's niggers, en Mars Dugal's own niggers; den dey wuz a settlement er free niggers en po' buckrahs down by de Wim'l'ton Road, en Mars Dugal' had de only vimya'd in de naberhood. I reckon it ain' so much so nowadays, but befo' de wah, in slab'ry times, a nigger did n' mine goin' fi' er ten mile in a night, w'en dey wuz sump'n good ter eat at de yuther een'.

"So atter a w'ile Mars Dugal' begin ter miss his scuppernon's. Co'se he 'cuse' de niggers er it, but dey all 'nied it ter de las'. Mars Dugal' sot spring guns en steel traps, en he en deoberseah sot up nights once't er twice't, tel one night Mars Dugal'—he 'uz a monst'us keerless man—got his leg shot full er cow-peas. But somehow er nudder dey could n' nebber ketch none er de niggers. I dunner how it happen, but it happen des like I tell you, en de grapes kep'on a-goin' des de same.

"But bimeby ole Mars Dugal' fix' up a plan ter stop it. Dey wuz a conjuh 'oman livin' down 'mongs' de free niggers on de Wim'l'ton Road, en all de darkies fum Rockfish ter Beaver Crick wuz feared er her. She could wuk de mos' powerfulles' kin' er goopher,—could make people hab fits, er rheumatiz, er make 'em des dwinel away en die; en dey say she went out ridin' de niggers at night, fer she wuz a witch 'sides bein' a cunjuh 'oman. Mars Dugal' hearn 'bout Aun' Peggy's doin's, en begun ter 'flect whe'r er no he could n' git her ter he'p him keep de niggers off'n de grapevimes. One day in the spring er de year, ole miss pack' up a basket er chick'n en poun'-cake, en a bottle er scuppernon' wine, en Mars Dugal' tuk it in his buggy en driv ober ter Aun' Peggy's cabin. He tuk de basket in, en had a long talk wid Aun' Peggy.

"De nex' day Aun' Peggy come up ter de vimya'd. Der niggers seed her slippin' 'roun', en dey soon foun' out what she 'uz doin' dere. Mars Dugal' had hi'ed her ter goopher de grapevimes. She sa'ntered 'roun' 'mongs' de vimes, en tuk a leaf fum dis one, en a grape-hull fum dat one, en a grape-seed fum anudder one; en den a little twig fum here, en a little pinch er dirt fum dere,—en put it all in a big black bottle, wid a snake's toof en a speckle' hen's gall en some ha'rs fum a black cat's tail, en den fill' de bottle wid scuppernon' wine. W'en she got de goopher all ready en fix', she tuk'n went out in de woods en buried it under de root uv a red oak tree, en den come back en tole one er de niggers she done goopher de grapevimes, en a'er a nigger w'at eat dem grapes 'ud be sho ter die inside'n twel' mont's.

"Atter dat de niggers let de scuppernon's 'lone, en Mars Dugal' did n' hab no 'casion ter fine no mo' fault; en de season wuz mos' gone, w'en a strange gemman stop at de plantation one night ter see Mars Dugal' on some business; en his coachman, seein' de scuppernon's growin' so nice en sweet, slip 'roun' behine de smoke-house, en et all de scuppernon's he could hole. Nobody did n' notice it at de time, but dat night, on de way home, de gemman's hoss runned away en kill' de coachman. W'en we hearn de noos, Aun' Lucy, de cook, she up'n say she seed de strange nigger eat'n' er de scuppernon's behine de smoke-house; en den we knowed de goopher had b'en er wukin'. Den one er de nigger chilluns runned away fum de quarters one day, en got in de scuppernon's, en died de nex' week. W'ite folks say he die' er de fevuh, but de niggers knowed it wuz de goopher. So you k'n be sho de darkies did n' hab much ter do wid dem scuppernon' vimes.

"W'en de scuppernon' season 'uz ober fer dat year, Mars Dugal' foun' he had made fifteen hund'ed gallon er wine; en one er de niggers hearn him laffin' wid de oberseah fit ter kill, en sayin' dem fifteen hund'ed gallon er wine wuz monst'us good intrus' on de ten dollars he laid out on de vimya'd. So I 'low ez he paid Aun' Peggy ten dollars fer to goopher de grapevimes.

"De goopher did n' wuk no mo' tel de nex' summer, w'en 'long to'ds de middle er de season one er de fiel' han's died; en ez dat lef' Mars Dugal' sho't er han's, he went off ter town fer ter buy anudder. He fotch de noo nigger home wid 'im. He wuz er ole nigger, er de color er a gingy-cake, en ball ez a hossapple on de top er his head. He was a peart ole nigger, do', en could do a big day's wuk.

"Now it happen dat one er de niggers on de nex' plantation, one er ole Mars Henry Brayboy's niggers, had runned away de day befo', en tuk ter de swamp, en ole Mars Dugal' en some er de yuther nabor w'ite folks had gone out wid dere guns en dere dogs fer ter he'p 'em hunt fer de nigger; en de han's on our own plantation wuz all so fluste-rated dat we fuhgot ter tell de noo han' 'bout de goopher on de scup-pernon' vimes. Co'se he smell de grapes en see de vimes, an atter dahk de fus' thing he done wuz ter slip off ter de grapevimes 'dout sayin' nuffin ter nobody. Nex' mawnin' he tole some er de niggers 'bout de fine bait er scuppernon' he et de night befo'.

"W'en dey tole 'im 'bout de goopher on de grapevimes, he 'uz dat tarrified dat he turn pale, en look des like he gwine ter die right in his tracks. De oberseah come up en axed w'at 'uz de matter; en w'en dey tole 'im Henry be'n eatin' er de scuppernon's, en got de goopher on 'im, he gin Henry a big drink er w'iskey, en 'low dat de nex' rainy day he take 'im ober ter Aun' Peggy's, en se ef she would n' take de goopher off'n him, seein' ez he did n' know nuffin erbout it tel he done et de grapes.

"Sho nuff, it rain de nex' day, en de oberseah went ober ter Aun' Peggy's wid Henry. En Aun' Peggy say dat bein' ez Henry did n' know 'bout de goopher, en et de grapes in ign'ance er de conseq'ences, she reckon she mought be able fer ter take de goopher off'n him. So she fotch out er bottle wid some cunjuh medicine in it, en po'd some out in a go'd fer Henry ter drink. He manage ter git it down; he say it tas'e like whiskey wid sump'n bitter in it. She 'lowed dat 'ud keep de goopher off'n him tel de spring; but w'en de sap begin ter rise in de grapevimes he ha' ter come en see her ag'in, en she tell him w'at e's ter do.

"Nex' spring, w'en de sap commence' ter rise in de scuppernon' vime, Henry tuk a ham one night. Whar'd he git de ham? *I* doan know; dey wa'n't no hams on de plantation 'cep'n' w'at 'uz in de smoke-house, but I never see Henry 'bout de smoke-house. But ez I wuz a-sayin', he tuk de ham ober ter Aun' Peggy's; en Aun' Peggy tole 'im dat w'en Mars Dugal' begin ter prune de grapevimes, he mus' go en take 'n scrape off de sap whar it ooze out'n de cut een's er de vimes, en 'n'int his ball head wid it; en ef he do dat once't a year de goopher would n' wuk agin 'im long ez he done it. En bein' ez he fotch her de ham, she fix' it so he kin eat all de scuppernon' he want.

"So Henry 'n'int his head wid de sap out'n de big grapevime des ha'f way 'twix' de quarters en de big house, en de goopher nebber wuk agin him dat summer. But de beatenes' thing you eber see happen ter Henry. Up ter dat time he wuz ez ball ez a sweeten' 'tater, but des ez soon ez de young leaves begun ter come out on de grapevimes, de ha'r begun ter grow out on Henry's head, en by de middle er de summer he had de bigges' head er ha'r on de plantation. Be o' dat, Henry had tol'able good ha'r 'roun' de aidges, but soon ez de young grapes begun ter come, Henry's ha'r begun to quirl all up in little balls, des like dis yer reg'lar grapy ha'r, en by de time de grapes got ripe his head look des like a bunch er grapes. Combin' it did n' do no good; he wuk at it ha'f de night wid er Jim Crow,[1] en think he git it straighten' out, but in de mawnin' de grapes 'ud be dere des de same. So he gin it up, en tried ter keep de grapes down by havin' his ha'r cut sho't.

"But dat wa'nt de quares' thing 'bout de goopher. When Henry come ter de plantation, he wuz gittin' a little ole an stiff in de j'ints. But dat summer he got des ez spry en libely ez any young nigger on de plantation; fac', he got so biggity dat Mars Jackson, de oberseah, ha' ter th'eaten ter whip 'im, ef he did n' stop cuttin' up his didos en behave hisse'f. But de mos' cur'ouses' thing happen' in de fall, when de sap begin ter go down in de grapevimes. Fus', when de grapes 'uz gethered, de knots begun ter straighten out'n Henry's ha'r; en w'en de leaves begin ter fall, Henry's ha'r 'mence' ter drap out; en when de vimes 'uz bar', Henry's head wuz baller 'n it wuz in de spring, en he begin ter git ole en stiff in de j'ints ag'in, en paid no mo' 'tention ter de gals dyoin' er de whole winter. En nex' spring, w'en he rub de sap on ag'in, he got young ag'in, en so soopl en libely dat none er de young niggers on de plantation could n' jump, ner dance, ner hoe ez much cotton ez Henry. But in de fall er de year his grapes 'mence' ter straighten out, en his j'ints ter git stiff, en his ha'r drap off, en de rheumatiz begin ter wrastle wid 'im.

"Now, ef you'd 'a' knowed ole Mars Dugal' McAdoo, you'd 'a'

[1] A small card, resembling a currycomb in construction, and used by negroes in the rural districts instead of a comb. (Chesnutt's note.)

knowed dat it ha' ter be a mighty rainy day when he could n' fine sump'n fer his niggers ter do, en it ha' ter be a mighty little hole he couldn' crawl thoo, en ha' ter be a monst'us cloudy night when a dollar git by him in de dahkness; en w'en he see how Henry git young in de spring en ole in de fall, he 'lowed ter hisse'f ez how he could make mo' money out'n Henry dan by wukkin' him in de cotton-fiel'. 'Long de nex' spring, atter de sap 'mence' ter rise, en Henry 'n'int 'is head en sta'ted fer ter git young en soopl, Mars Dugal' up 'n tuk Henry ter town, en sole 'im fer fifteen hunder' dollars. Co'se de man w'at bought Henry did n' know nuffin 'bout de goopher, en Mars Dugal' did n' see no 'casion fer ter tell 'im. Long to'ds de fall, w'en de sap went down, Henry begin ter git ole ag'in same ez yuzhal, en his noo marster begin ter git skeered les'n he gwine ter lose his fifteen-hunder'-dollar nigger. He sent fer a mighty fine doctor, but de med'cine did n' 'pear ter do no good; de goopher had a good holt. Henry tole de doctor 'bout de goopher, but de doctor des laff at 'im.

"One day in de winter Mars Dugal' went ter town, en wuz santerin' 'long de Main Street, when who should he meet but Henry's noo marster. Dey said 'Hoddy,' en Mars Dugal' ax 'im ter hab a seegyar; en atter dey run on awhile 'bout de craps en de weather, Mars Dugal' 'ax 'im, sorter keerless, like ez ef he des thought of it,—

" 'How you like de nigger I sole you las' spring?'

"Henry's marster shuck his head en knock de ashes off'n his seegyar.

" 'Spec' I made a bad bahgin when I bought dat nigger. Henry done good wuk all de summer, but sence de fall set in he 'pears ter be sorter pinin' away. Dey ain' nuffin pertickler de matter wid 'im—leastways de doctor say so—'cep'n' a tech er de rheumatiz; but his ha'r is all fell out, en ef he don't pick up his strenk mighty soon, I spec' I'm gwine ter lose 'im.'

"Dey smoked on awhile, en bimeby ole mars say, 'Well, a bahgin 's a bahgin, but you en me is good fren's, en I doan wan' ter see you lose all de money you paid fer dat nigger; en ef w'at you say is so, en I ain't 'sputin' it, he ain't wuf much now. I 'spec's you wukked him too ha'd dis summer, er e'se de swamps down here don't agree wid de san'-hill nigger. So you des lemme know, en ef he gits any wusser I'll be willin' ter gib yer five hund'ed dollars fer 'im, en take my chances on his livin'.'

"Sho 'nuff, when Henry begun ter draw up wid de rheumatiz en it look like he gwine ter die fer sho, his noo marster sen' feer Mars Dugal', en Mars Dugal' gin him what he promus, en brung Henry home ag'in. He tuk good keer uv 'im dyoin' er de winter,—give 'im w'iskey

ter rub his rheumatiz, en terbacker ter smoke, en all he want ter eat,—
'caze a nigger w'at he could make a thousan' dollars a year off'n did
n' grow on eve'y huckleberry bush.

"Nex' spring, w'en de sap ris en Henry's ha'r commence' ter sprout,
Mars Dugal' sole 'im ag'in, down in Robeson County dis time; en he
kep' dat sellin' business up fer five year er mo'. Henry nebber say nuffin 'bout de goopher ter his noo marsters, 'caze he know he gwine
ter be tuk good keer uv de nex' winter, w'en Mars Dugal' buy him back.
En Mars Dugal' made 'nuff money off'n Henry ter buy anudder plantation ober on Beaver Crick.

"But 'long 'bout de een' er dat five year dey come a stranger ter stop
at de plantation. De fus' day he 'uz dere he went out wid Mars Dugal' en
spent all de mawnin' lookin' ober de vimya'd, en atter dinner dey
spent all de evenin' playin' kya'ds. De niggers soon 'skiver' dat he wuz a
Yankee, en dat he come down ter Norf C'lina fer ter l'arn de w'ite
folks how to raise grapes en make wine. He promus Mars Dugal' he
c'd make de grapevimes b'ar twice't ez many grapes, en dat de noo
winepress he wuz a-sellin' would make mo' d'n twice't ez many gal-
lons er wine. En ole Mars Dugal' des drunk it all in, des 'peared ter be
bewitch' wid dat Yankee. W'en de darkies see dat Yankee runnin'
'roun' de vimya'd en diggin' under de grapevimes, dey shuk dere heads,
en 'lowed dat dey feared Mars Dugal' losin' his min'. Mars Dugal' had
all de dirt dug away fum under de roots er all de scuppernon' vimes,
an' let 'em stan' dat away fer a week er mo'. Den dat Yankee made
de niggers fix up a mixtry er lime en ashes en manyo, en po' it 'roun' de
roots er de grpaevimes. Den he 'vise Mars Dugal' fer ter trim de vimes
close't, en Mars Dugal' tuck 'n done eve'ything de Yankee tole him ter
do. Dyoin' all er dis time, mind yer, dis yer Yankee wuz libbin' off'n de
fat er de lan', at de big house, en playin' kya'ds wid Mars Dugal' eve'y
night; en de say Mars Dugal' los' mo'n a thousan' dollars dyoin' er de
week dat Yankee wuz a-ruinin' de grapevimes.

"W'en de sap ris nex' spring, ole Henry 'n'inted his head ez yuzhal,
en his ha'r 'mence' ter grow des de same ez it done eve'y year. De
scuppernon' vimes growed monst's fas', en de leaves wuz greener en
thicker dan dey eber be'n dyoin' my rememb'ance; en Henry's ha'r
growed out thicker dan eber, en he 'peared to git younger 'n younger,
en soopler 'n soopler; en seein' ez he wuz sho't er han's dat spring,
havin' tuk in consid'able noo groun', Mars Dugal' 'cluded he wouldn'
sell Henry 'tel he git de crap in en de cotton chop'. So he kep' Henry on
de plantation.

"But 'long 'bout time fer de grapes ter come on de scuppernon' vimes, dey 'peared ter come a change ober 'em; de leaves withered en swivel' up, en de young grapes turn' yaller, en bimeby eve'ybody on de plantation could see dat de whole vimya'd wuz dyin'. Mars Dugal' tuk'n water de vimes en done all he could, but 't wa'n' no use: dat Yankee had done bus' de watermillyum. One time de vimes picked up a bit, en Mars Dugal' 'lowed dey wuz gwine ter come out ag'in; but dat Yankee done dug too close under de roots, en prune de branches too close ter de vime, en all dat lime en ashes done burn' de life out'n de vimes, en dey des kep' a-with'in' en a-swivelin'.

"All dis time de goopher wuz a-wukkin'. When de vimes sta'ted ter wither, Henry 'mence' ter complain er his rheumatiz; en when de leaves begin ter dry up, his ha'r 'mence' ter drap out. When de vimes fresh' up a bit, Henry 'd git peart ag'in, en when de vimes wither' ag'in, Henry 'd git ole ag'in, en des kep' gittin' mo' en mo' fitten fer nuffin; he des pined away, en pined away, en fine'ly tuk ter his cabin; en when de big vime whar he got de sap ter 'n'int his head withered en turned yaller en died, Henry died too,—des went out sorter like a cannel. Dey did n't 'pear ter be nuffin de matter wid 'im, 'cep'n' de rheumatiz, but his strenk des dwinel' away 'tel he did n' hab ernuff lef' ter draw his bref. De goopher had got de under holt, en th'owed Henry dat time fer good en all.

"Mars Dugal' tuk on might'ly 'bout losin' his vimes en his nigger in de same year; en he swo' dat ef he could git holt er dat Yankee he'd wear 'im ter a frazzle, en den chaw up de frazzle; en he'd done it, too, for Mars Dugal' 'uz a monst'us brash man w'en he once git started. He sot de vimya'd out ober ag'in, but it wuz th'ee er fo' year befo' de vimes got ter b'arin' any scuppernon's.

"W'en de wah broke out, Mars Dugal' raise' a comp'ny, en went off ter fight de Yankees. He say he wuz mighty glad dat wah come, en he des want ter kill a Yankee fer eve'y dollar he los' 'long er dat grape-raisin' Yankee. En I 'spec' he would 'a' done it, too, ef de Yankees hadn' s'picioned sump'n, en killed him fus'. Atter de s'render ole miss move' ter town, de niggers all scattered 'way fum de plantation, en de vimya'd ain' be'n cultervated sence."

"Is that story true?" asked Annie doubtfully, but seriously, as the old man concluded his narrative.

"It's des ez true ez I'm a-settin' here, miss. Dey's a easy way ter prove it: I kin lead de way right ter Henry's grave ober yander in de plantation buryin'-groun'. En I tell yer w'at, marster, I would n' 'vise you to buy dis yer ole vimya'd, 'caze de goopher's on it yit, en dey ain' no tellin' w'en it's gwine ter crap out."

"But I thought you said all the old vines died."

"Dey did 'pear ter die, but a few un 'em come out ag'in, en is mixed in 'mongs de yuthers. I ain' skeered ter eat de grapes, 'caze I knows de old vimes fum de noo ones; but wid strangers dey ain' no tellin' w'at mought happen. I wouldn' 'vise yer ter buy dis vimya'd."

I bought the vineyard, nevertheless, and it has been for a long time in a thriving condition, and is often referred to by the local press as a striking illustration of the opportunities open to Northern capital in the development of Southern industries. The luscious scuppernong holds first rank among our grapes, though we cultivate a great many other varieties, and our income from grapes packed and shipped to the Northern markets is quite considerable. I have not noticed any developments of the goopher in the vineyard, although I have a mild suspicion that our colored assistants do not suffer from want of grapes during the season.

I found, when I bought the vineyard, that Uncle Julius had occupied a cabin on the place for many years, and derived a respectable revenue from the product of the neglected grapevines. This, doubtless, accounted for his advice to me not to buy the vineyard, though whether it inspired the goopher story I am unable to state. I believe, however, that the wages I paid him for his services as coachman, for I gave him employment in that capacity, were more than an equivalent for anything he lost by the sale of the vineyard.

1899

Questions

1. What do the terms "goopher" and "conjure" mean?
2. In describing Patesville, North Carolina early in the story, the narrator states: "I learned later on that underneath its somnolent exterior the deeper currents of life—love and hatred, joy and despair, ambition and avarice, faith and friendship—flowed not less steadily than in livelier latitudes." Considering what occurs later in the story, in what sense is this statement prophetic?
3. Chesnutt, the first important black American author of fiction, wrote at a time when the "plantation tradition" prevailed in literary approaches to the Negro and the South. This tradition glorified the "Lost Cause," looked back nostalgically at slavery as a benign institution, and re-

garded the Negro as a childlike, cheerful, and loyal figure whose peccadillos could be excused because of his inherent ignorance. Chesnutt's narrator is a white man, and during the early part of his writing career Chesnutt's editors maintained the fiction that he too was white. Describe the narrator's character. What is his attitude toward the South? toward Negroes? toward Julius? What does the narrator imply when he says of Julius: "There was a shrewdness in his eyes, too, which was not altogether African. . ."?

4. Is Julius an example of the childlike, cheerful, and loyal Negroes of the plantation tradition? What stereotypes of the Negro does his story seem to confirm? Are these "Negro characteristics" paralleled by similar traits in the story's white characters? Describe the character of 'Mars Dugal'.

5. Various comments by both Julius and the narrator imply a comparison of Negro's life under slavery to his lot after the Civil War. What is the story's general assessment of life under slavery?

Paul Laurence Dunbar
We Wear the Mask

We wear the mask that grins and lies,
It hides our cheeks and shades our eyes,—
This debt we pay to human guile;
With torn and bleeding hearts we smile,
And mouth with myriad subtleties.   5

Why should the world be overwise,
In counting all our tears and sighs?
Nay, let them only see us, while
   We wear the mask.

We smile, but, O great Christ, our cries   10
To Thee from tortured souls arise.
We sing, but oh, the clay is vile
Beneath our feet, and long the mile;
But let the world dream otherwise,
   We wear the mask.   15

1895

Reprinted by permission of Dodd, Mead & Company, Inc. from *The Complete Poems of Paul Laurence Dunbar.*

Questions

1. Is this poem on a racial topic? To whom does Dunbar refer when he speaks of "we"? Would the poem have a coherent meaning if you were unaware of the fact that Dunbar is a black poet?
2. What, specifically, does "wear the mask" mean? Does the poem specify why "we wear the mask"?
3. What is the meaning of line 5? What are the "subtleties" concerned with?
4. What is the meaning of line 3? About whose guile does Dunbar speak?

Countee Cullen
For Paul Laurence Dunbar

Born of the sorrowful of heart,
   Mirth was a crown upon his head;
Pride kept his twisted lips apart
   In jest, to hide a heart that bled.

1925

Question

1. Discuss line 3. The accommodationist tradition with which Dunbar is often associated is usually seen as having robbed the black man of dignity. In what way could Dunbar be regarded as displaying pride? Does "We Wear the Mask" manifest the poet's "pride"?

Stephen Crane
The Knife

I

Si Bryant's place was on the shore of the lake, and his garden patch, shielded from the north by a bold little promontory and a higher ridge inland, was accounted the most successful and surprising in all Whilomville township. One afternoon Si was working in the garden patch, when Doctor Trescott's man, Peter Washington, came trudging slowly along the road, observing nature. He scanned the white man's fine agricultural results. "Take your eye off them there mellons, you rascal," said Si, placidly.

The negro's face widened in a grin of delight. "Well, Mist' Bryant, I raikon I ain't on'y make m'se'f covertous er-lookin' at dem yere mellums, sure 'nough. Dey suhtainly is grand."

"That's all right," responded Si, with affected bitterness of spirit. "That's all right. Just don't you admire 'em too much, that's all."

Peter chuckled and chuckled. "Ma Lode! Mist' Bryant, y-y-you don' think I'm gwine come prowlin' in dish yer gawden?"

"No, I know you han't," said Si, with solemnity. "B'cause, if you did, I'd shoot you so full of holes you couldn't tell yourself from a sponge."

"Um—no, seh! No, seh! I don' raikon you'll get chance at Pete, Mist' Bryant. No, seh. I'll take an' run 'long an' rob er bank 'fore I'll come foolishin' 'round *your* gawden, Mist' Bryant."

Bryant, gnarled and strong as an old tree, leaned on his hoe and laughed a Yankee laugh. His mouth remained tightly closed, but the sinister lines which ran from the sides of his nose to the meetings of his lips developed to form a comic oval, and he emitted a series of grunts, while his eyes gleamed merrily and his shoulders shook. Pete, on the contrary, threw back his head and guffawed thunderously. The effete joke in regard to an American negro's fondness for watermelons was still an admirable pleasantry to them, and this was not the first time they had engaged in badinage over it. In fact, this venerable survival had formed between them a friendship of casual roadside quality.

Afterward Peter went on up the road. He continued to chuckle until he was far away. He was going to pay a visit to old Alek Williams, a negro who lived with a large family in a hut clinging to the side of a mountain. The scattered colony of negroes which hovered near Whilomville was of interesting origin, being the result of some contrabands who had drifted as far north as Whilomville during the great civil war. The descendants of these adventurers were mainly conspicuous of their bewildering number and the facility which they possessed for adding even to this number. Speaking, for example, of the Jacksons—one couldn't hurl a stone into the hills about Whilomville without having it land on the roof of a hut full of Jacksons. The town reaped little in labour from these curious suburbs. There were a few men who came in regularly to work in gardens, to drive teams, to care for horses, and there were a few women who came in to cook or to wash. These latter had usually drunken husbands. In the main the colony loafed in high spirits, and the industrious minority gained no direct honour from their fellows, unless they spent their earnings on raiment, in which case they were naturally treated with distinction. On the whole, the hardships of these people were the wind, the rain, the snow, and any other physical difficulties which they could cultivate. About twice a year the lady philanthropists of Whilomville went up against them, and came away poorer in goods but rich in complacence. After one of these attacks the colony would preserve a comic air of rectitude for two days, and then relapse again to the genial irresponsibility of a crew of monkeys.

Peter Washington was one of the industrious class who occupied a position of distinction, for he surely spent his money on personal decoration. On occasion he would dress better than the Mayor of Whilomville himself, or at least in more colours, which was the main thing to the minds of his admirers. His ideal had been the late gallant

Henry Johnson, whose conquests in Watermelon Alley, as well as in the hill shanties, had proved him the equal if not the superior of any Pullman car porter in the country. Perhaps Peter had too much Virginia laziness and humour in him to be a wholly adequate successor to the fastidious Henry Johnson, but, at any rate, he admired his memory so attentively as to be openly termed a dude by envious people.

On this afternoon he was going to call on old Alek Williams because Alek's eldest girl was just turned seventeen and, to Peter's mind, was a triumph of beauty. He was not wearing his best clothes, because on his last visit Alek's half-breed hound Susie had taken occasion to forcefully extract a quite large and valuable part of the visitor's trousers. When Peter arrived at the end of the rocky field which contained old Alek's shanty he stooped and provided himself with several large stones, weighing them carefully in his hand, and finally continuing his journey with three stones of about eight ounces each. When he was near the house, three gaunt hounds, Rover and Carlo and Susie, came sweeping down upon him. His impression was that they were going to climb him as if he were a tree, but at the critical moment they swerved and went growling and snapping around him, their heads low, their eyes malignant. The afternoon caller waited until Susie presented her side to him; then he heaved one of his eight-ounce rocks. When it landed, her hollow ribs gave forth a drum-like sound, and she was knocked sprawling, her legs in the air. The other hounds at once fled in horror, and she followed as soon as she was able, yelping at the top of her lungs. The afternoon caller resumed his march.

At the wild expressions of Susie's anguish old Alek had flung open the door and come hastily into the sunshine. "Yah, you Suse, come erlong outa dat now. What fer you—Oh, how do, how do, Mist' Wash'ton—how do?"

"How do, Mist' Willums? I done foun' it necessa'y fer ter damnear-kill dish yer dawg a' yourn, Mist' Willums."

"Come in, come in, Mist' Wash'ton. Dawg no'count, Mist' Wash'ton." Then he turned to address the unfortunate animal. "Hu't, did it? Hu't? 'Pears like you gwine lun some saince by time somebody brek yer back. 'Pears like I gwine club yer inter er frazzle 'fore you fin' out some saince. G'w'on 'way f'm yah!"

As the old man and his guest entered the shanty a body of black children spread out in crescent-shape formation and observed Peter with awe. Fat old Mrs. Williams greeted him turbulently, while the eldest girl, Mollie, lurked in a corner and giggled with finished imbecility, gazing at the visitor with eyes that were shy and bold by turns. She seemed at times absurdly over-confident, at times foolishly afraid; but her giggle consistently endured. It was a giggle on which an irascible but right-minded judge would have ordered her forthwith to be buried alive.

Amid a great deal of hospitable gabbling, Peter was conducted to the best chair out of the three that the house contained. Enthroned therein, he made himself charming in talk to the old people, who beamed upon him joyously. As for Mollie, he affected to be unaware of her existence. This may have been a method for entrapping the sentimental interest of that young gazelle, or it may be that the giggle had worked upon him.

He was absolutely fascinating to the old people. They could talk like rotary snow-ploughs, and he gave them every chance, while his face was illumined with appreciation. They pressed him to stay for supper, and he consented, after a glance at the pot on the stove which was too furtive to be noted.

During the meal old Alek recounted the high state of Judge Hagenthorpe's kitchen garden, which Alek said was due to his unremitting industry and fine intelligence. Alek was a gardener, whenever impending starvation forced him to cease temporarily from being a lily of the field.

"Mist' Bryant he suhtainly got er grand gawden," observed Peter.

"Dat so, dat so, Mist' Wash'ton," assented Alek. "He got fine gawden."

"Seems like I nev' *did* see sech mellums, big as er bar'l, layin' dere I don't raikon an'body in dish yer county kin hol' it with Mist' Bryant when comes to mellums."

"Dat so, Mist' Wash'ton."

They did not talk of watermelons until their heads held nothing else, as the phrase goes. But they talked of watermelons until, when Peter started for home that night over a lonely road, they held a certain dominant position in his mind. Alek had come with him as far as the fence, in order to protect him from possible attack by the mongrels. There they had cheerfully parted, two honest men.

The night was dark, and heavy with moisture. Peter found it uncomfortable to walk rapidly. He merely loitered on the road. When opposite Si Bryant's place he paused and looked over the fence into the garden. He imagined he could see the form of a huge melon lying in dim stateliness not ten yards away. He looked at the Bryant house. Two windows, downstairs, were lighted. The Bryants kept no dog, old Si's favourite child having once been bitten by a dog, and having since died, within that year, of pneumonia.

Peering over the fence, Peter fancied that if any low-minded night prowler should happen to note the melon, he would not find it difficult to possess himself of it. This person would merely wait until the lights were out in the house, and the people presumably asleep. Then he would climb the fence, reach the melon in a few strides, sever the stem with his ready knife, and in a trice be back in the road with his prize. There need be no noise, and, after all, the house was some distance.

Selecting a smooth bit of turf, Peter took a seat by the roadside. From time to time he glanced at the lighted window.

II

When Peter and Alek had said good-bye, the old man turned back in the rocky field and shaped a slow course toward that high dim light which marked the little window of his shanty. It would be incorrect to say that Alek could think of nothing but watermelons. But it was true that Si Bryant's watermelon patch occupied a certain conspicuous position in his thoughts.

He sighed; he almost wished that he was again a conscienceless pickaninny, instead of being one of the most ornate, solemn, and look-at-me-sinner deacons that ever graced the handle of a collection basket. At this time it made him quite sad to reflect upon his granite integrity. A weaker man might perhaps bow his moral head to the temptation, but for him such a fall was impossible. He was a prince of the church, and if he had been nine princes of the church he could not have been more proud. In fact, religion was to the old man a sort of personal dignity. And he was on Sundays so obtrusively good that you could see his sanctity through a door. He forced it on you until you would have felt its influence even in a fore-castle.

It was clear in his mind that he must put watermelon thoughts from him, and after a moment he told himself, with much ostentation, that he had done so. But it was cooler under the sky than in the shanty, and as he was not sleepy, he decided to take a stroll down to Si Bryant's place and look at the melons from a pinnacle of spotless innocence. Reaching the road, he paused to listen. It would not do to let Peter hear him, because that graceless rapscallion would probably misunderstand him. But, assuring himself that Peter was well on his way, he set out, walking briskly until he was within four hundred yards of

Bryant's place. Here he went to the side of the road, and walked thereafter on the damp, yielding turf. He made no sound.

He did not go on to that point in the main road which was directly
opposite the watermelon patch. He did not wish to have his ascetic
contemplation disturbed by some chance wayfarer. He turned off along
a short lane which led to Si Bryant's barn. Here he reached a place
where he could see, over the fence, the faint shapes of the melons.

Alek was affected. The house was some distance away, there was no
dog, and doubtless the Bryants would soon extinguish their lights and
go to bed. Then some poor lost lamb of sin might come and scale the
fence, reach a melon in a moment, sever the stem with his ready
knife, and in a trice be back in the road with his prize. And this poor
lost lamb of sin might even be a bishop, but no one would ever know
it. Alek singled out with his eye a very large melon, and thought that
the lamb would prove his judgment if he took that one.

He found a soft place in the grass, and arranged himself comfortably. He watched the lights in the windows.

III

It seemed to Peter Washington that the Bryants absolutely consulted
their own wishes in regard to the time for retiring; but at last he
saw the lighted windows fade briskly from left to right, and after a
moment a window on the second floor blazed out against the darkness. Si was going to bed. In five minutes this window abruptly van-
ished, and all the world was night.

Peter spent the ensuing quarter-hour in no mental debate. His mind
was fixed. He was here, and the melon was there. He would have it.
But an idea of being caught appalled him. He thought of his position.
He was the beau of his community, honoured right and left. He pic-
tured the consternation of his friends and the cheers of his enemies if
the hands of the redoubtable Si Bryant should grip him in his shame.

He arose and, going to the fence, listened. No sound broke the stillness, save the rhythmical incessant clicking of myriad insects and the
gutteral chanting of the frogs in the reeds at the lake-side. Moved
by sudden decision, he climbed the fence and crept silently and swiftly
down upon the melon. His open knife was in his hand. There was the
melon, cool, fair to see, as pompous in its fatness as the cook in a mon-
astery.

Peter put out a hand to steady it while he cut the stem. But at the
instant he was aware that a black form had dropped over the fence
lining the lane in front of him and was coming stealthily toward him.

In a palsy of terror he dropped flat upon the ground, not having strength enough to run away. The next moment he was looking into the amazed and agonized face of old Alek Williams.

There was a moment of loaded silence, and then Peter was overcome by a mad inspiration. He suddenly dropped his knife and leaped upon Alek. "I got che!" he hissed. "I got che! I got che!" The old man sank down as limp as rags. "I got che! I got che! Steal Mist' Bryant's mellums, hey?"

Alek, in a low voice, began to beg. "Oh, Mist' Peter Wash'ton, don' go fer ter be too ha'd on er ole man! I nev' come yere fer ter steal 'em. 'Deed I didn't, Mist' Wash'ton! I come yere jes fer ter *feel* 'em. Oh, please, Mist' Wash'ton—"

"Come erlong outa yer, you ol' rip," said Peter, "an' don't trumple on dese yer baids. I gwine put you w'ah you won' ketch col' ".

Without difficulty he tumbled the whining Alek over the fence to the roadway and followed him with sheriff-like expedition. He took him by the scruff. "Come erlong, deacon. I raikon I gwine put you w'ah you kin pray, deacon. Come erlong, deacon."

The emphasis and reiteration of his layman's title in the church produced a deadly effect upon Alek. He felt to his marrow the heinous crime into which this treacherous night had betrayed him. As Peter marched his prisoner up the road toward the mouth of the lane, he continued his remarks: "Come erlong, deacon. Nev' see er man so anxious-like erbout er mellum-paitch, deacon. Seem like you jes' must see 'em er-growin' an' *feel* 'em, deacon. Mist' Bryant he'll be s'prised, deacon, findin' out you come fer ter *feel* his mellums. Come erlong, deacon. Mist' Bryant he espectin' some ole rip like you come soon."

They had almost reached the lane when Alek's cur Susie, who had followed her master, approached in the silence which attends dangerous dogs; and seeing indications of what she took to be war, she appended herself swiftly but firmly to the calf of Peter's left leg. The mêlée was short, but spirited. Alek had no wish to have his dog complicate his already serious misfortunes, and went manfully to the defence of his captor. He procured a large stone, and by beating this with both hands down upon the resounding skull of the animal, he induced her to quit her grip. Breathing heavily, Peter dropped into the long grass at the roadside. He said nothing.

"Mist' Wash'ton," said Alek at last, in a quavering voice, "I raikon I gwine wait yere see what you gwine do ter me."

Whereupon Peter passed into a spasmodic state, in which he rolled to and fro and shook.

'Mist' Wash'ton, I hope dish yer dog ain't goine an' give you fitses?"

Peter sat up suddenly. "No, she ain't," he answered; "but she gin me er big skeer; an' fer yer 'sistance with er cobblestone, Mist' Willums, I tell you what I gwine do—I tell you what I gwine do." He waited an impressive moment. "I gwine 'lease you!"

Old Alek trembled like a little bush in a wind. "Mist' Wash'ton?"

Quoth Peter, deliberately, "I gwine 'lease you."

The old man was filled with a desire to negotiate this statement at once, but he felt the necessity of carrying off the event without an appearance of haste. "Yes, seh; thank 'e, seh; thank 'e, Mist' Wash'ton. I raikon I ramble home pressenly."

He waited an interval, and then dubiously said, "Good evenin', Mist' Wash'ton."

"Good-evenin', deacon. Don' come foolin' roun' *feelin'* no mellums, and I say troof. Good-evenin', deacon."

Alek took off his hat and made three profound bows. "Thank 'e, seh. Thank 'e, seh. Thank 'e, seh."

Peter underwent another severe spasm, but the old man walked off toward his home with a humble and contrite heart.

IV

The next morning Alek proceeded from his shanty under the complete but customary illusion that he was going to work. He trudged manfully along until he reached the vicinity of Si Bryant's place. Then, by stages, he relapsed into a slink. He was passing the garden patch under full steam when, at some distance ahead of him, he saw Si Bryant leaning casually on the garden fence.

"Good-mornin', Alek."

"Good-mawnin', Mist' Bryant," answered Alek, with a new deference. He was marching on, when he was halted by a word—"Alek!"

He stopped. "Yes, seh."

"I found a knife this mornin' in th' road," drawled Si, "an' I thought maybe it was *yourn*."

Improved in mind by this divergence from the direct line of attack, Alek stepped up easily to look at the knife. "No, seh," he said, scanning it as it lay in Si's palm, while the cold steel-blue eyes of the white man looked down into his stomach, " 'tain't no knife er mine." But he knew the knife. He knew it as if it had been his mother. And at the same moment a spark flashed through his head and made wise his understanding. He knew everything. " 'Tain't much of er knife, Mist' Bryant," he said, deprecatingly.

" 'Tain't much of a knife, I know that," cried Si, in sudden heat, "but I found it this mornin' in my watermelon patch—hear?"

"Watahmellum paitch?" yelled Alek, not astounded.

"Yes, in my watermelon patch," sneered Si, "an' I think you know something about it, too!"

"Me?" cried Alek. "Me?"

"Yes—you!" said Si, with icy ferocity. "Yes—you!" He had become convinced that Alek was not in any way guilty, but he was certain that the old man knew the owner of the knife, and so he pressed him at first on criminal lines. "Alek, you might as well own up now. You've been meddlin' with my watermelons!"

"Me?" cried Alek again. "Yah's *ma* knife. I done cah'e it foh yeahs."

Byant changed his ways. "Look here, Alek," he said, confidentially: "I know you and you know me, and there ain't no use in any more skirmishin'. I know that *you* know whose knife that is. Now whose is it?"

This challenge was so formidable in character that Alek temporarily quailed and began to stammer. "Er—now—Mist' Bryant—you—you—frien' er mine—"

"I know I'm a friend of yours, but," said Bryant, inexorably, "who owns this knife?"

Alek gathered unto himself some remnants of dignity and spoke with reproach: "Mist' Bryant, dish yer knife ain' mine."

"No," said Bryant, "it ain't. But you know who it belongs to, an' I want you to tell me—quick."

"Well, Mist' Bryant," answered Alek, scratching his wool, "I won't say 's I *do* know who b'longs ter dish yer knife, an' I won't say 's I *don't*."

Bryant again laughed his Yankee laugh, but this time there was little humour in it. It was dangerous.

Alek, seeing that he had got himself into hot water by the fine diplomacy of his last sentence, immediately began to flounder and totally submerge himself. "No, Mist' Bryant," he repeated, "I won't say 's I *do* know who b'longs ter dish yer knife, an' I won't say 's I *don't*." And he began to parrot his fatal sentence again and again. It seemed wound about his tongue. He could not rid himself of it. Its very power to make trouble for him seemed to originate the mysterious Afric reason for its repetition.

"Is he a very close friend of yourn?" said Bryant, softly.

"F-frien'?" stuttered Alek. He appeared to weigh this question with much care. "Well, seems like he *was* er frien', an' then agin, it seems like he—"

"It seems like he *wasn't?*" asked Bryant.

"Yes, seh, jest so, jest so," cried Alek. "Sometimes it seems like he *wasn't*. Then again—" He stopped for profound meditation.

The patience of the white man seemed inexhaustible. At length his low and oily voice broke the stillness. "Oh, well, of course if he's a friend of yourn, Alek! You know I wouldn't want to make no trouble for a friend of your*n*."

"Yes, seh," cried the negro at once. "He's er frien' er mine. He is dat."

"Well, then, it seems as if about the only thing to do is for you to tell me his name so's I can send him his knife, and that's all there is to it."

Alek took off his hat, and in perplexity ran his hand over his wool. He studied the ground. But several times he raised his eyes to take a sly peep at the imperturbable visage of the white man. "Y-y-yes, Mist' Bryant.—I raikon dat's erbout all what kin be done. I gwine tell you who b'longs ter dish yer knife."

"Of course," said the smooth Bryant, "it ain't a very nice thing to have to do, but—"

"No, seh," cried Alek, brightly; "I'm gwine tell you, Mist' Bryant. I gwine tell you erbout dat knife. Mist' Bryant," he asked, solemnly, "does you know who b'longs ter dat knife?"

"No, I—"

"Well, I gwine tell. I gwine tell who. Mist' Bryant—" The old man drew himself to a stately pose and held forth his arm. "I gwine tell who. Mist' Bryant, *dish yer knife b'longs ter Sam Jackson!*"

Bryant was startled into indignation. "Who in hell is Sam Jackson?" he growled.

"He's a nigger," said Alek, impressively, "and he wuks in er lumberyawd up yere in Hoswego."

1899

Questions

1. What qualities are emphasized in the characterization of Si Bryant? Is he basically a sympathetic or unsympathetic figure? How would you describe the relationship he shares with Peter Washington? Is Bryant a bigot?

2. Why does Peter Washington entrap Alek Williams? Crane suggests that Washington was overcome by "a mad inspiration," but are there qualities in Williams' character and personality that would promote this inspiration?

3. What traditional stereotyped views of the Negro are embodied in the story? Does Crane seem to accept or reject such views? Does his use of the term "effete" to describe the "joke in regard to an American negro's fondness for watermelons" indicate whether or not he feels the joke involves an accurate perception of a racial characteristic?

4. Is Washington's treatment of Williams a reflection of the manner in which Negroes view themselves and fellow Negroes (note Williams' description of "Sam Jackson" at the story's conclusion)? or would such an approach to a story published in 1899 merely represent the modern reader's attempt to place the story in a contemporary context?

5. How many levels of deceit does the story embody? Does Peter Washington lie? Does Si Bryant lie?

6. Critic Robert W. Stallman compares the story to "Huckleberry Finn," "where Huck learns all about social guile. Fabrication, equivocation, deceit, the mask of the lie—these equip man for society and protect him from it. To lie is to be saved." Do you agree with Stallman's approach to the story? Why does Alek lie to save Peter?

Gwendolyn Brooks
The White Troops Had Their Orders But the Negroes Looked Like Men

They had supposed their formula was fixed.
They had obeyed instructions to devise
A type of cold, a type of hooded gaze.
But when the Negroes came they were perplexed.
These Negroes looked like men. Besides, it taxed   5
Time and the temper to remember those
Congenital iniquities that cause
Disfavor of the darkness. Such as boxed
Their feelings properly, complete to tags—
A box for dark men and a box for Other—   10
Would often find the contents had been scrambled.
Or even switched. Who really gave two figs?

Neither the earth nor heaven ever trembled.
And there was nothing startling in the weather.

1945

Questions

1. What traditional poetic form does Miss Brooks employ? How does her poem vary from the conventions of that form? Is the fact of innovation within a traditional form appropriate to the situation detailed in the poem?
2. The poem was published in 1945, at a time when the U. S. armed services were still segregated. What do you think the term "orders" means in the poem's title? Could the term refer to something other than orders issued by a commanding officer? What other words in the poem parallel "orders"?
3. To what does Miss Brooks refer in the expression "those / Congenital iniquities that cause / Disfavor of the darkness" (lines 6-8)?
4. What is meant by "boxed feelings" in lines 8-11?
5. How would you describe the tone of this poem? Is it angry? sad? amused? sarcastic?

James Baldwin
Equal in Paris

On the 19th of December, in 1949, when I had been living in Paris for a little over a year, I was arrested as a receiver of stolen goods and spent eight days in prison. My arrest came about through an American tourist whom I had met twice in New York, who had been given my name and address and told to look me up. I was then living on the top floor of a ludicrously grim hotel on the rue du Bac, one of those enormous dark, cold, and hideous establishments in which Paris abounds that seem to breathe forth, in their airless, humid, stone-cold halls, the weak light, scurrying chambermaids, and creaking stairs, an odor of gentility long long dead. The place was run by an ancient Frenchman dressed in an elegant black suit which was green with age, who cannot properly be described as bewildered or even as being in a state of shock, since he had really stopped breathing around 1910. There he sat at his desk in the weirdly lit, fantastically furnished lobby, day in and day out, greeting each one of his extremely impoverished and *louche* lodgers with a stately inclination of the head that he had no doubt been taught in some impossibly remote time was the proper way for a *propriétaire* to greet his guests. If it had not been for his

From *Notes of a Native Son.* Reprinted by permission of the Beacon Press, copyright © 1955 by James Baldwin.

daughter, an extremely hardheaded *tricoteuse*—the inclination of *her* head was chilling and abrupt, like the downbeat of an ax—the hotel would certainly have gone bankrupt long before. It was said that this old man had not gone farther than the door of his hotel for thirty years, which was not at all difficult to believe. He looked as though the daylight would have killed him.

I did not, of course, spend much of my time in this palace. The moment I began living in French hotels I understood the necessity of French cafés. This made it rather difficult to look me up, for as soon as I was out of bed I hopefully took notebook and fountain pen off to the upstairs room of the Flore, where I consumed rather a lot of coffee and, as evening approached, rather a lot of alcohol, but did not get much writing done. But one night, in one of the cafés of St. Germain des Près, I was discovered by this New Yorker and only because we found ourselves in Paris we immediately established the illusion that we had been fast friends back in the good old U.S.A. This illusion proved itself too thin to support an evening's drinking, but by that time it was too late. I had committed myself to getting him a room in my hotel the next day, for he was living in one of the nest of hotels near the Gare St. Lazare, where, he said, the *propriétaire* was a thief, his wife a repressed nymphomaniac, the chambermaids "pigs," and the rent a crime. Americans are always talking this way about the French and so it did not occur to me that he meant what he said or that he would take into his own hands the means of avenging himself on the French Republic. It did not occur to me, either, that the means which he *did* take could possibly have brought about such dire results, results which were not less dire for being also comic-opera.

It came as the last of a series of disasters which had perhaps been made inevitable by the fact that I had come to Paris originally with a little over forty dollars in my pockets, nothing in the bank, and no grasp whatever of the French language. It developed, shortly, that I had no grasp of the French character either. I considered the French an ancient, intelligent, and cultured race, which indeed they are. I did not know, however, that ancient glories imply, at least in the middle of the present century, present fatigue and, quite probably, paranoia; that there is a limit to the role of the intelligence in human affairs; and that no people come into possession of a culture without having paid a heavy price for it. This price they cannot, of course, assess, but it is revealed in their personalities and in their institutions. The very word "institutions," from my side of the ocean, where, it seemed to me, we suffered so cruelly from the lack of them, had a pleasant ring, as of safety and order and common sense; one had to come into contact with these institutions in order to understand that they were also outmoded, exasperating, completely impersonal, and very often cruel. Similarly, the personality which had seemed from a distance to be so large and free had to be dealt with before one could see that, if it was large, it was also inflexible and, for the foreigner, full of strange, high, dusty rooms which could not be inhabited. One had, in short, to come into contact with an alien culture in order to understand that a culture was not a community basket-weaving project, nor yet an act of God; was something neither desirable nor undesirable in itself, being inevitable, being nothing more or less than the recorded and visible effects on a body of people of the vicissitudes with which they had been forced to deal. And their great men are revealed as simply another of these vicissitudes, even if, quite against their will, the brief battle of their great men with them has left them richer.

When my American friend left his hotel to move to mine, he took with him, out of pique, a bedsheet belonging to the hotel and put it in his suitcase. When he arrived at my hotel I borrowed the sheet, since my own were filthy and the chambermaid showed no sign of bringing me any clean ones, and put it on my bed. The sheets belonging to *my* hotel I put out in the hall, congratulating myself on having thus forced on the attention of the Grand Hôtel du Bac the unpleasant state of its linen. Thereafter, since, as it turned out, we kept very different hours —I got up at noon, when, as I gathered by meeting him on the stairs one day, he was only just getting in—my new-found friend and I saw very little of each other.

On the evening of the 19th I was sitting thinking melancholy thoughts about Christmas and staring at the walls of my room. I imagine that I had sold something or that someone had sent me a Christmas present, for I remember that I had a little money. In those days in Paris, though I floated, so to speak, on a sea of acquaintances, I knew almost no one. Many people were eliminated from my orbit by virtue of the fact that they had more money than I did, which placed me, in my own eyes, in the humiliating role of a free-loader; and other people were eliminated by virtue of the fact that they enjoyed their poverty, shrilly insisting that this wretched round of hotel rooms, bad food, humiliating concierges, and unpaid bills was the Great Adventure. It couldn't, however, for me, end soon enough, this Great Adventure; there was a real question in my mind as to which would end soonest, the Great Adventure or me. This meant, however, that there were many evenings when I sat in my room, knowing that I couldn't work there, and not knowing what to do, or whom to see. On this particular evening I went down and knocked on the American's door.

There were two Frenchmen standing in the room, who immediately introduced themselves to me as policemen; which did not worry me. I had got used to policemen in Paris bobbing up at the most improbable times and places, asking to see one's *carte d'identit*. These policemen, however, showed very little interest in my papers. They were looking for something else. I could not imagine what this would be and, since I knew I certainly didn't have it, I scarcely followed the conversation they were having with my friend. I gathered that they were looking for some kind of gangster and since I wasn't a gangster and knew that gangsterism was not, insofar as he had one, my friend's style, I was sure that the two policemen would presently bow and say *Merci, messieurs*, and leave. For by this time, I remember very clearly, I was dying to have a drink and go to dinner.

I did not have a drink or go to dinner for many days after this, and when I did my outraged stomach promptly heaved everything up again. For now one of the policemen began to exhibit the most vivid interest in me and asked, very politely, if he might see my room. To which we mounted, making, I remember, the most civilized small talk on the way and even continuing it for some moments after we were in the room in which there was certainly nothing to be seen but the familiar poverty and disorder of that precarious group of people of whatever age, race, country, calling, or intention which Paris recognizes as *les étudiants* and sometimes, more ironically and precisely, as *les nonconformistes*. Then he moved to my bed, and in a terrible flash, not quite an instant before he lifted the bedspread, I understood what he was looking for. We looked at the sheet, on which I read, for the first time, lettered in the most brilliant scarlet I have ever seen, the name of the hotel from which it had been stolen. It was the first time the word *stolen* entered my mind. I had certainly seen the hotel monogram the day I put the sheet on the bed. It had simply meant nothing to me. In New York I had seen hotel monograms on everything from silver to soap and towels. Taking things from New York hotels was practically a custom, though, I suddenly realized, I had never known anyone to take a *sheet*. Sadly, and without a word to me, the inspector took the sheet from the bed, folded it under his arm, and we started back downstairs. I understood that I was under arrest.

And so we passed through the lobby, four of us, two of us very clearly criminal, under the eyes of the old man and his daughter, neither of whom said a word, into the streets where a light rain was falling. And I asked, in French, "But is this very serious?"

For I was thinking, it is, after all, only a sheet, not even new.

"No," said one of them. "It's not serious."

"It's nothing at all," said the other.

I took this to mean that we would receive a reprimand at the police station and be allowed to go to dinner. Later on I concluded that they were not being hypocritical or even trying to comfort us. They meant exactly what they said. It was only that they spoke another language.

In Paris everything is very slow. Also, when dealing with the bureaucracy, the man you are talking to is never the man you have to see. The man you have to see has just gone off to Belgium, or is busy with his family, or has just discovered that he is a cuckold; he will be in next Tuesday at three o'clock, or sometime in the course of the afternoon, or possibly tomorrow, or, possibly, in the next five minutes. But if he is coming in the next five minutes he will be far too busy to be able to see you today. So that I suppose I was not really astonished to learn at the commissariat that nothing could possibly be done about us before The Man arrived in the morning. But no, we could not go off and have dinner and come back in the morning. Of course he knew that we *would* come back—that was not the question. Indeed, there was no question: we would simply have to stay there for the night. We were placed in a cell which rather resembled a chicken coop. It was now about seven in the evening and I relinquished the thought of dinner and began to think of lunch.

I discouraged the chatter of my New York friend and this left me alone with my thoughts. I was beginning to be frightened and I bent all my energies, therefore, to keeping my panic under control. I began to realize that I was in a country I knew nothing about, in the hands of a people I did not understand at all. In a similar situation in New York I would have had some idea of what to do because I would have had some idea of what to expect. I am not speaking now of legality which, like most of the poor, I had never for an instant trusted, but of the temperament of the people with whom I had to deal. I had become very accomplished in New York at guessing and, therefore, to a limited extent manipulating to my advantage the reactions of the white world. But this was not New York. None of my old weapons could serve me here. I did not know what they saw when they looked at me. I knew very well what Americans saw when they looked at me and this allowed me to play endless and sinister variations on the role which they had assigned me; since I knew that it was, for them, of the utmost importance that they never be confronted with what, in their own personalities, made this role so necessary and gratifying to them, I knew that they could never call my hand or, indeed, afford to know what I was doing; so that I moved into every crucial situation with the deadly and rather desperate advantages of bitterly accumulated perception, of pride and contempt. This is an awful sword and shield to carry through the world, and the discovery that, in the game I was playing, I did myself a violence of which the world, at its most ferocious, would scarcely have been capable, was what had driven me out of New York. It was a strange feeling, in this situation, after a year in Paris, to discover that my weapons would never again serve me as they had.

It was quite clear to me that the Frenchmen in whose hands I found myself were no better or worse than their American counterparts. Certainly their uniforms frightened me quite as much, and their impersonality, and the threat, always very keenly felt by the poor, of violence, was as present in that commissariat as it had ever been for me in any police station. And I had seen, for example, what Paris policemen could do to Arab peanut vendors. The only difference here was that I did not understand these people, did not know what techniques their cruelty took, did not know enough about their personalities to see danger coming, to ward it off, did not know on what ground to meet it. That evening in the commissariat I was not a despised black man. They would simply have laughed at me if I had behaved like one. For them, I was an American. And here it was they who had the advantage, for that word, *Américain*, gave them some idea, far from inaccurate of what to expect from me. In order to corroborate none of their ironical expectations I said nothing and did nothing—which was not the way any Frenchman, white or black, would have reacted. The question thrusting up from the bottom of my mind was not *what* I was, but *who*. And this question, since a *what* can get by with skill but a *who* demands resources, was my first real intimation of what humility must mean.

In the morning it was still raining. Between nine and ten o'clock a black Citroën took us off to the Ile de la Cité, to the great, gray Préfecture. I realize now that the questions I put to the various policemen who escorted us were always answered in such a way as to corroborate what I wished to hear. This was not out of politeness, but simply out of indifference—or, possibly, an ironical pity—since each of the policemen knew very well that nothing would speed or halt the machine in which I had become entangled. They knew I did not know this and there was certainly no point in their telling me. In one way or another I would certainly come out at the other side—for they also knew that being found with a stolen bedsheet in one's possession was not a crime punishable by the guillotine. (They had the advantage over me there, too, for there were certainly moments later on when I was not so sure.) If I did *not* come out at the other side—well, that was just too bad. So, to my question, put while we were in the Citroën—"Will it be over today?"—I received a *"Oui, bien sûr."* He was not lying. As it turned out, the *procès-verbal* was over that day. Trying to be realistic I dismissed, in the Citroën, all thoughts of lunch and pushed my mind ahead to dinner.

At the Préfecture we were first placed in a tiny cell, in which it was almost impossible either to sit or to lie down. After a couple of hours of this we were taken down to an office, where, for the first time, I encountered the owner of the bedsheet and where the *procès-verbal* took place. This was simply an interrogation, quite chillingly clipped and efficient (so that there was, shortly, no doubt in one's own mind that one *should* be treated as a criminal), which was recorded by a secretary. When it was over, this report was given to us to sign. One had, of course no choice but to sign it, even though my mastery of written French was very far from certain. We were being held, according to the law in France, incommunicado, and all my angry demands to be allowed to speak to my embassy or to see a lawyer met with a stony *"Oui, oui. Plus tard."* The *procès-verbal* over, we were taken back to the cell, before which, shortly, passed the owner of the bedsheet. He said he hoped we had slept well, gave a vindictive wink, and disappeared.

By this time there was only one thing clear: that we had no way of controlling the sequence of events and could not possibly guess what this sequence would be. It seemed to me, since what I regarded as the high point—*the procès-verbal*—had been passed and since the hotel-keeper was once again in possession of his sheet, that we might reasonably expect to be released from police custody in a matter of hours. We had been detained now for what would soon be twenty-four hours, during which time I had learned only that the official charge against me was *receleur.* My mental shifting, between lunch and dinner, to say nothing of the physical lack of either of these delights, was beginning to make me dizzy. The steady chatter of my friend from New York, who was determined to keep my spirits up, made me feel murderous; I was praying that some power would release us from this freezing pile of stone before the impulse became the act. And I was beginning to wonder what was happening in that beautiful city, Paris, which lived outside these walls. I wondered how long it would take before anyone casually asked, "But where's Jimmy? He hasn't been around"—and realized, knowing the people I knew, that it would take several days.

Quite late in the afternoon we were taken from our cells; handcuffed, each to a separate officer; led through a maze of steps and corridors to the top of the building; fingerprinted; photographed. As in movies I had seen, I was placed against a wall, facing an old-fashioned camera, behind which stood one of the most completely cruel and indifferent faces I had ever seen, while someone next to me and, therefore, just outside my line of vision, read off in a voice from which all human feeling, even feeling of the most base description, had long since fled, what must be called my public characteristics—which, at that time and in that place, seemed anything but that. He might have been roaring to the hostile world secrets which I could barely, in the privacy of midnight, utter to myself. But he was only reading off my height, my features, my approximate weight, my color—that color which, in the United States, had often, odd as it may sound, been my salvation—the color of my hair, my age, my nationality. A light then flashed, the photographer and I staring at each other as though there was murder in our hearts, and then it was over. Handcuffed again, I was led downstairs to the bottom of the building, into a great enclosed shed in which had been gathered the very scrapings off the Paris streets. Old, old men, so ruined and old that life in them seemed really to prove the miracle of the quickening power of the Holy Ghost—for clearly their life was no longer their affair, it was no longer even their burden, they were simply the clay which had once been touched. And men not so old, with faces the color of lead and the consistency of oatmeal, eyes that made me think of stale *café-au-lait* spiked with arsenic, bodies which could take in food and water—any food and water—and pass it out, but which could not do anything more, except possibly, at midnight, along the riverbank where rats scurried, rape. And young men, harder and crueler than the Paris stones, older by far than I, their chronological senior by some five to seven years. And North Africans, old and young, who seemed the only living people in this place because they yet retained the grace to be bewildered. But they were not bewildered by being in this shed: they were simply bewildered because they were no longer in North Africa. There was a great hole in the center of this shed which was the common toilet. Near it, though it was impossible to get very far from it, stood an old man with white hair, eating a piece of camembert. It was at this point, probably, that thought, for me, stopped, that physiology, if one may say so, took over. I found myself incapable of saying a word, not because I was afraid I would cry but because I was afraid I would vomit. And I did not think any longer of the city of Paris but my mind flew back to that home from which I had fled. I was sure that I would never see it any more. And it must have seemed to me that my flight from home was the cruelest trick I had ever played on myself, since it had led me here, down to a lower point than any I could ever in my life have imagined—lower, far, than anything I had seen in that Harlem which I had so hated and so loved, the escape from which had soon become the greatest direction of my life. After we had been here an hour or so a functionary came and opened the door and called out our names. And I was sure that *this* was my release. But I was handcuffed again and led out of the Préfecture into the streets—it was dark now, it was still raining—and before the steps of the Préfecture stood the great police wagon, doors facing me wide open. The handcuffs were taken off, I entered the wagon, which was peculiarly constructed. It was divided by a narrow aisle, and on each side of the aisle was a series of narrow doors. These doors opened on a narrow cubicle, beyond which was a door which opened onto another narrow cubicle: three or four cubicles, each private, with a locking door. I was placed in one of them; I remember there was a small vent just above my head which let in a little light. The door of my cubicle was locked from the outside. I had no idea where this wagon was taking me and, as it began to move, I began to cry. I suppose I cried all the way to prison, the prison called Fresnes, which is twelve kilometers outside of Paris.

For reasons I have no way at all of understanding, prisoners whose last initial is A, B, or C are always sent to Fresnes; everybody else is sent to a prison called, rather cynically it seems to me, La Santé. I will, obviously, never be allowed to enter La Santé, but I was told by people who certainly seemed to know that it was infinitely more unbearable than Fresnes. This arouses in me, until today, a positive storm of curiosity concerning what I promptly began to think of as The Other Prison. My colleague in crime, occurring lower in the alphabet, had been sent there and I confess that the minute he was gone I missed him. I missed him because he was not French and because he was the only person in the world who knew that the story I told was true.

For, once locked in, divested of shoelaces, belt, watch, money, papers, nailfile, in a freezing cell in which both the window and the toilet were broken, with six other adventurers, the story I told of *l'affaire du drap de lit* elicited only the wildest amusement or the most suspicious disbelief. Among the people who shared my cell the first three days no one, it is true, had been arrested for anything much more serious—or, at least, not serious in my eyes. I remember that there was a boy who had stolen a knitted sweater from a *monoprix*, who would probably, it was agreed, receive a six-month sentence. There was an older man there who had been arrested for some kind of petty larceny. There were two North Africans, vivid, brutish, and beautiful, who alternated between gaiety and fury, not at the fact of their arrest but at the state of the cell. None poured as much emotional energy into the fact of their arrest as I did; they took it, as I would have liked to take it, as simply another unlucky happening in a very dirty world. For, though I had grown accustomed to thinking of myself as looking upon the world with a hard, penetrating eye, the truth was that they were far more realistic about the world than I, and more nearly right about it. The gap between us, which only a gesture I made could have bridged, grew steadily, during thirty-six hours, wider. I could not make any gesture simply because they frightened me. I was unable to accept my imprisonment as a fact, even as a temporary fact. I could not, even for a moment, accept my present companions as *my* companions. And they, of course, felt this and put it down, with perfect justice, to the fact that I was an American.

There was nothing to do all day long. It appeared that we would one day come to trial but no one knew when. We were awakened at seven-thirty by a rapping on what I believe is called the Judas, that small opening in the door of the cell which allows the guards to survey the prisoners. At this rapping we rose from the floor—we slept on straw pallets and each of us was covered with one thin blanket—and moved to the door of the cell. We peered through the opening into the center of the prison, which was, as I remember, three tiers high, all gray stone and gunmetal steel, precisely that prison I had seen in movies, except that, in the movies, I had not known that it was cold in prison. I had not known that when one's shoelaces and belt have been removed one is, in the strangest way, demoralized. The necessity of shuffling and the necessity of holding up one's trousers with one hand turn one into a rag doll. And the movies fail, of course, to give one any idea of what prison food is like. Along the corridor, at seven-thirty, came three men, each pushing before him a great garbage can, mounted on wheels. In the garbage can of the first was the bread—this was passed to one through the small opening in the door. In the can of the second was the coffee. In the can of the third was what was always called *la soupe*, a pallid paste of potatoes which had certainly been bubbling on the back of the prison stove long before that first, so momentous revolution. Naturally, it was cold by this time and, starving as I was, I could not eat it. I drank the coffee—which was not coffee—because it was hot, and spent the rest of the day, huddled in my blanket, munching on the bread. It was not the French bread one bought in bakeries. In the evening the same procession returned. At ten-thirty the lights went out. I had a recurring dream, each night, a nightmare which always involved my mother's fried chicken. At the moment I was about to eat it came the rapping at the door. Silence is really all I remember of those first three days, silence and the color gray.

I am not sure now whether it was on the third or the fourth day that I was taken to trial for the first time. The days had nothing, obviously, to distinguish them from one another. I remember that I was very much aware that Christmas Day was approaching and I wondered if I was really going to spend Christmas Day in prison. And I remember that the first trial came the day before Christmas Eve.

On the morning of the first trial I was awakened by hearing my name called. I was told, hanging in a kind of void between my mother's fried chicken and the cold prison floor, "*Vous préparez. Vous êtes extrait*"—which simply terrified me, since I did not know what interpretation to put on the word "*extrait*," and since my cellmates had been amusing themselves with me by telling terrible stories about the inefficiency of French prisons, an inefficiency so extreme that it had often happened that someone who was supposed to be taken out and tried found himself on the wrong line and was guillotined instead. The best way of putting my reaction to this is to say that, though I knew they were teasing me, it was simply not possible for me to totally *dis*believe them. As far as I was concerned, once in the hands of the law in France, anything could happen. I shuffled along with the others, who were *extrait* to the center of the prison, trying, rather, to linger in the office, which seemed the only warm spot in the whole world, and found myself again in that dreadful wagon, and was carried again to the Ile de la Cité, this time to the Palais de Justice. The entire day, except for ten minutes, was spent in one of the cells, first waiting to be tried, then waiting to be taken back to prison.

For I was *not* tried that day. By and by I was handcuffed and led through the halls, upstairs to the courtroom where I found my New York friend. We were placed together, both stage-whisperingly certain that this was the end of our ordeal. Nevertheless, while I waited for our case to be called, my eyes searched the courtroom, looking for a face I knew, hoping, anyway, that there was someone there who knew *me*, who would carry to someone outside the news that I was in trouble. But there was no one I knew there and I had had time to realize that there was probably only one man in Paris who could help me, an American patent attorney for whom I had worked as an office boy. He could have helped me because he had a quite solid position and some prestige and would have testified that, while working for him, I had handled large sums of money regularly, which made it rather unlikely that I would stoop to trafficking in bedsheets. However, he was somewhere in Paris, probably at this very moment enjoying a snack and a glass of wine and as far as the possibility of reaching him was concerned, he might as well have been on Mars. I tried to watch the proceedings and to make my mind a blank. But the proceedings were not reassuring. The boy, for example, who had stolen the sweater *did* receive a six-month sentence. It seemed to me that all the sentences meted out that day were excessive; though, again, it seemed that all the people who were sentenced that day had made, or clearly were going to make, crime their career. This seemed to be the opinion of the judge, who scarcely looked at the prisoners or listened to them; it seemed to be the opinion of the prisoners, who scarcely bothered to speak in their own behalf; it seemed to be the opinion of the lawyers, state lawyers for the most part, who were defending them. The great impulse of the courtroom seemed to be to put these people where they could not be seen—and not because they were offended at the crimes, unless, indeed, they were offended that the crimes were so petty, but because they did not wish to know that their society could be counted on to produce, probably in greater and greater numbers, a whole body of people for whom crime was the only possible career. Any society inevitably produces its criminals, but a society at once rigid and unstable can do nothing whatever to alleviate the poverty of its lowest members, cannot present to the hypothetical young man at the crucial moment that so-well-advertised right path. And the fact, perhaps, that the French are the earth's least sentimental people and must also be numbered among the most proud aggravates the plight of their lowest, youngest, and unluckiest members, for it means that the idea of rehabilitation is scarcely real to them. I confess that this attitude on their part raises in me sentiments of exasperation, admiration, and despair, revealing as it does, in both the best and the worst sense, their renowned and spectacular hard-headedness.

Finally our case was called and we rose. We gave our names. At the point that it developed that we were American the proceedings ceased, a hurried consultation took place between the judge and what I took to be several lawyers. Someone called out for an interpreter. The arresting officer had forgotten to mention our nationalities and there was, therefore, no interpreter in the court. Even if our French had been better than it was we would not have been allowed to stand trial without an interpreter. Before I clearly understood what was happening, I was handcuffed again and led out of the courtroom. The trial had been set back for the 27th of December.

I have sometimes wondered if I would *ever* have got out of prison if it had not been for the older man who had been arrested for the mysterious petty larceny. He was acquitted that day and when he returned to the cell—for he could not be released until morning—he found me sitting numbly on the floor, having just been prevented, by the sight of a man, all blood, being carried back to *his* cell on a stretcher, from seizing the bars and screaming until they let me out. The sight of the man on the stretcher proved, however, that screaming would not do much for me. The petty-larceny man went around asking if he could do anything in the world outside for those he was leaving behind. When he came to me I, at first, responded, "No, nothing"—for I suppose I had by now retreated into the attitude, the earliest I remember, that of my father, which was simply (since I had lost his God) that nothing could help me. And I suppose I will remember with gratitude until I die the fact that the man now insisted: *"Mais, êtes-vous sûr?"* Then it swept over me that he was going *outside* and he instantly became my first contact since the Lord alone knew how long with the outside world. At the same time, I remember, I did not really believe that he would help me. There was no reason why he should. But I gave him the phone number of my attorney friend and my own name.

So, in the middle of the next day, Christmas Eve, I shuffled downstairs again, to meet my visitor. He looked extremely well fed and sane and clean. He told me I had nothing to worry about any more. Only not even he could do anything to make the mill of justice grind any faster. He would, however, send me a lawyer of his acquaintance who would defend me on the 27th, and he would himself, along with several other people, appear as a character witness. He gave me a package of Lucky Strikes (which the turnkey took from me on the way upstairs) and said that, though it was doubtful that there would be any celebration in the prison, he would see to it that I got a fine Christmas dinner when I got out. And this, somehow, seemed very funny. I remember being astonished at the discovery that I was actually laughing. I was, too, I imagine, also rather disappointed that my hair had not turned white, that my face was clearly not going to bear any marks of tragedy, disappointed at bottom, no doubt, to realize, facing him in that room, that far worse things had happened to most people and that, indeed, to paraphrase my mother, if this was the worst thing that ever happened to me I could consider myself among the luckiest people ever to be born. He injected—my visitor—into my solitary nightmare common sense, the world, and the hint of blacker things to come.

The next day, Christmas, unable to endure my cell, and feeling that, after all, the day demanded a gesture, I asked to be allowed to go to Mass, hoping to hear some music. But I found myself, for a freezing hour and a half, locked in exactly the same kind of cubicle as in the wagon which had first brought me to prison, peering through a slot placed at the level of the eye at an old Frenchman, hatted, overcoated, muffled, and gloved, preaching in this language which I did not understand, to this row of wooden boxes, the story of Jesus Christ's love for men.

The next day, the 26th, I spent learning a peculiar kind of game, played with match-sticks, with my cellmates. For, since I no longer felt that I would stay in this cell forever, I was beginning to be able to make peace with it for a time. On the 27th I went again to trial and, as had been predicted, the case against us was dismissed. The story of the *drap de lit*, finally told, caused great merriment in the courtroom, whereupon my friend decided that the French were "great." I was chilled by their merriment, even though it was meant to warm me. It could only remind me of the laughter I had often heard at home, laughter which I had sometimes deliberately elicited. This laughter is the laughter of those who consider themselves to be at a safe remove from all the wretched, for whom the pain of the living is not real. I had heard it so often in my native land that I had resolved to find a place where I would never hear it any more. In some deep, black, stony, and liberating way, my life, in my own eyes, began during that first year in Paris, when it was borne in on me that this laughter is universal and never can be stilled.

1955

Questions

1. Early in the essay Baldwin comments that "no people come into posses-
    sion of a culture without having paid a heavy price for it." What price
    have the French paid? What is Baldwin's general view of French society
    and character? Does he find American society preferable to French?
2. Describe the progression of emotional attitudes through which Baldwin
    passes as "l'affaire du drap de lit" unfolds.
3. Baldwin possesses a unique ability to characterize a person in a few
    descriptive strokes, as, for example, in his portrait of the hotel-keeper's
    daughter: "an extremely hardheaded 'tricoteuse'—the inclination of
    "her" head was chilling and abrupt, like the downbeat of an ax. . . ."
    Point to other examples of Baldwin's concise characterizations.
4. What weapons for dealing with legal authority in New York did Baldwin
    find himself deprived of in Paris? What does he mean when he writes
    that "my color . . . in the United States, had often, odd as it may sound,
    been my salvation. . . ."?
5. Speaking of the American attorney who secured his liberty, Baldwin
    writes: "He injected—my visitor—into my solitary nightmare common
    sense, the world, and the hint of blacker things to come." What are the
    "blacker things to come" and why does the American attorney, in par-
    ticular, provide a hint of them?
6. Why was Baldwin living in Paris? What did the incident teach him about
    escape?

Langston Hughes
Dinner Guest: Me

I know I am
The Negro Problem
Being wined and dined,
Answering the usual questions
That come to white mind   5
Which seeks demurely
To probe in polite way
The why and wherewithal
Of darkness U.S.A.—
Wondering how things got this way   10
In current democratic night,
Murmuring gently
Over *fraises du bois*,
"I'm so ashamed of being white."

The lobster is delicious,   15
The wine divine,
And center of attention
At the damask table, mine.
To be a Problem on
Park Avenue at eight   20
Is not so bad.
Solutions to the Problem,
Of course, wait.

1967

Questions

1. What is the meaning of "darkness U.S.A." in line 9?
2. Are the polite liberals who are "ashamed of being white" the only object of mockery in the poem?
3. How would you characterize the poem's tone?
4. Hughes is sometimes regarded as a "versifier" rather than a "poet." Do you agree with this assessment? What characteristics of diction, meter, and style distinguish this selection from the preceding poem by Gwendolyn Brooks?

Eldridge Cleaver
The Muhammad Ali-
Patterson Fight

It is tempting to say that the Muhammad Ali–Floyd Patterson fight
was an "internal affair" of the Negro people. But how could that be, if
it is true that both fighters and the boxing game itself, like everything
else in America, are more or less owned and controlled by whites? The
fight was, ideologically, a pivotal event, reflecting the consolidation of
certain psychic gains of the Negro revolution. However, the diplo-
matic fiction of the "internal affair," no longer operative in international
politics, is also inoperative here. Both black and white America,
looking on, were sucked into the vortex of the event, feeling somehow
a profound relationship to what was being enacted in that ring. They
knew that a triumph and a defeat were taking place with consequences
for America, transcending the fortunes of the two men squaring off
in the ring to test their strength.

The simplistic version of the fight bandied about in the press was
that there was a "white hope" and a "black hope" riding on this fight.

The white hope for a Patterson victory was, in essence, a counterrevolutionary desire to force the Negro, now in rebellion and personified in the boxing world by Ali, back into his "place." The black hope, on the contrary, was to see Lazarus crushed, to see Uncle Tom defeated, to be given symbolic proof of the victory of the autonomous Negro over the subordinate Negro.

The broad support for Muhammad Ali among Negroes had nothing to do with the black Muslims' racist ideology. Even the followers of the late beloved Malcolm X, many of whom despise Muhammad Ali for the scurvy remarks he made about the fallen Malcolm, nevertheless favored him over Patterson as the lesser of two evils—because Ali was more in harmony with the furious psychic stance of the Negro today, while Patterson was an anachronism light years behind. In time of war, in the very center of the battle, the man of peace cannot command the ear of his people and he loses ground to the man of war. The revolutionary rage in the black man's soul today, which boiled over and burned Watts to the ground, means nothing if it doesn't mean business, and it was focused in cold, deadly hatred and contempt upon Floyd Patterson and the boot-licking art of the puppet in the style of his image.

There is no doubt that white America will accept a black champion, applaud and reward him, as long as there is no "white hope" in sight. But what white America demands in her black champions is a brilliant, powerful body and a dull, bestial mind—a tiger in the ring and a pussy-cat outside the ring. It is a hollow, cruel mockery to crown a man king in the boxing ring and then shove him about outside, going so far as to burn a cross on his front doorstep, as whites did when Floyd Patterson tried to integrate a neighborhood. "A man's home is his castle" is a saying not meant for Negroes; a Negro's castle exists only in his mind. And for a black king of boxing the boundaries of his kingdom are sharply circumscribed by the ropes around the ring. A slave in private life, a king in public—this is the life that every black champion has had to lead—until the coming of Muhammad Ali.

Muhammad Ali is the first "free" black champion ever to confront white America. In the context of boxing, he is a genuine revolutionary, the black Fidel Castro of boxing. To the mind of "white" white America, and "white" black America, the heavyweight crown has fallen into enemy hands, usurped by a pretender to the throne. Muhammad Ali is conceived as "occupying" the heavyweight kingdom in the name of a dark, alien power, in much the same way as Castro was conceived as a temporary interloper "occupying" Cuba. It made no difference that, when Patterson announced that he would beat Ali and return the crown to America, Ali protested vigorously, asking, "What does he mean? I'm an American too!" Floyd Patterson was the symbolic spearhead of a counterrevolutionary host, leader of the mythical legions of faithful darkies who inhabit the white imagination, whose assigned task it was to liberate the crown and restore it to its proper "place" in the Free World. Muhammad Ali, in crushing the Rabbit in twelve—after punishing him at will so there could be no doubt, so that the sports writers could not rob him of his victory on paper—inflicted a psychological chastisement on "white" white America similar in shock value to Fidel Castro's at the Bay of Pigs. If the Bay of Pigs can be seen as a straight right hand to the psychological jaw of white America, then Las Vegas was a perfect left hook to the gut.

Essentially, every black champion until Muhammad Ali has been a puppet, manipulated by whites in his private life to control his public image. His role was to conceal the strings from which he was suspended, so as to appear autonomous and self-motivated before the public. But with the coming of Muhammad Ali, the puppet-master was left with a handful of strings to which his dancing doll was no longer attached. For every white man, feeling himself superior to every black man, it was a serious blow to his self-image; because Muhammad Ali, by the very fact that he leads an autonomous private life, cannot fulfill the psychological needs of whites.

The heavyweight champion is a symbol of masculinity to the American male. And a black champion, as long as he is firmly fettered in his private life, is a fallen lion at every white man's feet. Through a curious psychic mechanism, the puniest white man experiences himself as a giant-killer, as a superman, a great white hunter leading a gigantic ape, the black champion tamed by the white man, around on a leash. But when the ape breaks away from the leash, beats with deadly fists upon his massive chest and starts talking to boot, proclaiming himself to be the greatest, spouting poetry, and annihilating every gunbearer the white hunter sics on him (the white hunter not being disposed to crawl into the ring himself), a very serious slippage takes place in the white man's self-image—*because that by which he defined himself no longer has a recognizable identity.* "If that black ape is a man," the white hunter asks himself, "then what am I?"

It was Sonny Liston who marked the coming of the autonomous Negro to boxing. But he was nonideological and so the scandal he caused could be handled, albeit with difficulty and pain. The mystique he exuded was that of a lone wolf who did not belong to his people or speak for them. He was for Liston and spoke only for Liston, and this was not out of harmony with the competitive ethic undergirding American culture. If every man is for himself, it was rational for Liston to be for *himself*. Although even this degree of autonomy in a Negro was bitterly resented, white America could tolerate it with less hysteria, with less of a sense of being threatened. But when the ideological Negro seized the heavyweight crown, no front of cool could conceal the ferocious emotional eruption in white America and among the embarrassed Uncle Toms, who were also experiencing an identity crisis. Yes, even old faithful Uncle Tom has a self-image. All men must have one or they start seeing themselves as women, women start seeing them as women, then women lose their own self-image, and soon nobody knows what they are themselves or what anyone else is—that is to say, the world starts looking precisely as it looks today. For there to be so deep an uproar over Muhammad Ali should indicate that there is something much more serious than a boxing title at stake, something cutting right to the center of the madness of our time.

The New Testament parable of Jesus raising Lazarus from the dead is interpreted by the Black Muslims as a symbolic parallel to the history of the Negro in America. By capturing black men in Africa and bringing them to slavery in America, the white devils *killed* the black man—killed him mentally, culturally, spiritually, economically, politically, and morally—transforming him into a "Negro," the symbolic Lazarus left in the "graveyard" of segregation and second-class citizenship. And just as Jesus was summoned to the cave to raise Lazarus from the dead, Elijah Muhammad had been summoned by God to lift up the modern Lazarus, the Negro, from his grave.

"Come out of her, my people!" cries Elijah Muhammad.

Cassius Clay, shedding his graveyard identity like an old dead skin, is one who heeded Elijah's call, repudiating the identity America gave him and taking on a new identity—Muhammad Ali. Floyd Patterson did not heed Elijah.

The America out of which Elijah Muhammad calls his people is indeed doomed, crumbling, burning, if not by the hand of God then by the hand of man, and this doomed America was partly buried in the boxing ring at Las Vegas when Muhammad Ali pounded a die-hard Lazarus into submission. With the America that is disappearing, the Lazarus-man created in the crucible of its hatred and pain is also vanishing. The victory of Muhammad Ali over Floyd Patterson marks the victory of a New World over an Old World, of life and light over Lazarus and the darkness of the grave. This is America recreating itself out of its own ruins. The pain is mighty for every American, black or white, because the task is gigantic and by no means certain of fulfillment. But there are strong men in this land and they will not be denied. Their task will not be ended until both Paul Bunyan and John Henry can look upon themselves and each other as men, the strength in the image of the one not being at the expense of the other.

Harsh, brutal, and vicious though it may be, no one can deny Muhammad Ali his triumph, and though you comb the ghettos of your desperate cities and beat the bushes of your black belts for another puppet who will succeed where the Rabbit failed, your search will be in vain. Because even as you search you, yourself, are being changed, and you will understand that you must continue to change or die. Yes, the Louisville Lip is a loudmouthed braggart. Yes, he is a Black Muslim racist, staunch enough in the need of his beliefs to divorce his wife for not adopting his religion; and firing his trainer, who taught him to "float like a butterfly and sting like a bee," for the same reason. But he is also a "free" man, determined not to be a white man's puppet even though he fights to entertain them; determined to be autonomous in his private life and a true king of his realm in public, and he is exactly that. A racist Black Muslim heavyweight champion is a bitter pill for racist white America to swallow. Swallow it—or throw the whole bit up, and hope that in the convulsions of your guts, America, you can vomit out the poisons of hate which have led you to a dead end in this valley of the shadow of death.

1968

Topics for General Discussion
and Written Reports on Chapter Two

1. Discuss the masks or protective self-images adopted by Negroes in the selections by Chesnutt, Dunbar, Crane, and Baldwin. What similarities do you find in these masks? What differences?

2. Contrast the response of the white world to Negro masks as it is reflected in the pieces by Chesnutt, Crane, Brooks, Hughes, and Cleaver. Which author seems most optimistic about the ability of whites to overcome the need for stereotyped preconceptions in dealing with blacks? Which writer appears to be most pessimistic?

3. Can you trace chronological changes in the approach to the topic of racial masks as reflected in these selections? What differences between the nineteenth-century selections by Chesnutt and Dunbar and the more modern pieces by Baldwin and Hughes might be attributed to changes in the prevailing popular American attitude toward race relations?

4. Write an essay in which you discuss the question of whether mask-wearing is a uniquely racial problem or whether it reflects some more universal problems of the human condition. You might also discuss some of the masks and images worn by college students.

Chapter Three
Brutality

THE LYNCHING

SILHOUETTE

THE SWIMMERS

THE CHICAGO "DEFENDER" SENDS A MAN
TO LITTLE ROCK, FALL, 1957

NIGHTMARE

Claude McKay
The Lynching

His spirit in smoke ascended to high heaven.
His father, by the cruelest way of pain,
Had bidden him to his bosom once again;
The awful sin remained still unforgiven.
All night a bright and solitary star   5
(Perchance the one that ever guided him,
Yet gave him up at last to Fate's wild whim)
Hung pitifully o'er the swinging char.
Day dawned, and soon the mixed crowds came to view
The ghastly body swaying in the sun: 10
The women thronged to look, but never a one
Showed sorrow in her eyes of steely blue;
And little lads, lynchers that were to be,
Danced round the dreadful thing in fiendish glee.

1922

From *Selected Poems of Claude McKay*, Twayne Publishers, Inc. Used by permission of the publisher.

Langston Hughes
Silhouette

Southern gentle lady,
Do not swoon.
They've just hung a black man
In the dark of the moon.

They've hung a black man   5
To a roadside tree
In the dark of the moon
For the world to see
How Dixie protects
Its white womanhood.   10

Southern gentle lady,
    Be good!
    Be good!

1948

Questions

1. Point out the words in McKay's poem which associate the black lynch victim with God. What terms in the poem associate whites with a counter force? Is the black victim intended to be seen as a Christ figure?
2. What is Hughes' essential attitude toward white Southern womanhood? How does his view of white womanhood compare with that found in McKay's "The Lynching"?
3. When, at the poem's conclusion, Hughes tells the white lady: "Be good! / Be good!" would you say he is advising her, enjoining her, or imploring her? What is the purpose of the last three lines?
4. Which poem do you think would be more effective in enlisting white support for such Congressional efforts as the Dyer Anti-Lynching Bill of 1922? Are these essentially propaganda poems or do they have other purposes to fulfill?

Allen Tate
The Swimmers

SCENE: *Montgomery County,*
Kentucky, July 1911

Kentucky water, clear springs: a boy fleeing
   To water under the dry Kentucky sun,
   His four little friends in tandem with him, seeing

Long shadows of grapevine wriggle and run
   Over the green swirl; mullein under the ear   5
   Soft as Nausicaä's palm; sullen fun

Savage as childhood's thin harmonious tear:
   O fountain, bosom source undying-dead
   Replenish me the spring of love and fear

And give me back the eye that looked and fled   10
   When a thrush idling in the tulip tree
   Unwound the cold dream of the copperhead.

—Along the creek the road was winding; we
  Felt the quicksilver sky. I see again
  The shrill companions of that odyssey: 15

Bill Eaton, Charlie Watson, "Nigger" Layne
  The doctor's son, Harry Duèsler who played
  The flute; and Tate, with water on the brain.

Dog-days: the dusty leaves where rain delayed
  Hung low on poison-oak and scuppernong,   20
  And we were following the active shade

Of water, that bells and bickers all night long.
  "No more'n a mile," Layne said. All five stood still.
  Listening, I heard what seemed at first a song;

Peering, I heard the hooves come down the hill.   25
  The posse passed, twelve horse; the leader's face
  Was worn as limestone on an ancient sill.

Then, as sleepwalkers shift from a hard place
  In bed, and rising to keep a formal pledge
  Descend a ladder into empty space,   30

We scuttled down the bank below a ledge
  And marched stiff-legged in our common fright
  Along a hog-track by the riffle's edge:

Into a world where sound shaded the sight
  Dropped the dull hooves again; the horsemen came   35
  Again, all but the leader. It was night

Momently and I feared: eleven same
  Jesus-Christers unmembered and unmade,
  Whose Corpse had died again in dirty shame.

The bank then levelling in a speckled glade,   40
  We stopped to breathe above the swimming-hole;
  I gazed at its reticulated shade

Recoiling in blue fear, and felt it roll
  Over my ears and eyes and lift my hair
  Like seaweed tossing on a sunk atoll.   45

I rose again. Borne on the copper air
  A distant voice green as a funeral wreath
  Against a grave: "That dead nigger there."

The melancholy sheriff slouched beneath
    A giant sycamore; shaking his head   50
    He plucked a sassafras twig and picked his teeth:

"We come too late." He spoke to the tired dead
    Whose ragged shirt soaked up the viscous flow
    Of blood in which It lay discomfited.

A butting horse-fly gave one ear a blow   55
    And glanced off, as the sheriff kicked the rope
    Loose from the neck and hooked it with his toe

Away from the blood.—I looked back down the slope:
    The friends were gone that I had hoped to greet.—
    A single horseman came at a slow lope   60

And pulled up at the hanged man's horny feet;
    The sheriff noosed the feet, the other end
    The stranger tied to his pommel in a neat

Slip-knot. I saw the Negro's body bend
    And straighten, as a fish-line cast transverse   65
    Yields to the current that it must subtend.

The sheriff's Goddamn was a murmured curse
    Not for the dead but for the blinding dust
    That boxed the cortège in a cloudy hearse

And dragged it towards our town. I knew I must   70
    Not stay till twilight in that silent road;
    Sliding my bare feet into the warm crust,

I hopped the stonecrop like a panting toad
    Mouth open, following the heaving cloud
    That floated to the court-house square its load   75

Of limber corpse that took the sun for shroud.
    There were three figures in the dying sun
    Whose light were company where three was crowd.

My breath crackled the dead air like a shotgun
    As, sheriff and the stranger disappearing,   80
    The faceless head lay still. I could not run

Or walk, but stood. Alone in the public clearing
    This private thing was owned by all the town,
    Though never claimed by us within my hearing.

1952

Questions

1. Identify the verse form employed by Tate.
2. What words and images does Tate employ to emphasize the contrast between the innocent swimming party and the brutal lynch party? What human link between the two parties is suggested in the words "sullen fun / Savage as childhood's thin harmonious tear" (lines 6-7)?
3. Nausicaä in line 6 was a princess who assisted Odysseus, and in line 15 Tate uses the term "that odyssey." In what sense was the young speaker involved in an odyssey?
4. What is "the cold dream of the copperhead" in line 12?
5. What references does Tate employ to associate the lynching with the crucifixion of Christ?
6. What is the boy's attitude toward the town in the last stanza? How would you sum up the boy's response to the whole experience described in the poem?

Gwendolyn Brooks

The Chicago *Defender* Sends a Man to Little Rock, Fall, 1957

In Little Rock the people bear
Babes, and comb and part their hair
And watch the want ads, put repair
To roof and latch. While wheat toast burns
A woman waters multiferns.   5

Time upholds or overturns
The many, tight, and small concerns.

In Little Rock the people sing
Sunday hymns like anything,
Through Sunday pomp and polishing.   10
And after testament and tunes,
Some soften Sunday afternoons
With lemon tea and Lorna Doones.

I forecast
And I believe   15
Come Christmas Little Rock will cleave
To Christmas tree and trifle, weave,
From laugh and tinsel, texture fast.

In Little Rock is baseball; Barcarolle.
That hotness in July . . . the uniformed figures raw and
        implacable   20
And not intellectual,
Batting the hotness or clawing the suffering dust.
The Open Air Concert, on the special twilight green . . .
When Beethoven is brutal or whispers to ladylike air.
Blanket-sitters are solemn, as Johann troubles to lean   25
To tell them what to mean . . .
There is love, too, in Little Rock. Soft women softly
Opening themselves in kindness,
Or, pitying one's blindness,
Awaiting one's pleasure   30
In Azure
Glory with anguished rose at the root . . .
To wash away old semidiscomfitures.
They reteach purple and unsullen blue.
The wispy soils go. And uncertain   35
Half-havings have they clarified to sures.

In Little Rock they know
Not answering the telephone is a way of rejecting life,
That it is our business to be bothered, is our business
To cherish bores or boredom, be polite   40
To lies and love and many-faceted fuzziness.

I scratch my head, massage the hate-I-had.
I blink across my prim and pencilled pad.
The saga I was sent for is not down.
Because there is a puzzle in this town.   45
The biggest News I do not dare
Telegraph to the Editor's chair:
"They are like people everywhere."
The angry Editor would reply
In hundred harryings of Why.   50

And true, they are hurling spittle, rock,
Garbage and fruit in Little Rock.
And I saw coiling storm a-writhe
On bright madonnas. And a scythe
Of men harassing brownish girls.   55
(The bows and barrettes in the curls
And braids declined away from joy.)

I saw a bleeding brownish boy . . .
The lariat lynch-wish I deplored.
The loveliest lynchee was our Lord.   60

1960

Questions

In 1957 Gwendolyn Brooks, first Negro poet to win the Pulitzer Prize, was sent by the Chicago "Defender," a leading Afro-American newspaper, to cover the crisis surrounding the integration of Little Rock, Arkansas public schools. The crisis involved widespread harassment of Negro children attempting to attend previously all-white schools and ultimately resulted in President Eisenhower's dispatching federal troops to preserve order in the city. Little Rock rapidly became an important symbol, integrationists seeing it as a symbol of federal determination to integrate public schools and segregationists seeing it as a symbol of stubborn resistance.

1. What "puzzle in this town" (line 45) did Miss Brooks discover?
2. What is the relevance of the concluding line to the entire poem? What previous religious references do you find in the poem? Does the last line help to explain Miss Brooks' ambivalent attitude toward the people of Little Rock?
3. What is the meaning of lines 53-54: "And I saw coiling storm a-writhe / On bright madonnas"? Why doesn't Miss Brook employ racial designations when she speaks of the people of Little Rock and their values or when she describes those who harass "brownish girls" (line 55)? How would you characterize her general attitude towards whites? Is it indignant? puzzled? hurt? forgiving?
4. What is the meaning of stanza 7 (lines 37-47)? Is this section of the poem concerned with specifically white values?

Malcolm X
excerpt from "Nightmare" in the Autobiography of Malcolm X

When my mother was pregnant with me, she told me later, a party of hooded Ku Klux Klan riders galloped up to our home in Omaha, Nebraska, one night. Surrounding the house, brandishing their shotguns and rifles, they shouted for my father to come out. My mother went to the front door and opened it. Standing where they could see her pregnant condition, she told them that she was alone with her three small children, and that my father was away, preaching, in Milwaukee. The Klansmen shouted threats and warnings at her that we had better get out of town because "the good Christian white people" were not going to stand for my father's "spreading trouble" among the "good" Negroes of Omaha with the "back to Africa" preachings of Marcus Garvey.

My father, the Reverend Earl Little, was a Baptist minister, a dedicated organizer for Marcus Aurelius Garvey's U.N.I.A. (Universal Negro Improvement Association). With the help of such disciples as my father, Garvey, from his headquarters in New York City's Harlem, was raising the banner of black-race purity and exhorting the Negro masses to return to their ancestral African homeland—a cause which had made Garvey the most controversial black man on earth.

Still shouting threats, the Klansmen finally spurred their horses and galloped around the house, shattering every window pane with their gun butts. Then they rode off into the night, their torches flaring, as suddenly as they had come.

My father was enraged when he returned. He decided to wait until I was born—which would be soon—and then the family would move. I am not sure why he made this decision, for he was not a frightened Negro, as most then were, and many still are today. My father was a big, six-foot-four, very black man. He had only one eye. How he had lost the other one I have never known. He was from Reynolds, Georgia, where he had left school after the third or maybe fourth grade. He believed, as did Marcus Garvey, that freedom, independence and self-respect could never be achieved by the Negro in America, and that therefore the Negro should leave America to the white man and return to his African land of origin. Among the reasons my father had decided to risk and dedicate his life to help disseminate this philosophy among his people was that he had seen four of his six brothers die by violence, three of them killed by white men, including one by lynching. What my father could not know then was that the remaining three, including himself, only one, my Uncle Jim, would die in bed, of natural causes. Northern white police were later to shoot my Uncle Oscar. And my father was finally himself to die by the white man's hands.

It has always been my belief that I, too, will die by violence. I have done all that I can to be prepared.

I was my father's seventh child. He had three children by a previous marriage—Ella, Earl, and Mary, who lived in Boston. He had met and married my mother in Philadelphia, where their first child, my oldest full brother, Wilfred, was born. They moved from Philadelphia to Omaha, where Hilda and then Philbert were born.

I was next in line. My mother was twenty-eight when I was born on May 19, 1925, in an Omaha hospital. Then we moved to Milwaukee, where Reginald was born. From infancy, he had some kind of hernia condition which was to handicap him physically for the rest of his life.

Louise Little, my mother, who was born in Grenada, in the British West Indies, looked like a white woman. Her father *was* white. She had straight black hair, and her accent did not sound like a Negro's. Of this white father of hers, I know nothing except her shame about it. I remember hearing her say she was glad that she had never seen him. It was, of course, because of him that I got my reddish-brown "mariny" color of skin, and my hair of the same color. I was the lightest child in our family. (Out in the world later on, in Boston and New York, I was among the millions of Negroes who were insane enough to feel that it was some kind of status symbol to be light-complexioned —that one was actually fortunate to be born thus. But, still later, I learned to hate every drop of that white rapist's blood that is in me.)

Our family stayed only briefly in Milwaukee, for my father wanted to find a place where he could raise our own food and perhaps build a business. The teaching of Marcus Garvey stressed becoming independent of the white man. We went next, for some reason, to Lansing, Michigan. My father bought a house and soon, as had been his pattern, he was doing free-lance Christian preaching in local Negro Baptist churches, and during the week he was roaming about spreading word of Marcus Garvey.

He had begun to lay away savings for the store he had always wanted to own when, as always, some stupid local Uncle Tom Negroes began to funnel stories about his revolutionary beliefs to the local white people. This time, the get-out-of-town threats came from a local hate society called The Black Legion. They wore black robes instead of white. Soon, nearly everywhere my father went, Black Legionnaries were reviling him as an "uppity nigger" for wanting to own a store, for living outside the Lansing Negro district, for spreading unrest and dissension among "the good niggers."

As in Omaha, my mother was pregnant again, this time with my youngest sister. Shortly after Yvonne was born came the nightmare night in 1929, my earliest vivid memory. I remember being suddenly snatched awake into a frightening confusion of pistol shots and shouting and smoke and flames. My father had shouted and shot at the two white men who had set the fire and were running away. Our home was burning down around us. We were lunging and bumping and tumbling all over each other trying to escape. My mother, with the baby in her arms, just made it into the yard before the house crashed in, showering sparks. I remember we were outside in the night in our underwear, crying and yelling our heads off. The white police and firemen came and stood around watching as the house burned down to the ground.

My father prevailed on some friends to clothe and house us temporarily; then he moved us into another house on the outskirts of East Lansing. In those days Negroes weren't allowed after dark in East Lansing proper. There's where Michigan State University is located; I related all of this to an audience of students when I spoke there in January, 1963 (and had the first reunion in a long while with my younger brother, Robert, who was there doing postgraduate studies in psychology). I told them how East Lansing harassed us so much that we had to move again, this time two miles out of town, into the country. This was where my father built for us with his own hands a four-room house. This is where I really begin to remember things—this home where I started to grow up.

After the fire, I remember that my father was called in and questioned about a permit for the pistol with which he had shot at the white men who set the fire. I remember that the police was always dropping by our house, shoving things around, "just checking" or "looking for a gun." The pistol they were looking for—which they never found, and for which they wouldn't issue a permit—was sewed up inside a pillow. My father's .22 rifle and his shotgun, though, were right out in the open; everyone had them for hunting birds and rabbits and other game.

1965

Topics for General Discussion
and Written Reports on Chapter Three

1. With the exception of Tate's poem, all of the preceding accounts of brutal racial incidents are by Negroes. Discuss the varying authorial purposes you believe to be involved in these selections. It is obvious, for example, that McKay and Malcolm X are concerned chiefly with depicting the horror of the incident and indicting the inhumanity of white oppressors. But, while a similar aim may be involved in the selections by Hughes, Tate, and Brooks, it is also clear that these latter works have other purposes to fulfill.

2. Contrast the speaker's point of view in these selections. Does it seem relevant, for example, that the speaker in the Brooks poem is presumably a woman or that the incident in Tate's poem is seen from the point of view of a white boy?

3. Which one of the selections in Chapter Three seems most successful in depicting the horror and brutality of a racial incident? Discuss the details employed by the author to achieve a feeling of horror in the reader.

4. Which one of the preceding selections seems most successful in coming to grips with the motivation and outlook of the oppressor?

5. Which one of these works seems most ironic in outlook? Discuss evidence of irony in all the selections. Which selection appears to be the most bitter in outlook?

Chapter Four
If We Must Die

IF WE MUST DIE

A CONTRACT (FOR THE DESTRUCTION
AND REBUILDING OF PATERSON)

THE JOB

MALCOLM X

BLACK PANTHER

EVERYTHING THAT RISES MUST CONVERGE

CONCERNING VIOLENCE

Claude McKay
If We Must Die

If we must die—let it not be like hogs
Hunted and penned in an inglorious spot,
While round us bark the mad and hungry dogs,
Making their mock at our accursed lot.
If we must die—oh, let us nobly die,   5
So that our precious blood may not be shed
In vain; then even the monsters we defy
Shall be constrained to honor us though dead!
Oh, Kinsmen! We must meet the common foe;
Though far outnumbered, let us show us brave,   10
And for their thousand blows deal one deathblow!
What though before us lies the open grave?
Like men we'll face the murderous, cowardly pack,
Pressed to the wall, dying, but fighting back!

1922

From *Selected Poems of Claude McKay*, Twayne Publishers, Inc. Used by permission of the publisher.

Questions

1. What is McKay's chief concern in the poem? Is it the achievement of social justice? the denouncement of white oppression? or something else?
2. The poem was written in the 1920's, but what attitudes does it share with contemporary black militancy?
3. Black militants have sometimes been labeled "romanticists." Define the term "romanticism." Does the poem embody romantic elements?
4. Is the underlying philosophy offered by the poem appropriate to a context outside that of race relations?

LeRoi Jones

A Contract (for the destruction and rebuilding of Paterson)

Flesh, and cars, tar, dug holes beneath stone
a rude hierarchy of money, band saws cross out
music, feeling. Even speech, corrodes.
                         I came here
from where I sat boiling in my veins, cold fear   5
at the death of men, the death of learning, in
cold fear, at my own. Romantic vests of same death
blank at the corner, blank when they raise their fingers

Criss the hearts, in dark flesh staggered so marvelous
are their lies. So complete, their mastery, of these   10
stupid niggers. Loud spics kill each other, and will not

make the simple trip to Tiffany's. Will not smash their stainless
heads, against the simpler effrontery of so callous a code as gain.

You are no brothers, dirty woogies, dying under dried rinds, in
    massa's
droopy tuxedos. Cab Calloways of the soul, at the soul's juncture,   15
    a
music, they think will save them from our eyes. (In back of the
    terminal

where the circus will not go. At the backs of crowds, stooped
    and vulgar
breathing hate syllables, unintelligible rapes of all that linger in
our new world. Killed in white fedora hats, they stand so mute
    at what

whiter slaves did to my fathers. They muster silence. They pray   20
    at the
steps of abstract prisons, to be kings, when all is silence, when all
is stone. When even the stupid fruit of their loins is gold, or
    something
else they cannot eat.

1964

Questions

1. In his epic poem "Paterson," William Carlos Williams approaches that
    New Jersey city as a figure of the American "city of man." What signifi-
    cance is there in Jones' allusion to Williams' poem?
2. What is it that, according to the first stanza, has crossed out music and
    feeling and promoted death?
3. Who are the "dirty woogies" of line 14 and why does Jones refuse to
    acknowledge them as brothers?
4. In its approach to the ills of American society, is the poem nihilistic
    (consult a good dictionary for the meaning of this term) or does Jones
    recommend a positive course of action?
5. What difficulties do you encounter in reading this poem?

Ben Caldwell
The Job

Personnel interviewer, white
Applicant #1, negro woman
Applicant #2, negro man
Applicant #3, negro man
Applicant #4, negro woman
Applicant #5, negro man
Applicant #6, black man
Applicant #7, negro man (latecomer)

Scene 1. Bright lighted office interior. 8:45 A.M. is the time on the wall clock. A large white sign hangs from the light green wall, reading, "NEW YORK OFFICE FOR N.O.," in foot-high letters. Underneath, half the size, is "PROJECT NEGRO OPPORTUNITIES." A blond, blue-eyed male is seated at a grey steel desk. There is an unoccupied chair beside the desk. A tall file cabinet is close by. Six people stand in single file line. Pink filled-out application forms in their hands. First in line is a pretty dark-complexioned young lady. Straight-

First printed in *The Drama Review*, Volume 12, Number 4 (T40), Summer 1968. Copyright 1968 *The Drama Review*. Reprinted by permission. All rights reserved.

*ened hair gleaming. She wears a blue imitation leather coat, a brown
skirt, a pink blouse. Her facial expression is sad. Behind her, a young
man of about 20. He has on a black leather coat, white shirt, dark tie,
green corduroy trousers, brown suede shoes. He is trying so hard to
give the impression that he's cool, unconcerned, that he looks tense.
Like he's braced against a stiff wind. Behind him is a "cat" who would
be considered "clean" in the slang sense. His processed hair sparkles
electrically. He wears an olive green, continental cut, entertainer's
suit. Black patent leather shoes. The cuffs of his clean yellow shirt hang
far beneath his jacket sleeves. Large cuff links. Every now and then
he hums the melody of a current popular R & B tune, ("Cool Jerk")
and does a little step to relieve his boredom. Behind is a woman of
about 35. She has on a fur collared black wool coat, a printed scarf is
tied on her head. She looks bored, tired, disgusted. Behind her is a
slumped negro man who looks tired from years of hard life and working. He has worked in the clothes he's wearing. Behind him is a tall
black man. His hair long, bushy. His black sports coat is much too
small. His much-washed khaki trousers are too short. He has dirty
white sneakers on his big feet, he wears no sox. He carries a musical
instrument case (saxophone). Maybe he just seems big because the
clothes are not his. The line faces the blonde blue-eyed male. He ex-
amines and files some papers and cards from atop the desk. He then
looks up, nods, signaling the first applicant to come forward. She walks
to, and stands beside, the desk. The blonde stands to greet her, extending his hand.*

INTERVIEWER. Good-morning. Welcome to N.O. My name is Mr.
Foster. Won't you sit down. *They both sit. She hands him her application.* Before we begin I'd like to ask you some questions, and tell you
a little about N.O. Did the Welfare refer you to N.O.?

1, *southern accent.* Yes.

INTERVIEWER. Good. Now Project N.O. is a government sponsored
program designed to fill some of the gaps in our welfare programs.
Broad smile. We realize that just to offer financial assistance does not
solve or eliminate the problem. We realize that some of us have difficulty finding jobs because of educational limitations. The N.O. program
tackles both problems. We offer assistance—financial—and training so
that you may qualify for a better paying job. And with your newly
acquired skills you also achieve job security. Would you give me your
name, please?

1. May-ree Free-mun.

INTERVIEWER, *writing*. How old are you, Mary?

1. 20

INTERVIEWER. Are you married, Mary?

1. No.

INTERVIEWER. Do you have any children, Mary?

1. *Slightly indignant*. No, I don't.

INTERVIEWER. Do you live alone or with your folks, Mary?

1. I live with my folks.

INTERVIEWER. How far did you go in school?

1. I graduated.

INTERVIEWER. You mean from high school?

1. Yes.

INTERVIEWER. Where was that—I mean where did you go to school?

1. In Georgia.

INTERVIEWER. What part of Georgia? And the name of the school?

1. Backwoods, Georgia. And I went to Freeman Gosden-Charles Corell High.

INTERVIEWER. Oh, yes, I understand that's a very good school. Did you like going to school, Mary?

1, *shrugging shyly*. It was all right.

INTERVIEWER. Well, did you take any special courses?

1. No.

INTERVIEWER. What are some of your interests, Mary?

1, *puzzled*. *No answer*.

INTERVIEWER. I mean is there something you like to do more than anything else?

1. I like to cook. And sew. I used to want to be a artist.

INTERVIEWER, *scribbling in his note pad*. Oh, that's nice. What kind of work have you done in the past?

1. Factory.

INTERVIEWER. Did you like working in a factory?

1, *shrugs. Indecisive.*

INTERVIEWER. Do you like to work, Mary?

1. Yes, but the jobs didn't pay much money—and they was always layin' off.

INTERVIEWER. I see. Now what we're going to try to do for you is, first, have you tested. Then we're going to see if we can send you to a school—to learn how to cook and sew—so you can get a good job cooking or sewing. Something that you like to do. How does that sound to you?

1. Well, I already can sew good enough to get a job, I just wan . . .

INTERVIEWER. Wait a minute. While you're going to school the government will pay you a salary until you graduate. Ah, you're smiling. I guess it makes you happy to know that things aren't so hopeless after all! *Big Smile.* Yes, N.O. is here to give hope to the hopeless. To give you a second chance for that chance you missed. *Pause.* Now, Mary, I want you to sign these two papers.

He waits while she signs. Meanwhile, on the line, the woman looks, impatiently, at her watch. Asks an unheard question of the man in front of her. The strange man on the end of the line (#6) drops a wrapped object, accidently. It makes a loud metallic ring. He picks it up, unzips the instrument bag, and places the object inside . . .

INTERVIEWER. Now I want you to take this card and go to this address, tomorrow, 9 A.M., to be tested. Then you come back here to see me Wednesday. I hope we've helped you on the way to an everlasting job. Good luck!

1. Thank you.

She gets up to leave. Her disposition changed from the earlier gloom. The men turn to watch her walk out. One of the men makes a remark to her as she passes. She conspicuously ignores him. The INTERVIEWER *writes and files. Then signals the next applicant to come forward.*

Scene 2. The INTERVIEWER *is finishing with the next-to-last applicant. The wall clock states 11:40.*

INTERVIEWER. Now I'm sure that once you finish the training and get a good job—a good *steady* job—you and your wife won't fight, and she won't have to call the cops on you. Ha, ha, ha, ha, ha! Okay, Sam?

5. Ha, ha. Yeah, OK. Thank you fo' everything, Mr. Foster.

INTERVIEWER, *standing as the applicant does—extending his hand.* I want you to keep this job, Sam, so you can stay out of trouble. Okay?

5. Okay.

INTERVIEWER. Okay. Glad we could help you. Best of luck, Sam. *Sam nods his head and leaves.* INTERVIEWER *takes some papers to the file. Files them. Returns to desk to answer the phone.* Yes? Oh, hi Stan. No, not quite. So far only four or five. Got one more to go. Oh, you know, the usual. Yeh. What did you expect? Just another way of keeping them in line. Ha ha ha. Where're you having lunch? Oh, good, I'll meet you there in about 20 minutes. All right, bye.

He looks at the last applicant apprehensively, and motions him forward. He stands to greet him. Into the blonde's extended hand 6 shoves the application. They both sit.

INTERVIEWER. I'm sorry you had to wait so long, sir.

6. That's all right. We've waited so long a few more minutes don't matter.

The INTERVIEWER *looks puzzled at this reply, and more so when he looks at the application. He smiles a nervous smile. He gestures.*

INTERVIEWER. Sir, you haven't filled out your application.

6. I know.

INTERVIEWER. Why is that, sir?

6. There is no reason to fill it out.

INTERVIEWER. Aren't you looking for a job?

6. No. I have a job.

INTERVIEWER, *further puzzled and at a loss for words. The applicant's intense glare unnerves him even more. He makes a "conversation piece" of the instrument case.*

INTERVIEWER. You have a job? Oh! Are you a musician?

6. Yes.

INTERVIEWER, *trying to sound interested instead of uneasy.* Oh! What do you play.

6. I play the truth.

INTERVIEWER. The truth? Is that an instrument? I don't understand! . . . What is this? Is this some sort of joke?

6, *just stares at him.*

We're here to help you. There's no information on this application and there's nothing I can do if . . .

6. I don't want you to do anything. Or I should say "*we.*" I have a job. I'm doing what all my people should be doing.

INTERVIEWER. I don't understand you, but I have a job to do. What's your name, sir?

6. Just call me Black Nigger—that's what you'd like to do, Whitey!

INTERVIEWER, *excited.* I thought so! One of those "black nationalist" characters! Look here, I can understand your anger, and even your bitterness—and I sympathize—but what you're doing is unreasonable. You're doing nothing to help yourself or your people. We're here to help *you* people. We're doing all we can to change the shameful conditions that have existed for too long. People like you make things worse. Now if you came here for a job, good—if not . . .

6. *During the speech he places his instrument case on his lap and opens it. He places his hands on the instrument.* I told you I didn't come here to get a job. I have a job. I came to do a job. I FEEL LIKE PLAYING! *He rises, quickly, and swings the instrument, striking the* INTERVIEWER *on the head, it makes a loud thump. The* INTERVIEWER *screams, loudly. Blood is running down his face, onto his white shirt. He runs to the file cabinet and frantically rummages through the cards.*

INTERVIEWER, *hysterical.* Wait! Wait! I know I can find you something! A good job! A good paying, steady, job! You don't have to do this!

6. Yeah! I feel like playing! Like swinging! How you like this JAZZ!?

The applicant swings again, striking him on the arms and hands. He sounds like a preacher preaching a sermon. We should have done this long time ago! *All* niggers should be doing this! Instead of begging and being killed. Kiss your ass when they should be kicking your ass! And trying to be like you! Hoping you'd treat us as men. Hoping you'd stop killing us. Hoping you'd accept us! But all you offer is jobs! We want our freedom and all you offer is jobs and integration! You've turned us wrongside out! You forced me into this role! Your clothes don't fit me! Your ways don't fit me! I'm not myself! I'm not a killer. *Whop!* I can't be myself till the world is free of you! *Whop! His blow knocks the* INTERVIEWER *to his knees.* I tried and I waited. But all you want is for us to be your slaves! That's all you want! I won't be your slave! *Whop!* I must save myself!

INTERVIEWER, *bubbling, babbling, gurgling, blood-choked sounds!* Oh, god, don't let them kill me! Don't let them kill me! Please don't kill me. *Trying to move away, on his knees.*

6. God ain't gon' answer you—your god is dead!

INTERVIEWER. AAaaaaaaaaaaaaaaaaaaalp! Please, god!

6. Understand how it feels to be beaten! *Whop!* Understand how it feels to beg! *Whop!* Understand how it feels to hope when there's no hope! *Whop!* So many of us died waiting and hoping! Placing faith in your lies and promises! So many of us never even had reason to hope! They shoulda been doing this! *Whop!* Understand how it feels to have your life taken from you! *WHAM!* There's no hope for you! There's no hope for you now!

He strikes again just as the phone rings. He pulls the desk in front of the apparently dead body. He puts his instrument back into the case. The phone continues to ring. He hurries to leave and bumps into a young man entering.

7. Oh! Excuse me! Is anybody here?

6. There's no one here! There's no one here!

7, *looking around.* Must be out to lunch! I guess I'll wait. I don't have anything to do. And I need a job, bad!

6 exits. 7 stands waiting.

Curtain.

Recorded music: Charlie Parker's "Now is the Time."

1968

Questions

1. To what does Caldwell's title refer? What is the slang meaning of the word "job"?
2. What is the attitude of the white interviewer toward the Negro applicants? Is he merely obtuse or does the play suggest a more sinister character to his attitude toward Negroes? Why is the interviewer uneasy on first meeting Applicant Number Six?
3. Note the interviewer's use of pronouns. What point does Caldwell seem to be making with these pronouns? Why does Caldwell italicize the word "you" when the interviewer tells Applicant Number Six "We're here to help **you** people"?
4. On what grounds does Caldwell indict federal programs such as "Project Negro Opportunities"?
5. Analyze the various references to money. What significance does money have in the play?
6. What significance is there in the fact that Applicant Number Six wears ill-fitting clothes? What, specifically, is the job that Number Six already has?

Gwendolyn Brooks
Malcolm X

For Dudley Randall

Original.
Ragged-round.
Rich-robust.

He had the hawk-man's eyes.
We gasped. We saw the maleness.   5
The maleness raking out and making gutteral the air
and pushing us to walls.

And in a soft and fundamental hour
a sorcery devout and vertical
beguiled the world.   10

He opened us—
who was a key,

who was a man.

1967

Questions

1. What sounds are emphasized in the first section of the poem? What notion does the term "Ragged-round" suggest? What sounds are emphasized in the second section?

2. What personal characteristics of Malcolm X are contrasted between sections two and three? What is the meaning of "a sorcery devout and vertical" in line 9?

3. What is Miss Brooks' final estimate of Malcolm X? Does the poem endorse his black nationalism?

4. Does the brief selection from Malcolm X's "Autobiography" which concludes Chapter Three suggest any of the black leader's personal characteristics underscored in Miss Brooks' poem?

Langston Hughes
Black Panther

Pushed into the corner
Of the hobnailed boot,
Pushed into the corner of the
"I-don't-want-to-die" cry,
Pushed into the corner of   5
"I don't want to study war no more,"
Changed into "Eye for eye,"
The Panther in his desperate boldness
Wears no disguise,
Motivated by the truest   10
Of the oldest
Lies.

1967

Questions

1. What is meant by the term "the corner / Of the hobnailed boot" (lines 1-2)?
2. What does Hughes mean when he writes that "The Panther in his desperate boldness / Wears no disguise" (lines 8-9)?
3. What is "the truest / Of the oldest / Lies" (lines 10-12) that motivates the Black Panther?
4. Before his death in 1967 Langston Hughes was sometimes criticized by more militant spokesmen for being too "cool" or restrained in his approach to racial injustice. Do you think this poem validates that criticism?

Flannery O'Connor
Everything That Rises Must Converge

Her doctor had told Julian's mother that she must lose twenty pounds on account of her blood pressure, so on Wednesday nights Julian had to take her downtown on the bus for a reducing class at the Y. The reducing class was designed for working girls over fifty, who weighed from 165 to 200 pounds. His mother was one of the slimmer ones, but she said ladies did not tell their age or weight. She would not ride the buses by herself at night since they had been integrated, and because the reducing class was one of her few pleasures, necessary for her health, and *free*, she said Julian could at least put himself out to take her, considering all she did for him. Julian did not like to consider all she did for him, but every Wednesday night he braced himself and took her.

She was almost ready to go, standing before the hall mirror, putting on her hat, while he, his hands behind him, appeared pinned to the door frame, waiting like Saint Sebastian for the arrows to begin

Reprinted with the permission of Farrar, Strauss & Giroux, Inc. from *Everything That Rises Must Converge* by Flannery O'Connor. Copyright © 1961 by the Estate of Mary Flannery O'Connor.

piercing him. The hat was new and had cost her seven dollars and a half. She kept saying, "Maybe I shouldn't have paid that for it. No, I shouldn't have. I'll take it off and return it tomorrow. I shouldn't have bought it."

Julian raised his eyes to heaven. "Yes, you should have bought it," he said. "Put it on and let's go." It was a hideous hat. A purple velvet flap came down on one side of it and stood up on the other; the rest of it was green and looked like a cushion with the stuffing out. He decided it was less comical than jaunty and pathetic. Everything that gave her pleasure was small and depressed him.

She lifted the hat one more time and set it down slowly on top of her head. Two wings of gray hair protruded on either side of her florid face, but her eyes, sky-blue, were as innocent and untouched by experience as they must have been when she was ten. Were it not that she was a widow who had struggled fiercely to feed and clothe and put him through school and who was supporting him still, "until he got on his feet," she might have been a little girl that he had to take to town.

"It's all right, it's all right," he said. "Let's go." He opened the door himself and started down the walk to get her going. The sky was a dying violet and the houses stood out darkly against it, bulbous liver-colored monstrosities of a uniform ugliness though no two were alike. Since this had been a fashionable neighborhood forty years ago, his mother persisted in thinking they did well to have an apartment in it. Each house had a narrow collar of dirt around it in which sat, usually, a grubby child. Julian walked with his hands in his pockets, his head down and thrust forward and his eyes glazed with the determination to make himself completely numb during the time he would be sacrificed to her pleasure.

The door closed and he turned to find the dumpy figure, surmounted by the atrocious hat, coming toward him. "Well," she said, "you only live once and paying a little more for it, I at least won't meet myself coming and going."

"Some day I'll start making money," Julian said gloomily—he knew he never would—"and you can have one of those jokes whenever you take the fit." But first they would move. He visualized a place where the nearest neighbors would be three miles away on either side.

"I think you're doing fine," she said, drawing on her gloves. "You've only been out of school a year. Rome wasn't built in a day."

She was one of the few members of the Y reducing class who arrived in hat and gloves and who had a son who had been to college.

"It takes time," she said, "and the world is in such a mess. This hat looked better on me than any of the others, though when she brought it out I said, 'Take that thing back. I wouldn't have it on my head,' and she said, 'Now wait till you see it on,' and when she put it on me, I said, 'We-ull,' and she said, 'If you ask me, that hat does something for you and you do something for the hat, and besides,' she said, 'with that hat, you won't meet yourself coming and going.' "

Julian thought he could have stood his lot better if she had been selfish, if she had been an old hag who drank and screamed at him. He walked along, saturated in depression, as if in the midst of his martyrdom he had lost his faith. Catching sight of his long, hopeless, irritated face, she stopped suddenly with a grief-stricken look, and pulled back on his arm. "Wait on me," she said. "I'm going back to the house and take this thing off and tomorrow I'm going to return it. I was out of my head. I can pay the gas bill with that seven-fifty."

He caught her arm in a vicious grip. "You are not going to take it back," he said. "I like it."

"Well," she said, "I don't think I ought . . ."

"Shut up and enjoy it," he muttered, more depressed than ever.

"With the world in the mess it's in," she said, "it's a wonder we can enjoy anything. I tell you, the bottom rail is on the top."

Julian sighed.

"Of course," she said, "if you know who you are, you can go anywhere." She said this every time he took her to the reducing class. "Most of them in it are not our kind of people," she said, "but I can be gracious to anybody. I know who I am."

"They don't give a damn for your graciousness," Julian said savagely. "Knowing who you are is good for one generation only. You haven't the foggiest idea where you stand now or who you are."

She stopped and allowed her eyes to flash at him. "I most certainly do know who I am," she said, "and if you don't know who you are, I'm ashamed of you."

"Oh hell," Julian said.

"Your great-grandfather was a former governor of this state," she said. "Your grandfather was a prosperous landowner. Your grandmother was a Godhigh."

"Will you look around you," he said tensely, "and see where you are now?" and he swept his arm jerkily out to indicate the neighborhood, which the growing darkness at least made less dingy.

"You remain what you are," she said. "Your great-grandfather had a plantation and two hundred slaves."

"There are no more slaves," he said irritably.

"They were better off when they were," she said. He groaned to see that she was off on that topic. She rolled onto it every few days like a train on an open track. He knew every stop, every junction, every swamp along the way, and knew the exact point at which her conclusion would roll majestically into the station: "It's ridiculous. It's simply not realistic. They should rise, yes, but on their own side of the fence."

"Let's skip it," Julian said.

"The ones I feel sorry for," she said, "are the ones that are half white. They're tragic."

"Will you skip it?"

"Suppose we were half white. We would certainly have mixed feelings."

"I have mixed feelings now," he groaned.

"Well let's talk about something pleasant," she said. "I remember going to Grandpa's when I was a little girl. Then the house had double stairways that went up to what was really the second floor—all the cooking was done on the first. I used to like to stay down in the kitchen on account of the way the walls smelled. I would sit with my nose pressed against the plaster and take deep breaths. Actually the place belonged to the Godhighs but your grandfather Chestny paid the mortgage and saved it for them. They were in reduced circumstances," she said, "but reduced or not, they never forgot who they were."

"Doubtless that decayed mansion reminded them," Julian muttered. He never spoke of it without contempt or thought of it without longing. He had seen it once when he was a child before it had been sold. The double stairways had rotted and been torn down. Negroes were living it in. But it remained in his mind as his mother had known it. It appeared in his dreams regularly. He would stand on the wide porch, listening to the rustle of oak leaves, then wander through the high-ceilinged hall into the parlor that opened onto it and gaze at the worn rugs and faded draperies. It occurred to him that it was he, not she, who could have appreciated it. He preferred its thread-bare elegance to anything he could name and it was because of it that all the neighborhoods they had lived in had been a torment to him—whereas she had hardly known the difference. She called her insensitivity "being adjustable."

"And I remember the old darky who was my nurse, Caroline. There was no better person in the world. I've always had a great respect for my colored friends," she said. "I'd do anything in the world for them and they'd . . ."

"Will you for God's sake get off that subject?" Julian said. When he got on a bus by himself, he made it a point to sit down beside a Negro, in reparation as it were for his mother's sins.

"You're mighty touchy tonight," she said. "Do you feel all right?"

"Yes I feel all right," he said. "Now lay off."

She pursed her lips. "Well, you certainly are in a vile humor," she observed. "I just won't speak to you at all."

They had reached the bus stop. There was no bus in sight and Julian, his hands still jammed in his pockets and his head thrust forward, scowled down the empty street. The frustration of having to wait on the bus as well as ride on it began to creep up his neck like a hand. The presence of his mother was borne in upon him as she gave a pained sigh. He looked at her bleakly. She was holding herself very erect under the preposterous hat, wearing it like a banner of her imaginary dignity. There was in him an evil urge to break her spirit. He suddenly unloosened his tie and pulled it off and put it in his pocket.

She stiffened. "Why must you look like *that* when you take me to town?" she said. "Why must you deliberately embarrass me?"

"If you'll never learn where you are," he said, "you can at least learn where I am."

"You look like a—thug," she said.

"Then I must be one," he murmured.

"I'll just go home," she said. "I will not bother you. If you can't do a little thing like that for me . . ."

Rolling his eyes upward, he put his tie back on. "Restored to my class," he muttered. He thrust his face toward her and hissed, "True culture is in the mind, the *mind*," he said, and tapped his head, "the mind."

"It's in the heart," she said, "and in how you do things and how you do things is because of who you *are*."

"Nobody in the damn bus cares who you are."

"I care who I am," she said icily.

The lighted bus appeared on top of the next hill and as it approached they moved out into the street to meet it. He put his hand under her elbow and hoisted her up on the creaking step. She entered with a little smile, as if she were going into a drawing room where everyone had been waiting for her. While he put in the tokens, she sat down on one of the broad front seats for three which faced the aisle. A thin woman with protruding teeth and long yellow hair was sitting on the end of it. His mother moved up beside her and left room for Julian beside herself. He sat down and looked at the floor across the aisle where a pair of thin feet in red and white canvas sandals were planted.

His mother immediately began a general conversation meant to attract anyone who felt like talking. "Can it get any hotter?" she said and removed from her purse a folding fan, black with a Japanese scene on it, which she began to flutter before her.

"I reckon it might could," the woman with the protruding teeth said, "but I know for a fact my apartment couldn't get no hotter."

"It must get the afternoon sun," his mother said. She sat forward and looked up and down the bus. It was half filled. Everybody was white. "I see we have the bus to ourselves," she said. Julian cringed.

"For a change," said the woman across the aisle, the owner of the red and white canvas sandals. "I come on one the other day and they were thick as fleas—up front and all through."

"The world is in a mess everywhere," his mother said. "I don't know how we've let it get in this fix."

"What gets my goat is all those boys from good families stealing automobile tires," the woman with the protruding teeth said. "I told my boy, I said you may not be rich but you been raised right and if I ever catch you in any such mess, they can send you on to the reformatory. Be exactly where you belong."

"Training tells," his mother said. "Is your boy in high school?"

"Ninth grade," the woman said.

"My son just finished college last year. He wants to write but he's selling typewriters until he gets started," his mother said.

The woman leaned forward and peered at Julian. He threw her such a malevolent look that she subsided against the seat. On the floor across the aisle there was an abandoned newspaper. He got up and got it and opened it out in front of him. His mother discreetly continued the conversation in a lower tone but the woman across the aisle said in a loud voice, "Well that's nice. Selling typewriters is close to writing. He can go right from one to the other."

"I tell him," his mother said, "that Rome wasn't built in a day."

Behind the newspaper Julian was withdrawing into the inner compartment of his mind where he spent most of his time. This was a kind of mental bubble in which he established himself when he could not bear to be a part of what was going on around him. From it he could see out and judge but in it he was safe from any kind of penetration from without. It was the only place where he felt free of the general idiocy of his fellows. His mother had never entered it but from it he could see her with absolute clarity.

The old lady was clever enough and he thought that if she had started from any of the right premises, more might have been expected of her. She lived according to the laws of her own fantasy world, outside of which he had never seen her set foot. The law of it was to sacrifice herself for him after she had first created the necessity to do so by making a mess of things. If he had permitted her sacrifices, it was only because her lack of foresight had made them necessary. All of her life had been a struggle to act like a Chestny without the Chestny goods, and to give him everything she thought a Chestny ought to have; but since, said she, it was fun to struggle, why complain? And when you had won, as she had won, what fun to look back on the hard times! He could not forgive her that she had enjoyed the struggle and that she thought *she* had won.

What she meant when she said she had won was that she had brought him up successfully and had sent him to college and that he had turned out so well—good looking (her teeth had gone unfilled so that his could be straightened), intelligent (he realized he was too intelligent to be a success), and with a future ahead of him (there was of course no future ahead of him). She excused him gloominess on the grounds that he was still growing up and his radical ideas on his lack of practical experience. She said he didn't yet know a thing about "life," that he hadn't even entered the real world—when already he was as disenchanted with it as a man of fifty.

The further irony of all this was that in spite of her, he had turned out so well. In spite of going to only a third-rate college, he had, on his own initiative, come out with a first-rate education; in spite of growing up dominated by a small mind, he had ended up with a large one; in spite of all her foolish views, he was free of prejudice and unafraid to face facts. Most miraculous of all, instead of being blinded by love for her as she was for him, he had cut himself emotionally free of her and could see her with complete objectivity. He was not dominated by his mother.

The bus stopped with a sudden jerk and shook him from his meditation. A woman from the back lurched forward with little steps and barely escaped falling in his newspaper as she righted herself. She got off and a large Negro got on. Julian kept his paper lowered to watch. It gave him a certain satisfaction to see injustice in daily operation. It confirmed his view that with a few exceptions there was no one worth knowing within a radius of three hundred miles. The Negro was well dressed and carried a briefcase. He looked around and then sat down on the other end of the seat where the woman with the red and white canvas sandals was sitting. He immediately unfolded a newspaper and obscured himself behind it. Julian's mother's elbow at once prodded insistently into his ribs. "Now you see why I won't ride on these buses by myself," she whispered.

The woman with the red and white canvas sandals had risen at the same time the Negro sat down and had gone further back in the bus and taken the seat of the woman who had got off. His mother leaned forward and cast her an approving look.

Julian rose, crossed the aisle, and sat down in the place of the woman with the canvas sandals. From this position, he looked serenely across at his mother. Her face had turned an angry red. He stared at her, making his eyes the eyes of a stranger. He felt his tension suddenly lift as if he had openly declared war on her.

He would have liked to get in conversation with the Negro and to talk with him about art or politics or any subject that would be above the comprehension of those around them, but the man remained entrenched behind his paper. He was either ignoring the change of seating or had never noticed it. There was no way for Julian to convey his sympathy.

His mother kept her eyes fixed reproachfully on his face. The woman with the protruding teeth was looking at him avidly as if he were a type of monster new to her.

"Do you have a light?" he asked the Negro.

Without looking away from his paper, the man reached in his pocket and handed him a packet of matches.

"Thanks," Julian said. For a moment he held the matches foolishly. A NO SMOKING sign looked down upon him from over the door. This alone would not have deterred him; he had no cigarettes. He had quit smoking some months before because he could not afford it. "Sorry," he muttered and handed back the matches. The Negro lowered the paper and gave him an annoyed look. He took the matches and raised the paper again.

His mother continued to gaze at him but she did not take advantage of his momentary discomfort. Her eyes retained their battered look. Her face seemed to be unnaturally red, as if her blood pressure had risen. Julian allowed no glimmer of sympathy to show on his face. Having got the advantage, he wanted desperately to keep it and carry it through. He would have liked to teach her a lesson that would last her a while, but there seemed no way to continue the point. The Negro refused to come out from behind his paper.

Julian folded his arms and looked stolidly before him, facing her but as if he did not see her, as if he had ceased to recognize her existence. He visualized a scene in which, the bus having reached their stop, he would remain in his seat and when she said, "Aren't you going to get off?" he would look at her as at a stranger who had rashly addressed him. The corner they got off on was usually deserted, but it was well lighted and it would not hurt her to walk by herself the four blocks to the Y. He decided to wait until the time came and then decide whether or not he would let her get off by herself. He would have to be at the Y at ten to bring her back, but he could leave her wondering if he was going to show up. There was no reason for her to think she could always depend on him.

He retired again into the high-ceilinged room sparsely settled with large pieces of antique furniture. His soul expanded momentarily but then he became aware of his mother across from him and the vision shriveled. He studied her coldly. Her feet in little pumps dangled like a child's and did not quite reach the floor. She was training on him an exaggerated look of reproach. He felt completely detached from her. At that moment he could with pleasure have slapped her as he would have slapped a particularly obnoxious child in his charge.

He began to imagine various unlikely ways by which he could teach her a lesson. He might make friends with some distinguished Negro professor or lawyer and bring him home to spend the evening. He would be entirely justified but her blood pressure would rise to 300. He could not push her to the extent of making her have a stroke, and moreover, he had never been successful at making any Negro friends. He had tried to strike up an acquaintance on the bus with some of the better types, with ones that looked like professors or ministers or lawyers. One morning he had sat sown next to a distinguished-looking dark brown man who had answered his questions with a sonorous solemnity but who had turned out to be an undertaker. Another day he had sat down beside a cigar-smoking Negro with a diamond ring on his finger, but after a few stilted pleasantries, the Negro had rung the buzzer and risen, slipping two lottery tickets into Julian's hand as he climbed over him to leave.

He imagined his mother lying desperately ill and his being able to secure only a Negro doctor for her. He toyed with that idea for a few minutes and then dropped it for a momentary vision of himself participating as a sympathizer in a sit-in demonstration. This was possible but he did not linger with it. Instead, he approached the ultimate horror. He brought home a beautiful suspiciously Negroid woman. Prepare yourself, he said. There is nothing you can do about it. This is the woman I've chosen. She's intelligent, dignified, even good, and she's suffered and she hasn't thought it *fun*. Now persecute us, go ahead and persecute us. Drive her out of here, but remember, you're driving me too. His eyes were narrowed and through the indignation he had generated, he saw his mother across the aisle, purple-faced, shrunken to the dwarf-like proportions of her moral nature, sitting like a mummy beneath the ridiculous banner of her hat.

He was tilted out of his fantasy again as the bus stopped. The door opened with a sucking hiss and out of the dark a large, gaily dressed, sullen-looking colored woman got on with a little boy. The child, who might have been four, had on a short plaid suit and a Tyrolean hat with a blue feather in it. Julian hoped that he would sit down beside him and that the woman would push in beside his mother. He could think of no better arrangement.

As she waited for her tokens, the woman was surveying the seating possibilities—he hoped with the idea of sitting where she was least wanted. There was something familiar-looking about her but Julian could not place what it was. She was a giant of a woman. Her face was set not only to meet opposition but to seek it out. The downward tilt of her large lower lip was like a warning sign: DON'T TAMPER WITH ME. Her bulging figure was encased in a green crepe dress and her feet overflowed in red shoes. She had on a hideous hat. A purple velvet flap came down on one side of it and stood up on the other; the rest of it was green and looked like a cushion with the stuffing out. She carried a mammoth red pocketbook that bulged throughout as if it were stuffed with rocks.

To Julian's disappointment, the little boy climbed up on the empty seat beside his mother. His mother lumped all children, black and white, into the common category, "cute," and she thought little Negroes were on the whole cuter than little white children. She smiled at the little boy as he climbed on the seat.

Meanwhile the woman was bearing down upon the empty seat beside Julian. To his annoyance, she squeezed herself into it. He saw his mother's face change as the woman settled herself next to him and he realized with satisfaction that this was more objectionable to her than it was to him. Her face seemed almost gray and there was a look of dull recognition in her eyes, as if suddenly she had sickened at some awful confrontation. Julian saw that it was because she and the woman had, in a sense, swapped sons. Though his mother would not realize the symbolic significance of this, she would feel it. His amusement showed plainly on his face.

The woman next to him muttered something unintelligible to herself. He was conscious of a kind of bristling next to him, a muted growling like that of an angry cat. He could not see anything but the red pocketbook upright on the bulging green thighs. He visualized the woman as she had stood waiting for her tokens—the ponderous figure, rising from the red shoes upward over the solid hips, the mammoth bosom, the haughty face, to the green and purple hat.

His eyes widened.

The vision of the two hats, identical, broke upon him with the radiance of a brilliant sunrise. His face was suddenly lit with joy. He could not believe that Fate had thrust upon his mother such a lesson. He gave a loud chuckle so that she would look at him and see that he saw. She turned her eyes on him slowly. The blue in them seemed to have turned a bruised purple. For a moment he had an uncomfortable sense of her innocence, but it lasted only a second before principle rescued him. Justice entitled him to laugh. His grin hardened until it said to her as plainly as if he were saying aloud: Your punishment exactly fits your pettiness. This should teach you a permanent lesson.

Her eyes shifted to the woman. She seemed unable to bear looking at him and to find the woman preferable. He became conscious again of the bristling presence at his side. The woman was rumbling like a volcano about to become active. His mother's mouth began to twitch slightly at one corner. With a sinking heart, he saw incipient signs of recovery on her face and realized that this was going to strike her suddenly as funny and was going to be no lesson at all. She kept her eyes on the woman and an amused smile came over her face as if the woman were a monkey that had stolen her hat. The little Negro was looking up at her with large fascinated eyes. He had been trying to attract her attention for some time.

"Carver!" the woman said suddenly. "Come heah!"

When he saw that the spotlight was on him at last, Carver drew his feet up and turned himself toward Julian's mother and giggled.

"Carver!" the woman said. "You heah me? Come heah!"

Carver slid down from the seat but remained squatting with his back against the base of it, his head turned slyly around toward Julian's mother, who was smiling at him. The woman reached a hand across the aisle and snatched him to her. He righted himself and hung backwards on her knees, grinning at Julian's mother. "Isn't he cute?" Julian's mother said to the woman with the protruding teeth.

"I reckon he is," the woman said without conviction.

The Negress yanked him upright but he eased out of her grip and shot across the aisle and scrambled, giggling wildly, onto the seat beside his love.

"I think he likes me," Julian's mother said, and smiled at the woman. It was the smile she used when she was being particularly gracious to an inferior. Julian saw everything lost. The lesson had rolled off her like rain on a roof.

The woman stood up and yanked the little boy off the seat as if she were snatching him from contagion. Julian could feel the rage in her at having no weapon like his mother's smile. She gave the child a sharp slap across his leg. He howled once and then thrust his head into her stomach and kicked his feet against her shins. "Be-have," she said vehemently.

The bus stopped and the Negro who had been reading the newspaper got off. The woman moved over and set the little boy down with a thump between herself and Julian. She held him firmly by the knee. In a moment he put his hands in front of his face and peeped at Julian's mother through his fingers.

"I see yooooooooo!" she said and put her hand in front of her face and peeped at him.

The woman slapped his hand down. "Quit yo' foolishness," she said, "before I knock the living Jesus out of you!"

Julian was thankful that the next stop was theirs. He reached up and pulled the cord. The woman reached up and pulled it at the same time. Oh my God, he thought. He had the terrible intuition that when they got off the bus together, his mother would open her purse and give the little boy a nickel. The gesture would be as natural to her as breathing. The bus stopped and the woman got up and lunged to the front, dragging the child, who wished to stay on, after her. Julian and his mother got up and followed. As they neared the door, Julian tried to relieve her of her pocketbook.

"No," she murmured, "I want to give the little boy a nickel."

"No!" Julian hissed. "No!"

She smiled down at the child and opened her bag. The bus door opened and the woman picked him up by the arm and descended with him, hanging at her hip. Once in the street she set him down and shook him.

Julian's mother had to close her purse while she got down the bus step but as soon as her feet were on the ground, she opened it again and began to rummage inside. "I can't find but a penny," she whispered, "but it looks like a new one."

"Don't do it!" Julian said fiercely between his teeth. There was a streetlight on the corner and she hurried to get under it so that she could better see into her pocketbook. The woman was heading off rapidly down the street with the child still hanging backward on her hand.

"Oh little boy!" Julian's mother called and took a few quick steps and caught up with them just beyond the lamppost. "Here's a bright new penny for you," and she held out the coin, which shone bronze in the dim light.

The huge woman turned and for a moment stood, her shoulders lifted and her face frozen with frustrated rage, and stared at Julian's mother. Then all at once she seemed to explode like a piece of machinery that had been given one ounce of pressure too much. Julian saw the black fist swing out with the red pocketbook. He shut his eyes and cringed as he heard the woman shout. "He don't take nobody's pennies!" When he opened his eyes, the woman was disappearing down the street with the little boy staring wide-eyed over her shoulder. Julian's mother was sitting on the sidewalk.

"I told you not to do that," Julian said angrily. "I told you not to do that!"

He stood over her for a minute, gritting his teeth. Her legs were stretched out in front of her and her hat was on her lap. He squatted down and looked her in the face. It was totally expressionless. "You got exactly what you deserved," he said. "Now get up."

He picked up her pocketbook and put what had fallen out back in it. He picked the hat up off her lap. The penny caught his eye on the sidewalk and he picked that up and let it drop before her eyes into the purse. Then he stood up and leaned over and held his hands out to pull her up. She remained immobile. He sighed. Rising above them on either side were black apartment buildings, marked with irregular rectangles of light. At the end of the block a man came out of a door and walked off in the opposite direction. "All right," he said, "suppose somebody happens by and wants to know why you're sitting on the sidewalk?"

She took the hand and, breathing hard, pulled heavily up on it and then stood for a moment, swaying slightly as if the spots of light in the darkness were circling around her. Her eyes, shadowed and confused, finally settled on his face. He did not try to conceal his irritation. "I hope this teaches you a lesson," he said. She leaned forward and her eyes raked his face. She seemed trying to determine his identity. Then, as if she found nothing familiar about him, she started off with a headlong movement in the wrong direction.

"Aren't you going on to the Y?" he asked.

"Home," she muttered.

"Well, are we walking?"

For answer she kept going. Julian followed along, his hands behind him. He saw no reason to let the lesson she had had go without backing it up with an explantion of its meaning. She might as well be made to understand what had happened to her. "Don't think that was just an uppity Negro woman," he said. "That was the whole colored race which will no longer take your condescending pennies. That was your black double. She can wear the same hat as you, and to be sure," he added gratuitously (because he thought it was funny), "it looked better on her than it did on you. What all this means," he said, "is that the old world is gone. The old manners are obsolete and your graciousness is not worth a damn." He thought bitterly of the house that had been lost for him. "You aren't who you think you are," he said.

She continued to plow ahead, paying no attention to him. Her hair had come undone on one side. She dropped her pocketbook and took no notice. He stooped and picked it up and handed it to her but she did not take it.

"You needn't act as if the world had come to an end," he said, "because it hasn't. From now on you've got to live in a new world and face a few realities for a change. Buck up," he said, "it won't kill you."

She was breathing fast.

"Let's wait on the bus," he said.

"Home," she said thickly.

"I hate to see you behave like this," he said. "Just like a child. I should be able to expect more of you." He decided to stop where he was and make her stop and wait for a bus. "I'm not going any further," he said, stopping. "We're going on the bus."

She continued to go on as if she had not heard him. He took a few steps and caught her arm and stopped her. He looked into her face and caught his breath. He was looking into a face he had never seen before. "Tell Grandpa to come get me," she said.

He stared, stricken.

"Tell Caroline to come get me," she said.

Stunned, he let her go and she lurched forward again, walking as if one leg were shorter than the other. A tide of darkness seemed to be sweeping her from him. "Mother!" he cried. "Darling, sweetheart, wait!" Crumpling, she fell to the pavement. He dashed forward and fell at her side, crying, "Mamma, Mamma!" He turned her over. Her face was fiercely distorted. One eye, large and staring, moved slightly to the left as if it had become unmoored. The other remained fixed on him, raked his face again, found nothing and closed.

"Wait here, wait here!" he cried and jumped up and began to run for help toward a cluster of lights he saw in the distance ahead of him. "Help, help!" he shouted, but his voice was thin, scarcely a thread of sound. The lights drifted farther away the faster he ran and his feet moved numbly as if they carried him nowhere. The tide of darkness seemed to sweep him back to her, postponing from moment to moment his entry into the world of guilt and sorrow.

1961

Questions

1. Why is so much attention devoted to the hat worn by Julian's mother? Why does Julian insist that she not return it to the store where she had purchased it? What significance is there in the fact that the Negro woman who boards the bus wears a similar hat?
2. Who was Saint Sebastian, the saint to whom Julian compares himself at the story's outset? Where else in the story does the notion of martyrdom appear?
3. How would you describe Julian's estimate of his own character? Is this estimate markedly different from that which Miss O'Connor intends that the reader arrive at? Is Julian ever treated with irony by the author?
4. Discuss the characterization of Julian's mother. What unpleasant traits are emphasized in her description? Are there any admirable elements in her nature? Does she, as she contends, "know who I am"? Why does Julian resent his mother? Is he correct when he claims that he sees her with "complete objectivity"? Julian constantly speaks of "teaching her a lesson," but precisely what lesson does he want her to learn?
5. What is Julian's attitude toward Negroes? What reasons do you suspect lay behind the fact that "he had never been successful at making any Negro friends"?
6. What terms are used to characterize the Negro woman on the bus?

What in her description foreshadows the blow she administers at the story's conclusion? Why does she angrily insist that Carver, the Negro boy, "Come heah!"?

7.   What do you think the incident of the penny and the retaliation it provokes is intended to reveal? Do you think Miss O'Connor intends that the reader agree with Julian's summary: "What all this means . . . is that the old world is gone. The old manners are obsolete and your graciousness is not worth a damn"?

8.   What is the meaning of the story's concluding sentence?

Frantz Fanon
from "Concerning Violence" in *The Wretched of the Earth*

The colonial world is a world cut in two. The dividing line, the frontiers are shown by barracks and police stations. In the colonies it is
the policeman and the soldier who are the official, instituted go-be-
tweens, the spokesmen of the settler and his rule of oppression. In
capitalist societies the educational system, whether lay or clerical,
the structure of moral reflexes handed down from father to son, the
exemplary honesty of workers who are given a medal after fifty
years of good and loyal service, and the affection which springs from
harmonious relations and good behavior—all these aesthetic expressions of respect for the established order serve to create around
the exploited person an atmosphere of submission and of inhibition
which lightens the task of policing considerably. In the capitalist countries a multitude of moral teachers, counselors and "bewilderers"

Translated from the French by Constance Farrington. Reprinted by permission of Grove Press, Inc. Copyright © 1963 by Presence Africaine.

separate the exploited from those in power. In the colonial countries, on the contrary, the policeman and the soldier, by their immediate presence and their frequent and direct action maintain contact with the native and advise him by means of rifle butts and napalm not to budge. It is obvious here that the agents of government speak the language of pure force. The intermediary does not lighten the oppression, nor seek to hide the domination; he shows them up and puts them into practice with the clear conscience of an upholder of the peace; yet he is the bringer of violence into the home and into the mind of the native.

The zone where the natives live is not complementary to the zone inhabited by the settlers. The two zones are opposed, but not in the service of a higher unity. Obedient to the rules of pure Aristotelian logic, they both follow the principle of reciprocal exclusivity. No conciliation is possible, for of the two terms, one is superfluous. The settlers' town is a strongly built town, all made of stone and steel. It is a brightly lit town; the streets are covered with asphalt, and the garbage cans swallow all the leavings, unseen, unknown and hardly thought about. The settler's feet are never visible, except perhaps in the sea; but there you're never close enough to see them. His feet are protected by strong shoes although the streets of his town are clean and even, with no holes or stones. The settler's town is a well-fed town, an easygoing town; its belly is always full of good things. The settlers' town is a town of white people, of foreigners.

The town belonging to the colonized people, or at least the native town, the Negro village, the medina, the reservation, is a place of ill fame, peopled by men of evil repute. They are born there, it matters little where or how; they die there, it matters not where, nor how. It is a world without spaciousness; men live there on top of each other, and their huts are built one on top of the other. The native town is a hungry town, starved of bread, of meat, of shoes, of coal, of light. The native town is a crouching village, a town on its knees, a town wallowing in the mire. It is a town of niggers and dirty Arabs. The look that the native turns on the settler's town is a look of lust, a look of envy; it expresses his dream of possession—all manner of possession: to sit at the settler's table, to sleep in the settler's bed, with his wife if possible. The colonized man is an envious man. And this the settler knows very well; when their glances meet he ascertains bitterly, always on the defensive, "They want to take our place." It is true, for there is no native who does not dream at least once a day of setting himself up in the settler's place.

This world divided into compartments, this world cut in two is inhabited by two different species. The originality of the colonial context is that economic reality, inequality, and the immense difference of ways of life never come to mask the human realities. When you examine at close quarters the colonial context, it is evident that what parcels out the world is to begin with the fact of belonging to or not belonging to a given race, a given species. In the colonies the economic substructure is also a superstructure. The cause is the consequence; you are rich because you are white, you are white because you are rich. This is why Marxist analysis should always be slightly stretched every time we have to do with the colonial problem.

Everything up to and including the very nature of precapitalist society, so well explained by Marx, must here be thought out again. The serf is in essence different from the knight, but a reference to divine right is necessary to legitimize this statutory difference. In the colonies, the foreigner coming from another country imposed his rule by means of guns and machines. In defiance of his successful transplantation, in spite of his appropriation, the settler still remains a foreigner. It is neither the act of owning factories, nor estates, nor a bank balance which distinguishes the governing classes. The governing race is first and foremost those who come from elsewhere, those who are unlike the original inhabitants, "the others."

The violence which has ruled over the ordering of the colonial world, which has ceaselessly drummed the rhythm for the destruction of native social forms and broken up without reserve the systems of reference of the economy, the customs of dress and external life, that same violence will be claimed and taken over by the native at the moment when, deciding to embody history in his own person, he surges into the forbidden quarters. To wreck the colonial world is henceforward a mental picture of action which is very clear, very easy to understand and which may be assumed by each one of the individuals which constitute the colonized people. To break up the colonial world does not mean that after the frontiers have been abolished lines of communication will be set up between the two zones. The destruction of the colonial world is no more and no less than the abolition of one zone, its burial in the depths of the earth or its expulsion from the country.

The natives' challenge to the colonial world is not a rational confrontation of points of view. It is not a treatise on the universal, but the untidy affirmation of an original idea propounded as an absolute. The colonial world is a Manichean world. It is not enough for the settler

to delimit physically, that is to say with the help of the army and the police force, the place of the native. As if to show the totalitarian character of colonial exploitation the settler paints the native as a sort of
quintessence of evil.* Native society is not simply described as a society
lacking in values. It is not enough for the colonist to affirm that
those values have disappeared from, or still better never existed in, the
colonial world. The native is declared insensible to ethics; he represents not only the absence of values, but also the negation of values. He
is, let us dare to admit, the enemy of values, and in this sense he is
the absolute evil. He is the corrosive element, destroying all that comes
near him; he is the deforming element, disfiguring all that has to do
with beauty or morality; he is the depository of maleficent powers, the
unconscious and irretrievable instrument of blind forces. Monsieur
Meyer could thus state seriously in the French National Assembly that
the Republic must not be prostituted by allowing the Algerian people to become part of it. All values, in fact, are irrevocably poisoned
and diseased as soon as they are allowed in contact with the colonized
race. The customs of the colonized people, their traditions, their myths
—above all, their myths—are the very sign of that poverty of spirit
and of their constitutional depravity. That is why we must put the
DDT which destroys parasites, the bearers of disease, on the same level
as the Christian religion which wages war on embryonic heresies and
instincts, and on evil as yet unborn. The recession of yellow fever and
the advance of evangelization form part of the same balance sheet.
But the triumphant *communiqués* from the missions are in fact a source
of information concerning the implantation of foreign influences in
the core of the colonized people. I speak of the Christian religion, and
no one need be astonished. The Church in the colonies is the white people's Church, the foreigner's Church. She does not call the native to
God's ways but to the ways of the white man, of the master, of the
oppressor. And as we know, in this matter many are called but few
chosen.

At times this Manicheism goes to its logical conclusion and dehu-
manizes the native, or to speak plainly, it turns him into an animal. In
fact, the terms the settler uses when he mentions the native are zoologi-
cal terms. He speaks of the yellow man's reptilian motions, of the stink
of the native quarter, of breeding swarms, of foulness, of spawn, of
gesticulations. When the settler seeks to describe the native fully in
exact terms he constantly refers to the bestiary. The European rarely

* We have demonstrated the mechanism of this Manichean world in *Black Skin,
White Masks* (New York: Grove Press, 1967).

hits on a picturesque style; but the native, who knows what is in the mind of the settler, guesses at once what he is thinking of. Those hordes of vital statistics, those hysterical masses, those faces bereft of all humanity, those distended bodies which are like nothing on earth, that mob without beginning or end, those children who seem to belong to nobody, that laziness stretched out in the sun, that vegetative rhythm of life—all this forms part of the colonial vocabulary. General de Gaulle speaks of "the yellow multitudes" and François Mauriac of the black, brown, and yellow masses which soon will be unleashed. The native knows all this, and laughs to himself every time he spots an allusion to the animal world in the other's words. For he knows that he is not an animal; and it is precisely at the moment he realizes his humanity that he begins to sharpen the weapons with which he will secure its victory.

1961

Topics for General Discussion
and Written Reports on Chapter Four

1. What attitudes are shared by McKay, Jones, and Caldwell in regard to militancy? Where do they differ? Do you feel the selections by Jones, Caldwell, and Brooks could be regarded as positive responses to McKay's exhortation: "oh, let us nobly die"?

2. What criticisms of anger and militancy are implicit in the works by Hughes and O'Connor?

3. Discuss the passage from Fanon as a commentary on the selections in Chapter Four. What ideas in these selections are illuminated by Fanon? How do the Hughes and O'Connor pieces function as rejoinders to Fanon?

4. Fanon has exerted significant influence on both black and white radicals in their approach to the American racial dilemma. "The Wretched of the Earth," the book by Fanon which contains the chapter "Concerning Violence," deals largely with the Algerian fight for independence from French colonial rule. Do you feel that the preceding selection from that chapter has relevance to America's race problem, or, more specifically, to the problems of the black urban ghetto?

Chapter Five
The Barrier

SONG OF PRAISE

THE BARRIER

MELLOW

A MATTER OF PRINCIPLE

SON IN THE AFTERNOON

from BLACK LIKE ME

Countee Cullen
Song of Praise

Who lies with his milk-white maiden,
Bound in the length of her pale gold hair,
Cooled by her lips with the cold kiss laden,
He lies, but he loves not there.

Who lies with his nut-brown maiden,   5
Bruised to the bone by her sin-black hair,
Warmed with the wine that her full lips trade in,
He lies, and his love lies there.

1927

Claude McKay
The Barrier

I must not gaze at them although
Your eyes are dawning day;
I must not watch you as you go
Your sun-illumined way.

I hear but I must never heed   5
The fascinating note,
Which, fluting like a river reed,
Comes from your trembling throat.

I must not see upon your face
Love's softly glowing spark;   10
For there's the barrier of race,
You're fair and I am dark.

1922

From *Selected Poems of Claude McKay*, Twayne Publishers, Inc. Used by permission of the publisher.

Langston Hughes
Mellow

Into the laps
of black celebrities
white girls fall
like pale plums from a tree
beyond a high tension wall   5
wired for killing
which makes it
more thrilling.

1951

Questions

1. How would you characterize the speaker's attitude toward the "milk-white maiden" in Cullen's poem?
2. What is the meaning of line 6 in "Song of Praise"? Why is the term "sin-black" used to describe the nut-brown maiden's hair?
3. How does the speaker's attitude toward the fair lady in "The Barrier" differ from Cullen's attitude toward the milk-white maiden in the previous poem?
4. How would you describe the mood of McKay's poem? Is it bitter? desolate? angry?
5. Contrast the attitude toward white girls in Hughes' "Mellow" with that manifested in McKay's "The Barrier" and Cullen's "Song of Praise." What attitude does the term "pale plums" (line 4) suggest?
6. What is the tone of Hughes' poem? Is it angry? scornful? amused? In particular, what effect does the pat rime in the last three lines have on the poem's tone?
7. The three preceding poems offer a variety of emotional response to the topic of cross-racial sexual relationship, but by no means exhaust the ways in which one might react to the topic. What other emotional responses might be brought to the subject? (Compare the attitude in these poems to that found in the following short story by John A. Williams or in William Melvin Kelley's "The Only Man on Liberty Street.") Which one of the three poems seems to you most "contemporary" in its attitude toward interracial sex?

Charles W. Chesnutt
A Matter of Principle

I

"What our country needs most in its treatment of the race problem,"
observed Mr. Cicero Clayton at one of the monthly meetings of the
Blue Vein Society, of which he was a prominent member, "is a clearer
conception of the brotherhood of man."

The same sentiment in much the same words had often fallen from
Mr. Clayton's lips,—so often, in fact, that the younger members of
the society sometimes spoke of him—among themselves of course—as
"Brotherhood Clayton." The sobriquet derived its point from the application he made of the principle involved in this oft-repeated proposition.

The fundamental article of Mr. Clayton's social creed was that he
himself was not a negro.

"I know," he would say, "that the white people lump us all together
as negroes, and condemn us all to the same social ostracism. But I
don't accept this classification, for my part, and I imagine that, as the
chief party in interest, I have a right to my opinion. People who belong by half or more of their blood to the most virile and progressive
race of modern times have as much right to call themselves white as
others have to call them negroes."

Mr. Clayton spoke warmly, for he was well informed, and had thought much upon the subject; too much, indeed, for he had not been able to escape entirely the tendency of too much concentration upon one subject to make even the clearest minds morbid.

"Of course we can't enforce our claims, or protect ourselves from being robbed of our birthright; but we can at least have principles, and try to live up to them the best we can. If we are not accepted as white, we can at any rate make it clear that we object to being called black. Our protest cannot fail in time to impress itself upon the better class of white people; for the Anglo-Saxon race loves justice, and will eventually do it, where it does not conflict with their own interests."

Whether or not the fact that Mr. Clayton meant no sarcasm, and was conscious of no inconsistency in this eulogy, tend to establish the racial identity he claimed may safely be left to the discerning reader.

In living up to his creed Mr. Clayton declined to associate to any considerable extent with black people. This was sometimes a little inconvenient, and occasionally involved a sacrifice of some pleasure for himself and his family, because they would not attend entertainments where many black people were likely to be present. But they had a social refuge in a little society of people like themselves; they attended, too, a church, of which nearly all the members were white, and they were connected with a number of the religious and benevolent associations open to all good citizens, where they came into contact with the better class of white people, and were treated, in their capacity of members, with a courtesy and consideration scarcely different from that accorded to other citizens.

Mr. Clayton's racial theory was not only logical enough, but was in his own case backed up by substantial arguments. He had begun life with a small patrimony, and had invested his money in a restaurant, which by careful and judicious attention had gown from a cheap eating-house into the most popular and successful confectionery and catering establishment in Groveland. His business occupied a double store on Oakwood Avenue. He owned houses and lots, and stocks and bonds, had good credit at the banks, and lived in a style befitting his income and business standing. In person he was of olive complexion, with slightly curly hair. His features approached the Cuban or Latin-American type rather than the familiar broad characteristics of the mulatto, this suggestion of something foreign being heightened by a Vandyke beard and a carefully waxed and pointed mustache. When he walked to church on Sunday mornings with his daughter Alice, they were a couple of such striking appearance as surely to attract attention.

Miss Alice Clayton was queen of her social set. She was young, she was handsome. She was nearly white; she frankly confessed her sorrow that she was not entirely so. She was accomplished and amiable, dressed in good taste, and had for her father by all odds the richest colored man—the term is used with apologies to Mr. Clayton, explaining that it does not necessarily mean a negro—in Groveland. So pronounced was her superiority that really she had but one social rival worthy of the name,—Miss Lura Watkins, whose father kept a prosperous livery stable and lived in almost as good style as the Claytons. Miss Watkins, while good-looking enough, was not so young nor quite so white as Miss Clayton. She was popular, however, among their mutual acquaintances, and there was a good-natured race between the two as to which should make the first and best marriage.

Marriages among Miss Clayton's set were serious affairs. Of course marriage is always a serious matter, whether it be a success or a failure, and there are those who believe that any marriage is better than no marriage. But among Miss Clayton's friends and associates matrimony took on an added seriousness because of the very narrow limits within which it could take place. Miss Clayton and her friends, by reason of their assumed superiority to black people, or perhaps as much by reason of a somewhat morbid shrinking from the curiosity manifested toward married people of strongly contrasting colors, would not marry black men, and except in rare instances white men would not marry them. They were therefore restricted for a choice to the young men of their own complexion. But these, unfortunately for the girls, had a wider choice. In any State where the laws permit freedom of the marriage contract, a man, by virtue of his sex, can find a wife of whatever complexion he prefers; of course he must not always ask too much in other respects, for most women like to better their social position when they marry. To the number thus lost by "going on the other side," as the phrase went, add the worthless contingent whom no self-respecting woman would marry, and the choice was still further restricted; so that it had become fashionable, when the supply of eligible men ran short, for those of Miss Clayton's set who could afford it to go traveling, ostensibly for pleasure, but with the serious hope that they might meet their fate away from home.

Miss Clayton had perhaps a larger option than any of her associates. Among such men as there were she could have taken her choice. Her beauty, her position, her accomplishments, her father's wealth, all made her eminently desirable. But, on the other hand, the same things rendered her more difficult to reach, and harder to please. To get access to her heart, too, it was necessary to run the gauntlet of her parents, which, until she had reached the age of twenty-three, no one had succeeded in doing safely. Many had called, but none had been chosen.

There was, however, one spot left unguarded, and through it Cupid, a veteran sharpshooter, sent a dart. Mr. Clayton had taken into his service and into his household a poor relation, a sort of cousin several times removed. This boy—his name was Jack—had gone into Mr. Clayton's service at a very youthful age,—twelve or thirteen. He had helped about the housework, washed the dishes, swept the floors, taken care of the lawn and the stable for three or four years, while he attended school. His cousin had then taken him into the store, where he had swept the floor, washed the windows, and done a class of work that kept fully impressed upon him the fact that he was a poor dependent. Nevertheless he was a cheerful lad, who took what he could get and was properly grateful, but always meant to get more. By sheer force of industry and affability and shrewdness, he forced his employer to promote him in time to a position of recognized authority in the establishment. Any one outside of the family would have perceived in him a very suitable husband for Miss Clayton; he was of about the same age, or a year or two older, was as fair of complexion as she, when she was not powdered, and was passably good-looking, with a bearing of which the natural manliness had been no more warped than his training and racial status had rendered inevitable; for he had early learned the law of growth, that to bend is better than to break. He was sometimes sent to accompany Miss Clayton to places in the evening, when she had no other escort, and it is quite likely that she discovered his good points before her parents did. That they should in time perceive them was inevitable. But even then, so accustomed were they to looking down upon the object of their former bounty, that they only spoke of the matter jocularly.

"Well, Alice," her father would say in his bluff way, "you'll not be absolutely obliged to die an old maid. If we can't find anything better for you, there's always Jack. As long as he doesn't take to some other girl, you can fall back on him as a last chance. He'd be glad to take you to get into the business."

Miss Alice had considered the joke a very poor one when first made, but by occasional repetition she became somewhat familiar with it. In time it got around to Jack himself, to whom it seemed no joke at all.

He had long considered it a consummation devoutly to be wished, and when he became aware that the possibility of such a match had occurred to the other parties in interest, he made up his mind that the idea should in due course of time become an accomplished fact. He had even suggested as much to Alice, in a casual way, to feel his ground; and while she had treated the matter lightly, he was not without hope that she had been impressed by the suggestion. Before he had had time, however, to follow up this lead, Miss Clayton, in the spring of 187–, went away on a visit to Washington.

The occasion of her visit was a presidential inauguration. The new President owed his nomination mainly to the votes of the Southern delegates in the convention, and was believed to be correspondingly well disposed to the race from which the Southern delegates were for the most part recruited. Friends of rival and unsuccessful candidates for the nomination had more than hinted that the Southern delegates were very substantially rewarded for their support at the time when it was given; whether this was true or not the parties concerned know best. At any rate the colored politicians did not see it in that light, for they were gathered from near and far to press their claims for recognition and patronage. On the evening following the White House inaugural ball, the colored people of Washington gave an "inaugural" ball at a large public hall. It was under the mangement of their leading citizens, among them several high officials holding over from the last administration, and a number of professional and business men. This ball was the most noteworthy social event that colored circles up to that time had ever known. There were many visitors from various parts of the country. Miss Clayton attended the ball, the honors of which she carried away easily. She danced with several partners, and was introduced to innumerable people whom she had never seen before, and whom she hardly expected ever to meet again. She went away from the ball, at four o'clock in the morning, in a glow of triumph, and with a confused impression of senators and representatives and lawyers and doctors of all shades, who had sought an introduction, led her through the dance, and overwhelmed her with compliments. She returned home the next day but one, after the most delightful week of her life.

II

One afternoon, about theee weeks after her return from Washington, Alice received a letter through the mail. The envelope bore the words "House of Representatives" printed in one corner, and in the opposite corner, in a bold running hand, a Congressman's frank, "Hamilton M. Brown, M.C." The letter read as follows:—

House of Representatives,

Washington, D. C., March 30, 187–.

Miss Alice Clayton, Groveland.

Dear Friend (if I may be permitted to call you so after so brief an acquaintance),—I remember with sincerest pleasure our recent meeting at the inaugaral ball, and the sensation created by your beauty, your amiable manners, and your graceful dancing. Time has so strengthened the impression I then received, that I should have felt inconsolable had I thought it impossible ever to again behold the charms which had brightened the occasion of our meeting and eclipsed by their brilliancy the leading belles of the capital. I had hoped, however, to have the pleasure of meeting you again, and circumstances have fortunately placed it in my power to do so at an early date. You have doubtless learned that the contest over the election in the Sixth Congressional District of South Carolina has been decided in my favor, and that I now have the honor of representing my native State at the national capital. I have just been appointed a member of a special committee to visit and inspect the Sault River and the Straits of Mackinac, with reference to the needs of lake navigation. I have made arrangements to start a week ahead of the other members of the committee, whom I am to meet in Detroit on the 20th. I shall leave here on the 2d, and will arrive in Groveland on the 3d, by the 7.30 evening express. I shall remain in Groveland several days, in the course of which I shall be pleased to call, and renew the acquaintance so auspiciously begun in Washington, which it is my fondest hope may ripen into a warmer friendship.

If you do not regard my visit as presumptuous, and do not write me in the meanwhile forbidding it, I shall do myself the pleasure of waiting on you the morning after my arrival in Groveland.

With renewed expressions of my sincere admiration and profound esteem, I remain,

Sincerely yours,

Hamilton M. Brown, M.C.

To Alice, and especially to her mother, this bold and flowery letter had very nearly the force of a formal declaration. They read it over again and again, and spent most of the afternoon discussing it. There were few young men in Groveland eligible as husbands for so superior a person as Alice Clayton, and an addition to the number would be very acceptable. But the mere fact of his being a Congressman was not sufficient to qualify him; there were other considerations.

"I've never heard of this Honorable Hamilton M. Brown," said Mr. Clayton. The letter had been laid before him at the supper-table. "It's strange, Alice, that you haven't said anything about him before. You must have met lots of swell folks not to recollect a Congressman."

"But he wasn't a Congressman then," answered Alice; "he was only a claimant. I remember Senator Bruce, and Mr. Douglass; but there were so many doctors and lawyers and politicians that I couldn't keep track of them all. Still I have a faint impression of a Mr. Brown who danced with me."

She went into the parlor and brought out the dancing programme she had used at the Washington ball. She had decorated it with a bow of blue ribbon and preserved it as a souvenir of her visit.

"Yes," she said, after examining it, "I must have danced with him. Here are the initials—'H.M.B.' "

"What color is he?" asked Mr. Clayton, as he plied his knife and fork.

"I have a notion that he was rather dark—darker than any one I had ever danced with before."

"Why did you dance with him?" asked her father. "You weren't obliged to go back on your principles because you were away from home."

"Well, father, 'when you're in Rome'—you know the rest. Mrs. Clearweather introduced me to several dark men, to him among others. They were her friends, and common decency required me to be courteous."

"If this man is black, we don't want to encourage him. If he's the right sort, we'll invite him to the house."

"And make him feel at home," added Mrs. Clayton, on hospitable thoughts intent.

"We must ask Sadler about him to-morrow," said Mr. Clayton, when he had drunk his coffee and lighted his cigar. "If he's the right man he shall have cause to remember his visit to Groveland. We'll show him that Washington is not the only town on earth."

The uncertainty of the family with regard to Mr. Brown was soon removed. Mr. Solomon Sadler, who was supposed to know everything worth knowing concerning the colored race, and everybody of importance connected with it, dropped in after supper to make an evening call. Sadler was familiar with the history of every man of negro ancestry who had distinguished himself in any walk of life. He could give the pedigree of Alexander Pushkin, the titles of scores of Dumas's novels (even Sadler had not time to learn them all), and could recite the whole of Wendell Phillips's lecture on Toussaint l'Ouverture. He claimed a personal acquaintance with Mr. Frederick Douglass, and had been often in Washington, where he was well known and well received in good colored society.

"Let me see," he said reflectively, when asked for information about the Honorable Hamilton M. Brown. "Yes, I think I know him. He studied at Oberlin just after the war. He was about leaving there when I entered. There were two H. M. Browns there—a Hamilton M. Brown and a Henry M. Brown. One was stout and dark and the other was slim and quite light; you could scarcely tell him from a dark white man. They used to call them 'light Brown' and 'dark Brown.' I didn't know either of them except by sight, for they were there only a few weeks after I went in. As I remember them, Hamilton was the fair one—a very good-looking, gentlemanly fellow, and, as I heard, a good student and a fine speaker."

"Do you remember what kind of hair he had?" asked Mr. Clayton.

"Very good indeed; straight, as I remember it. He looked something like a Spaniard or a Portuguese."

"Now that you describe him," said Alice, "I remember quite well dancing with such a gentleman; and I'm wrong about my 'H.M.B.' The dark man must have been some one else; there are two others on my card that I can't remember distinctly, and he was probably one of those."

"I guess he's all right, Alice," said her father when Sadler had gone away. "He evidently means business, and we must treat him *white*. Of course he must stay with us; there are no hotels in Groveland while he is here. Let's see—he'll be here in three days. That isn't very long, but I guess we can get ready. I'll write a letter this afternoon—or you write it, and invite him to the house, and say I'll meet him at the depot. And you may have *carte blanche* for making the preparations."

"We must have some people to meet him."

"Certainly; a reception is the proper thing. Sit down immediately and write the letter and I'll mail it first thing in the morning, so he'll get it before he has time to make other arrangements. And you and your mother put your heads together and make out a list of guests, and I'll have the invitations printed to-morrow. We will show the darkeys of Groveland how to entertain a Congressman."

It will be noted that in moments of abstraction or excitement Mr. Clayton sometimes relapsed into forms of speech not entirely consistent with his principles. But some allowance must be made for his atmosphere; he could no more escape from it than the leopard can change his spots, or the—In deference to Mr. Clayton's feelings the quotation will be left incomplete.

Alice wrote the letter on the spot and it was duly mailed, and sped on its winged way to Washington.

The preparations for the reception were made as thoroughly and elaborately as possible on so short a notice. The invitations were issued; the house was cleaned from attic to cellar; an orchestra was engaged for the evening; elaborate floral decorations were planned and the flowers ordered. Even the refreshments, which ordinarily, in the household of a caterer, would be mere matter of familiar detail, became a subject of serious consultation and study.

The approaching event was a matter of very much interest to the fortunate ones who were honored with invitations, and this for several reasons. They were anxious to meet this sole representative of their race in the —th Congress, and as he was not one of the old-line colored leaders, but a new star risen on the political horizon, there was a special curiosity to see who he was and what he looked like. Moreover, the Claytons did not often entertain a large company, but when they did, it was on a scale commensurate with their means and position, and to be present on such an occasion was a thing to remember and to talk about. And, most important consideration of all, some remarks dropped by members of the Clayton family had given rise to the rumor that the Congressman was seeking a wife. This invested his visit with a romantic interest, and gave the reception a practical value; for there were other marriageable girls besides Miss Clayton, and if one was left another might be taken.

III

On the evening of April 3d, at fifteen minutes of six o'clock, Mr. Clayton, accompanied by Jack, entered the livery carriage waiting at his gate and ordered the coachman to drive to the Union Depot. He had taken Jack along, partly for company, and partly that Jack might relieve the Congressman of any trouble about his baggage, and make himself useful in case of emergency. Jack was willing enough to go, for he had foreseen in the visitor a rival for Alice's hand,—indeed he had heard more or less of the subject for several days,—and was glad to make a reconnaissance before the enemy arrived upon the field of battle. He had made—at least he had thought so—considerable progress with Alice during the three weeks since her return from Washington, and once or twice Alice had been perilously near the tender stage. This visit had disturbed the situation and threatened to ruin his chances; but he did not mean to give up without a struggle.

Arrived at the main entrance, Mr. Clayton directed the carriage to wait, and entered the station with Jack. The Union Depot at Groveland was an immense oblong structure, covering a dozen parallel tracks and furnishing terminal passenger facilities for half a dozen railroads. The tracks ran east and west, and the depot was entered from the south, at about the middle of the building. On either side of the entrance, the waiting-rooms, refreshment rooms, baggage and express departments, and other administrative offices, extended in a row for the entire length of the building; and beyond them and parallel with them stretched a long open space, separated from the tracks by an iron fence or *grille*. There were two entrance gates in the fence, at which tickets must be shown before access could be had to trains, and two other gates, by which arriving passengers came out.

My Clayton looked at the blackboard on the wall underneath the station clock, and observed that the 7.30 train from Washington was five minutes late. Accompanied by Jack he walked up and down the platform until the train, with the usual accompaniment of panting steam and clanging bell and rumbling trucks, pulled into the station, and drew up on the third or fourth track from the iron railing. Mr. Clayton stationed himself at the gate nearest the rear end of the train, reasoning that the Congressman would ride in a parlor car, and would naturally come out by the gate nearest the point at which he left the train.

"You'd better go and stand by the other gate, Jack," he said to his companion, "and stop him if he goes out that way."

The train was well filled and a stream of passengers poured through. Mr. Clayton scanned the crowd carefully as they approached the gate, and scrutinized each passenger as he came through, without seeing any one that met the description of Congressman Brown as given by Sadler, or any one that could in his opinion be the gentleman for whom he was looking. When the last one had passed through he was left to the conclusion that his expected guest had gone out by the other gate. Mr. Clayton hastened thither.

"Didn't he come out this way, Jack?" he asked.

"No, sir," replied the young man, "I haven't seen him."

"That's strange," mused Mr. Clayton, somewhat anxiously. "He would hardly fail to come without giving us notice. Surely we must have missed him. We'd better look around a little. You go that way and I'll go this."

Mr. Clayton turned and walked several rods along the platform to the men's waiting-room, and standing near the door glanced around to see if he could find the object of his search. The only colored person in the room was a stout and very black man, wearing a broadcloth suit and a silk hat, and seated a short distance from the door. On the seat by his side stood a couple of valises. On one of them, the one nearest him, on which his arm rested, was written, in white letters, plainly legible,—

"H. M. Brown, M. C.

"Washington, D. C."

Mr. Clayton's feelings at this discovery can better be imagined than described. He hastily left the waiting-room, before the black gentleman, who was looking the other way, was even aware of his presence, and, walking rapidly up and down the platform, communed with himself upon what course of action the situation demanded. He had invited to his house, had come down to meet, had made elaborate preparations to entertain on the following evening, a light-colored man,—a white man by his theory, an acceptable guest, a possible husband for his daughter, an avowed suitor for her hand. If the Congressman had turned out to be brown, even dark brown, with fairly good hair, though he might not have desired him as a son-in-law, yet he could have welcomed him as a guest. But even this softening of the blow was denied him, for the man in the waiting-room was palpably, aggressively black, with pronounced African features and woolly hair, without apparently a single drop of redeeming white blood. Could he, in the face of his well-known principles, his lifelong rule of conduct, take this negro into his home and introduce him to his friends? Could he subject his wife and daughter to the rude shock of such a disappointment? It would be bad enough for them to learn of the ghastly mistake, but to have him in the house would be twisting the arrow in the wound.

Mr. Clayton had the instincts of a gentleman, and realized the delicacy of the situation. But to get out of his difficulty without wounding the feelings of the Congressman required not only diplomacy but dispatch. Whatever he did must be done promptly; for if he waited many minutes the Congressman would probably take a carriage and be driven to Mr. Clayton's residence.

A ray of hope came for a moment to illumine the gloom of the situation. Perhaps the black man was merely sitting there, and not the owner of the valise! For there were two valises, one on each side of the supposed Congressman. For obvious reasons he did not care to make the inquiry himself, so he looked around for his companion, who came up a moment later.

"Jack," he exclaimed excitedly, "I'm afraid we're in the worst kind of a hole, unless there's some mistake! Run down to the men's waiting-room and you'll see a man and a valise, and you'll understand what I mean. Ask that darkey if he is the Honorable Mr. Brown, Congressman from South Carolina. If he says yes, come back right away and let me know, without giving him time to ask any questions, and put your wits to work to help me out of the scrape."

"I wonder what's the matter?" said Jack to himself, but did as he was told. In a moment he came running back.

"Yes, sir," he announced; "he says he's the man."

"Jack," said Mr. Clayton desperately, "if you want to show your appreaciation of what I've done for you, you must suggest some way out of this. I'd never dare to take that negro to my house, and yet I'm obliged to treat him like a gentleman."

Jack's eyes had worn a somewhat reflective look since he had gone to make the inquiry. Suddenly his face brightened with intelligence, and then, as a newsboy ran into the station calling his wares, hardened into determination.

"Clarion, special extry 'dition! All about de epidemic er dipt'eria!" clamored the newsboy with shrill childish treble, as he made his way toward the waiting-room. Jack darted after him, and saw the man to whom he had spoken buy a paper. He ran back to his employer, and dragged him over toward the ticket-seller's window.

"I have it, sir!" he exclaimed, seizing a telegraph blank and writing rapidly, and reading aloud as he wrote. "How's this for a way out?"—

"DEAR SIR,—I write you this note here in the depot to inform you of an unfortunate event which has interfered with my plans and those of my family for your entertainment while in Groveland. Yesterday my daughter Alice complained of a sore throat, which by this afternoon had developed into a case of malignant diphtheria. In consequence our house has been quarantined; and while I have felt myself obliged to come down to the depot, I do not feel that I ought to expose you to the possibility of infection, and I therefore send you this by another hand. The bearer will conduct you to a carriage which I have ordered placed at your service, and unless you should prefer some other hotel, you will be driven to the Forest Hill House, where I beg you will consider yourself my guest during your stay in the city, and make the fullest use of every convenience it may offer. From present indications I fear no one of our family will be able to see you, which we shall regret beyond expression, as we have made elaborate arrangements for your entertainment. I still hope, however, that you may enjoy your visit, as there are many places of interest in the city, and many friends will doubtless be glad to make your acquaintance.

"With assurances of my profound regret, I am

Sincerely yours,

"CICERO CLAYTON."

"Splendid!" cried Mr. Clayton. "You've helped me out of a horrible scrape. Now, go and take him to the hotel and see him comfortably located, and tell them to charge the bill to me."

"I suspect, sir," suggested Jack, "that I'd better not go up to the house, and you'll have to stay in yourself for a day or two, to keep up appearances. I'll sleep on the lounge at the store, and we can talk business over the telephone."

"All right, Jack, we'll arrange the details later. But for Heaven's sake get him started, or he'll be calling a hack to drive up to the house. I'll go home on a street car."

"So far so good," sighed Mr. Clayton to himself as he escaped from the station. "Jack is a deuced clever fellow, and I'll have to do something more for him. But the tug-of-war is yet to come. I've got to bribe a doctor, shut up the house for a day or two, and have all the ill-humor of two disappointed women to endure until this negro leaves town. Well, I'm sure my wife and Alice will back me up at any cost. No sacrifice is too great to escape having to entertain him; of course I have no prejudice against his color,—he can't help that,—but it is the *principle* of the thing. If we received him it would be a concession fatal to all my views and theories. And I am really doing him a kindness, for I'm sure that all the world could not make Alice and her mother treat him with anything but cold politeness. It'll be a great mortification to Alice, but I don't see how else I could have got out of it."

He boarded the first car that left the depot, and soon reached home. The house was lighted up, and through the lace curtains of the parlor windows he could see his wife and daughter, elegantly dressed, waiting to receive their distinguished visitor. He rang the bell impatiently, and a servant opened the door.

"The gentleman didn't come?" asked the maid.

"No," he said as he hung up his hat. This brought the ladies to the door.

"He didn't come?" they exclaimed. "What's the matter?"

"I'll tell you," he said. "Mary," this to the servant, a white girl, who stood in open-eyed curiosity, "we shan't need you any more to-night."

Then he went into the parlor, and, closing the door, told his story. When he reached the point where he had discovered the color of the honorable Mr. Brown, Miss Clayton caught her breath, and was on the verge of collapse.

"That nigger," said Mrs. Clayton indignantly, "can never set foot in this house. But what did you do with him?"

Mr. Clayton quickly unfolded his plan, and described the disposition he had made of the Congressman.

"It's an awful shame," said Mrs. Clayton. "Just think of the trouble and expense we have gone to! And poor Alice'll never get over it, for everybody knows he came to see her and that he's smitten with her. But you've done just right; we never would have been able to hold up our heads again if we had introduced a black man, even a Congressman, to the people that are invited here to-morrow night, as a sweetheart of Alice. Why, she wouldn't marry him if he was President of the United States and plated with gold an inch thick. The very idea!"

"Well," said Mr. Clayton, "then we've got to act quick. Alice must wrap up her throat—by the way, Alice, how *is* your throat?"

"It's sore," sobbed Alice, who had been in tears almost from her father's return, "and I don't care if I do have diphtheria and die, no, I don't!" and she wept on.

"Wrap up your throat and go to bed, and I'll go over to Doctor Pillsbury's and get a diphtheria card to nail up on the house. In the morning, first thing, we'll have to write notes recalling the invitations for to-morrow evening, and have them delivered by messenger boys. We were fools for not finding out all about this man from some one who knew, before we invited him here. Sadler don't know more than half he thinks he does, anyway. And we'll have to do this thing thoroughly, or out motives will be misconstrued, and people will say we are prejudiced and all that, when it is only a matter of principle with us."

The programme outlined above was carried out to the letter. The invitations were recalled, to the great disappointment of the invited guests. The family physician called several times during the day. Alice remained in bed, and the maid left without notice, in such a hurry that she forgot to take her best clothes.

Mr. Clayton himself remained at home. He had a telephone in the house, and was therefore in easy communication with his office, so that the business did not suffer materially by reason of his absence from the store. About ten o'clock in the morning a note came up from the hotel, expressing Mr. Brown's regrets and sympathy. Toward noon Mr. Clayton picked up the morning paper, which he had not theretofore had time to read, and was glancing over it casually, when his eye fell upon a column headed "A Colored Congressman." He read the article with astonishment that rapidly turned to chagrin and dismay. It was an interview describing the Congressman as a tall and shapely man, about thirty-five years old, with an olive complexion not noticeably darker than many a white man's, straight hair, and eyes as black as sloes.

"The bearing of this son of South Carolina reveals the polished manners of the Southern gentleman, and neither from his appearance nor his conversation would one suspect that the white blood which flows in his veins in such preponderating measure had ever been crossed by that of a darker race," wrote the reporter, who had received instructions at the office that for urgent business considerations the lake shipping interest wanted Representative Brown treated with marked consideration.

There was more of the article, but the introductory portion left Mr. Clayton in such a state of bewilderment that the paper fell from his hand. What was the meaning of it? Had he been mistaken? Obviously so, or else the reporter was wrong, which was manifestly improbable. When he had recovered himself somewhat, he picked up the newspaper and began reading where he had left off.

"Representative Brown traveled to Groveland in company with Bishop Jones of the African Methodist Jerusalem Church, who is *en route* to attend the general conference of his denomination at Detroit next week. The bishop, who came in while the writer was interviewing Mr. Brown, is a splendid type of the pure negro. He is said to be a man of great power among his people, which may easily be believed after one has looked upon his expressive countenance and heard him discuss the questions which affect the welfare of his church and his race."

Mr. Clayton stared at the paper. " 'The bishop,' " he repeated, " 'is a splendid type of the pure negro.' I must have mistaken the bishop for the Congressman! But how in the world did Jack get the thing balled up? I'll call up the store and demand an explanation of him."

"Jack," he asked, "what kind of a looking man was the fellow you gave the note to at the depot?"

"He was a very wicked-looking fellow, sir," came back the answer. "He had a bad eye, looked like a gambler, sir. I am not surprised that you didn't want to entertain him, even if he was a Congressman."

"What color was he—that's what I want to know—and what kind of hair did he have?"

"Why, he was about my complexion, sir, and had straight black hair."

The rules of the telephone company did not permit swearing over the line. Mr. Clayton broke the rules.

"Was there any one else with him?" he asked when he had relieved his mind.

"Yes, sir, Bishop Jones of the African Methodist Jerusalem Church was sitting there with him; they had traveled from Washington together. I drove the bishop to his stopping-place after I had left Mr. Brown at the hotel. I didn't suppose you'd mind."

Mr. Clayton fell into a chair, and indulged in thoughts unutterable.

He folded up the paper and slipped it under the family Bible, where it was least likely to be soon discovered.

"I'll hide the paper, anyway," he groaned. "I'll never hear the last of this till my dying day, so I may as well have a few hours' respite. It's too late to go back, and we've got to play the farce out. Alice is really sick with disappointment, and to let her know this now would only make her worse. May be he'll leave town in a day or two, and then she'll be in condition to stand it. Such luck is enough to disgust a man with trying to do right and live up to his principles."

Time hung a little heavy on Mr. Clayton's hands during the day. His wife was busy with the housework. He answered several telephone calls about Alice's health, and called up the store occasionally to ask how the business was getting on. After lunch he lay down on a sofa and took a nap, from which he was aroused by the sound of the doorbell. He went to the door. The evening paper was lying on the porch, and the newsboy, who had not observed the diphtheria sign until after he had rung, was hurrying away as fast as his legs would carry him.

Mr. Clayton opened the paper and looked it through to see if there was any reference to the visiting Congressman. He found what he sought and more. An article on the local page contained a résumé of the information given in the morning paper, with the following additional paragraph:

"A reporter, who called at the Forest Hill this morning to interview Representative Brown, was informed that the Congressman had been invited to spend the remainder of his time in Groveland as the guest of Mr. William Watkins, the proprietor of the popular livery establishment on Main Street. Mr. Brown will remain in the city several days, and a reception will be tendered him at Mr. Watkins's on Wednesday evening."

"That ends it," sighed Mr. Clayton. "The dove of peace will never again rest on my roof-tree."

But why dwell longer on the sufferings of Mr. Clayton, or attempt to describe the feelings or chronicle the remarks of his wife and daughter when they learned the facts in the case?

As to Representative Brown, he was made welcome in the hospitable home of Mr. William Watkins. There was a large and brilliant assemblage at the party on Wednesday evening, at which were displayed the costumes prepared for the Clayton reception. Mr. Brown took a fancy to Miss Lura Watkins, to whom, before the week was over, he became engaged to be married. Meantime poor Alice, the innocent victim of circumstances and principles, lay sick abed with a supposititious case of malignant diphtheria, and a real case of acute disappointment and chagrin.

"Oh, Jack!" exclaimed Alice, a few weeks later, on the way home from evening church in company with the young man, "what a dreadful thing it all was! And to think of that hateful Lura Watkins marrying the Congressman!"

The street was shaded by trees at the point where they were passing, and there was no one in sight. Jack put his arm around her waist, and, leaning over, kissed her.

"Never mind, dear," he said soothingly, "you still have your 'last chance' left, and I'll prove myself a better man than the Congressman."

Occasionally, at social meetings, when the vexed question of the future of the colored race comes up, as it often does, for discussion, Mr. Clayton may still be heard to remark sententiously:—

"What the white people of the United States need most, in dealing with this problem, is a higher conception of the brotherhood of man. For of one blood God made all the nations of the earth."

1899

Questions

1. Exactly what is the principle of Mr. Clayton that is referred to in the story's title? What does he mean by "brotherhood" in his familiar speech on the topic?
2. Point out examples of Chesnutt's humorous word play surrounding such terms as "colored," "negro," "black," "white," "brown," and other designations of color.
3. What are some other sources of humor in the story?
4. Aside from its concern with light skin color, what other preoccupations of the black bourgeoisie are mocked in the story?
5. Chesnutt is described in Edward Margolies' "Native Sons" as "apparently so light-complexioned that he could easily have 'passed'" and, despite its humorous tone, the story must have touched on topics the author had considered seriously. Do you find any traces of bitterness in the story?
6. Why doesn't Chesnutt display the same mocking attitude toward the social ambitions of Jack that he does toward those of the Clayton family?

John A. Williams
Son in the Afternoon

It was hot. I tend to be a bitch when it's hot. I goosed the little Ford over
Sepulveda Boulevard toward Santa Monica until I got stuck in the traffic
that pours from L.A. into the surrounding towns. I'd had a very lousy
day at the studio.

I was—still am—a writer and this studio had hired me to check
scripts and films with Negroes in them to make sure the Negro movie-
goer wouldn't be offended. The signs were already clear one day the
whole of American industry would be racing pellmell to get a Negro,
showcase a spade. I was kind of a pioneer. I'm a *Negro* writer, you
see. The day had been tough because of a couple of verbs—slink and
walk. One of those Hollywood hippies had done a script calling for a
Negro waiter to slink away from the table where a dinner party was
glaring at him. I said the waiter should walk, not slink, because later on
he becomes a hero. The Hollywood hippie, who understood it all because he had some colored friends, said that it was essential to the plot
that the waiter slink. I said you don't slink one minute and become a
hero the next; there has to be some consistency. The Negro actor I
was standing up for said nothing either way. He had played Uncle

Tom roles so long that he had become Uncle Tom. But the director agreed with me.

Anyway . . . hear me out now. I was on my way to Santa Monica to pick up my mother, Nora. It was a long haul for such a hot day. I had planned a quiet evening: a nice shower, fresh clothes, and then I would have dinner at the Watkins and talk with some of the musicians on the scene for a quick taste before they cut to their gigs. After, I was going to the Pigalle down on Figueroa and catch Earl Grant at the organ, and still later, if nothing exciting happened, I'd pick up Scottie and make it to the Lighthouse on the Beach or to the Strollers and listen to some of the white boys play. I liked the long drive, especially while listening to Sleepy Stein's show on the radio. Later, much later of course, it would be home, back to Watts.

So you see, this picking up Nora was a little inconvenient. My mother was a maid for the Couchmans. Ronald Couchman was an architect, a good one I understood from Nora who has a fine sense for this sort of thing; you don't work in some hundred-odd houses during your life without getting some idea of the way a house should be laid out. Couchman's wife, Kay, was a playgirl who drove a white Jaguar from one party to another. My mother didn't like her too much; she didn't seem to care much for her son, Ronald, junior. There's something wrong with a parent who can't really love her own child, Nora thought. The Couchmans lived in a real fine residential section, of course. A number of actors lived nearby, character actors, not really big stars.

Somehow it is very funny. I mean that the maids and butlers knew everything about these people, and these people knew nothing at all about the help. Through Nora and her friends I knew who was laying whose wife; who had money and who *really* had money; I knew about the wild parties hours before the police, and who smoked marijuana, when, and where they got it.

To get to Couchman's driveway I had to go three blocks up one side of a palm-planted center strip and back down the other. The driveway bent gently, then swept back out of sight of the main road. The house, sheltered by slim palms, looked like a transplanted New England Colonial. I parked and walked to the kitchen door, skirting the growling Great Dane who was tied to a tree. That was the route to the kitchen door.

I don't like kitchen doors. Entering people's houses by them, I mean. I'd done this thing most of my life when I called at places where Nora worked to pick up the patched or worn sheets or the half-eaten roasts, the battered, tarnished silver—the fringe benefits of a housemaid. As a teen-ager I'd told Nora I was through with that crap; I was not going through anyone's kitchen door. She only laughed and said I'd learn. One day soon after, I called for her and without knocking walked right through the front door of this house and right on through the living room. I was almost out of the room when I saw feet behind the couch. I leaned over and there was Mr. Jorgensen and his wife making out like crazy. I guess they thought Nora had gone and it must have hit them sort of suddenly and they went at it like the hell-bomb was due to drop any minute. I've been that way too, mostly in the spring. Of course, when Mr. Jorgensen looked over his shoulder and saw me, you know what happened. I was thrown out and Nora right behind me. It was the middle of winter, the old man was sick and the coal bill three months overdue. Nora was right about those kitchen doors: I learned.

My mother saw me before I could ring the bell. She opened the door. "Hello," she said. She was breathing hard, like she'd been running or something. "Come in and sit down. I don't know *where* that Kay is. Little Ronald is sick and she's probably out gettin' drunk again." She left me then and trotted back through the house, I guess to be with Ronnie. I hated the combination of her white nylon uniform, her dark brown face and the wide streaks of gray in her hair. Nora had married this guy from Texas a few years after the old man had died. He was all right. He made out okay. Nora didn't have to work, but she just couldn't be still; she always had to be doing something. I suggested she quit work, but I had as much luck as her husband. I used to tease her about liking to be around those white folks. It would have been good for her to take an extended trip around the country visiting my brothers and sisters. Once she got to Philadelphia, she could go right out to the cemetery and sit awhile with the old man.

I walked through the Couchman home. I liked the library. I thought if I knew Couchman I'd like him. The room made me feel like that. I left it and went into the big living room. You could tell that Couchman had let his wife do that. Everything in it was fast, dart-like, with no sense of ease. But on the walls were several of Couchman's conceptions of buildings and homes. I guess he was a disciple of Wright. My mother walked rapidly through the room without looking at me and said, "Just be patient, Wendell. She should be here real soon."

"Yeah," I said, "with a snootful." I had turned back to the drawings when Ronnie scampered into the room, his face twisted with rage.

"Nora!" he tried to roar, perhaps the way he'd seen the parents of some of his friends roar at their maids. I'm quite sure Kay didn't shout at Nora, and I don't think Couchman would. But then no one shouts at Nora. "Nora, you come right back here this minute!" the little bastard shouted and stamped and pointed to a spot on the floor where Nora was supposed to come to roost. I have a nasty temper. Sometimes it lies dormant for ages and at other times, like when the weather is hot and nothing seems to be going right, it's bubbling and ready to explode. "Don't talk to *my* mother like that, you little—!" I said sharply, breaking off just before I cursed. I wanted him to be large enough for me to strike. "How'd you like for me to talk to *your* mother like that?"

The nine-year-old looked up at me in surprise and confusion. He hadn't expected me to say anything. I was just another piece of furniture. Tears rose in his eyes and spilled out onto his pale cheeks. He put his hands behind him, twisted them. He moved backwards, away from me. He looked at my mother with a "Nora, come help me" look. And sure enough, there was Nora, speeding back across the room, gathering the kid in her arms, tucking his robe together. I was too angry to feel hatred for myself.

Ronnie was the Couchman's only kid. Nora loved him. I suppose that was the trouble. Couchman was gone ten, twelve hours a day. Kay didn't stay around the house any longer than she had to. So Ronnie had only my mother. I think kids should have someone to love, and Nora wasn't a bad sort. But somehow when the six of us, her own children, were growing up we never had her. She was gone, out scuffling to get those crumbs to put into our mouths and shoes for our feet and praying for something to happen so that all the space in between would be taken care of. Nora's affection for us took the form of rushing out into the morning's five o'clock blackness to wake some silly bitch and get her coffee; took form in her trudging five miles home every night instead of taking the streetcar to save money to buy tablets for us, to use at school, we said. But the truth was that all of us liked to draw and we went through a writing tablet in a couple of hours every day. Can you imagine? There's not a goddamn artist among us. We never had the physical affection, the pat on the head, the quick, smiling kiss, the "gimmee a hug" routine. All of this Ronnie was getting.

Now he buried his little blond head in Nora's breast and sobbed. "There, there now," Nora said. "Don't you cry, Ronnie. Ol' Wendell is just jealous, and he hasn't much sense either. He didn't mean nuthin'."

I left the room. Nora had hit it of course, hit it and passed on. I looked back. It didn't look so incongruous, the white and black together, I mean. Ronnie was still sobbing. His head bobbed gently on Nora's shoulder. The only time I ever got that close to her was when she trapped me with a bearhug so she could whale the daylights out of me after I put a snowball through Mrs. Grant's window. I walked outside and lit a cigarette. When Ronnie was in the hospital the month before, Nora got me to run her way over to Hollywood every night to see him. I didn't like that worth a damn. All right, I'll admit it: it did upset me. All that affection I didn't get nor my brothers and sisters going to that little white boy who, without a doubt, when away from her called her the names he'd learned from adults. Can you imagine a nine-year-old kid calling Nora a "girl," "our girl?" I spat at the Great Dane. He snarled and then I bounced a rock off his fanny. "Lay down, you bastard," I muttered. It was a good thing he was tied up.

I heard the low cough of the Jaguar slapping against the road. The car was throttled down, and with a muted roar it swung into the driveway. The woman aimed it for me. I was evil enough not to move. I was tired of playing with these people. At the last moment, grinning, she swung the wheel over and braked. She bounded out of the car like a tennis player vaulting over a net.

"Hi," she said, tugging at her shorts.

"Hello."

"You're Nora's boy?"

"I'm Nora's son." Hell, I was as old as she was; besides, I can't stand "boy."

"Nora tells us you're working in Hollywood. Like it?"

"It's all right."

"You must be pretty talented."

We stood looking at each other while the dog whined for her attention. Kay had a nice body and it was well tanned. She was high, boy, was she high. Looking at her, I could feel myself going into my sexy bastard routine; sometimes I can swing it great. Maybe it all had to do with the business inside. Kay took off her sunglasses and took a good look at me. "Do you have a cigarette?"

I gave her one and lit it. "Nice tan," I said. Most white people I know think it's a great big deal if a Negro compliments them on their tans. It's a large laugh. You have all this volleyball about color and come summer you can't hold the white folks back from the beaches, anyplace where they can get some sun. And of course the blacker they get, the more pleased they are. Crazy. If there is ever a Negro revolt, it will come during the summer and Negroes will descend upon the beaches around the nation and paralyze the country. You can't conceal

cattle prods and bombs and pistols and police dogs when you're showing your birthday suit to the sun.

"You like it?" she asked. She was pleased. She placed her arm next
to mine. "Almost the same color," she said.

"Ronnie isn't feeling well," I said.

"Oh, the poor kid. I'm so glad we have Nora. She's such a charm.
I'll run right in and look at him. Do have a drink in the bar. Fix me one
too, will you?" Kay slipped inside and I went to the bar and poured
out two strong drinks. I made hers stronger than mine. She was back
soon. "Nora was trying to put him to sleep and she made me stay out."
She giggled. She quickly tossed off her drink. "Another, please?" While
I was fixing her drink she was saying how amazing it was for Nora to
have such a talented son. What she was really saying was that it was
amazing for a servant to have a son who was not also a servant. "Anything can happen in a democracy," I said. "Servants' sons drink with
madames and so on."

"Oh, Nora isn't a servant," Kay said. "She's part of the family."

Yeah, I thought. Where and how many times had I heard *that* before?

In the ensuing silence, she started to admire her tan again. "You
think it's pretty good, do you? You don't know how hard I worked to
get it." I moved close to her and held her arm. I placed my other arm
around her. She pretended not to see or feel it, but she wasn't trying to get away either. In fact she was pressing closer and the register
in my brain that tells me at the precise moment when I'm in, went off.
Kay was very high. I put both arms around her and she put both hers
around me. When I kissed her, she responded completely.

"Mom!"

"Ronnie, come back to bed," I heard Nora shout from the other
room. We could hear Ronnie running over the rug in the outer room.
Kay tried to get away from me, push me to one side, because we could
tell that Ronnie knew where to look for his Mom: he was running
right for the bar, where we were. "Oh, please," she said, "don't let
him see us." I wouldn't let her push me away. "Stop!" she hissed. "He'll
see us!" We stopped struggling just for an instant, and we listened to
the echoes of the word *see*. She gritted her teeth and renewed her efforts to get away.

Me? I had the scene laid right out. The kid breaks into the room, see,
and sees his mother in this real wriggly clinch with his colored guy
who's just shouted at him, see, and no matter how his mother explains

it away, the kid has the image—the colored guy and his mother—for the rest of his life, see?

That's the way it happened. The kid's mother hissed under her breath. "*You're crazy!*" and she looked at me as though she were seeing me or something about me for the very first time. I'd released her as soon as Ronnie, romping into the bar, saw us and came to a full, open-mouthed halt. Kay turned to me, but she couldn't speak.

Outside in the living room my mother called, "Wendell, where are you? We can go now."

I started to move past Kay and Ronnie. I felt many things, but I made myself think mostly, *There you little bastard, there.*

My mother thrust her face inside the door and said, "Good-bye, Mrs. Couchman. See you tomorrow. 'Bye, Ronnie."

"Yes," Kay said, sort of stunned. "Tomorrow." She was reaching for Ronnie's hand as we left, but the kid was slapping her hand away. I hurried quickly after Nora, hating the long drive back to Watts.

1962

Questions

1. What is the significance of the story's title? How do you think Williams wishes the reader to view Nora? Is she irresponsible in her treatment of her own children? Why does she continue to work as a servant in white households, against the urgings of her son and second husband?
2. What seems to be Wendell's estimate of himself? What is his attitude toward his job as a Hollywood writer? Is his attitude toward the white world ambivalent? Do you find significance in his "hating the long drive back to Watts"? Is Wendell ultimately a sympathetic figure?
3. Discuss the characterization of Kay. Is her portrait convincing?
4. What stereotyped notion of black-white sexual attitudes is Williams overturning in describing Wendell's treatment of Kay?
5. Williams is the author of a novel entitled "The Angry Ones" and "Son in the Afternoon" appeared in "The Angry Black," an anthology he edited in 1962. In what sense is this an "angry" story?

John Howard Griffin
from Black Like Me

NOVEMBER 24

I hitchhiked up toward the swamp country between Mobile and Montgomery. A magnificent cool day.

I walked some miles before a large, pleasant-faced man halted his light truck and told me to get in. When I opened the door I saw a shotgun propped against the seat next to his knee. I recalled it was considered sport among some elements in Alabama to hunt "nigs" and I backed away.

"Come on," he laughed. "That's for hunting deer."

I glanced again at his florid face, saw he looked decent and climbed into the leather seat beside him.

"Do you have any luck getting rides through here?" he asked.

"No sir. You're my first ride since Mobile."

I learned he was a married man, fifty-three years old, father of a family now grown and grandfather of two children. He was certainly, by the tone of his conversation, an active civic leader and respected member of his community. I began to hope that I had encountered a decent white.

"You married?" he asked.

"Yes sir."

"Any kids?"

"Yes sir—three."

"You got a pretty wife?"

"Yes sir."

He waited a moment and then with lightness, paternal amusement, "She ever had it from a white man?"

I stared at my black hands, saw the gold wedding band and mumbled something meaningless, hoping he would see my reticence. He overrode my feelings and the conversation grew more salacious. He told me how all of the white men in the region craved colored girls. He said he hired a lot of them both for housework and in his business. "And I guarantee you, I've had it in every one of them before they ever got on the payroll." A pause. Silence above humming tires on the hot-top road. "What do you think of that?"

"Surely some refuse," I suggested cautiously.

"Not if they want to eat—or feed their kids," he snorted. "If they don't put out, they don't get the job."

I looked out the window to tall pine trees rising on either side of the highway. Their turpentine odor mingled with the soaped smells of the man's khaki hunting clothes.

"You think that's pretty terrible, don't you?" he asked.

I knew I should grin and say, "Why no—it's just nature," or some other disarming remark to avoid provoking him.

"Don't you?" he insisted pleasantly.

"I guess I do."

"Why hell—everybody does it. Don't you know that?"

"No sir."

"Well, they sure as hell do. We figure we're doing you people a favor to get some white blood in your kids."

The grotesque hypocrisy slapped me as it does all Negroes. It is worth remembering when the white man talks of the Negro's lack of sexual morality, or when he speaks with horror about mongrelization and with fervor about racial purity. Mongrelization is already a widespread reality in the South—it has been exclusively the white man's contribution to the Southen Way of Life. His vast concern for "racial purity" obviously does not extend to all races.[1]

---

[1] Later I encountered many whites who freely admitted the same practices my companion described. In fairness, however, other Southern whites roundly condemned it and claimed it was not as typical as my informants suggested. None denied that it was widespread.

This aspect of Southern life does not hit the newspapers because, as my companion said, "Alabama nigger women are good about that— they won't never go to the cops or tell on you."

It was obvious what would happen if one of them tried it.

As I feared it would, my lack of "cooperation" nettled the driver. He took my silence, rightly, for disapproval.

"Where you from?" he asked.

"Texas."

"What're you doing down here?"

"Just traveling around, trying to find jobs."

"You're not down here to stir up trouble, are you?"

"Ohgodno."

"You start stirring up these niggers and we sure as hell know how to take care of you."

"I don't intend to."

"Do you know what we do to troublemakers down here?"

"No sir."

"We either ship them off to the pen or kill them."

He spoke in a tone that sickened me, casual, merciless. I looked at him. His decent blue eyes turned yellow. I knew that nothing could touch him to have mercy once he decided a Negro should be "taught a lesson." The immensity of it terrified me. But it caught him up like a lust now. He entertained it, his voice unctuous with pleasure and cruelty. The highway stretched deserted through the swamp forests. He nodded toward the solid wall of brush flying past our windows.

"You can kill a nigger and toss him into that swamp and no one'll ever know what happened to him."

"Yes sir . . ."

I forced myself to silence, forced myself to picture this man in his other roles. I saw him as he played with his grandchildren, as he stood up in church with open hymnal in hand, as he drank a cup of coffee in the morning before dressing and then shaved and talked with his wife pleasantly about nothing, as he visited with friends on the front porch Sunday afternoons. That was the man I had seen when I first got into the truck. The amiable, decent American was in all his features. This was the dark tangent in every man's belly, the sickness, the coldness, the mercilessness, the lust to cause pain or fear through self-power. Surely not even his wife or closest friends had ever seen him like this. It was a side he would show no one but his victims, or those who connived with him. The rest—what he really must be as a husband, devoted father and respected member of the community—I had to supply with my imagination. He showed me the lowest and I had to surmise the highest.

His face was set hard in an attempt to regain his equilibrium, when he pulled off the main highway and stopped on a dirt road that led into the jungle. We had engaged in a subtle battle of which I think he had only then become aware. He needed to salvage from it something. "This is where I turn off. I guess you want to stick to the highway."

I thanked him for the ride and opened the door. Before I could get out, he spoke again. "I'll tell you how it is here. We'll do business with you people. We'll sure as hell screw your women. Other than that, you're just *completely off the record as far as we're concerned*. And the quicker you people get that through your heads, the better off you'll be."

"Yes, sir . . ." I stepped out and closed the door. He drove down the side road scattering fine gravel behind his wheels. I listened until his truck was out of hearing distance. The heavy air of evening, putrid with swamp rot, smelled fragrant. I walked across the highway, sat on my duffel and waited for another car. None came. The woods issued no sound. I felt strangely safe, isolated, alone in the stillness of dusk turning to night. First stars appeared in darkening skies still pale and the earth's heat escaped upward.

1961

Topics for General Discussion
and Written Reports on Chapter Five

1. Various studies, such as Myrdal's "An American Dilemma" and Cash's "The Mind of the South," have shown that one of the most deep-rooted notions in white attitudes toward race is the belief that black males are especially attracted to white women. Do the preceding selections tend to endorse or counteract this notion?

2. What do the selections by black authors McKay, Hughes, and Williams and by white author Griffin say about the manner in which whites are attracted to black sexual partners?

3. Discuss the element of violence that runs through several of the selections in this chapter.

4. Discuss the variety of emotional tones it is possible for a writer to bring to the topic of cross-racial sexual attitudes.

5. Do you think Chesnutt's "A Matter of Principle" belongs in this chapter? How is it relevant to the other works which make up the chapter?

NAT TURNER, "THE CONFESSIONS"
AS REPORTED BY THOMAS R. GRAY

OF MR. BOOKER T. WASHINGTON AND OTHERS

O BLACK AND UNKNOWN BARDS

YET DO I MARVEL
SIMON THE CYRENIAN SPEAKS
MOOD

A BLACK MAN TALKS OF REAPING

THE ETHICS OF LIVING JIM CROW

POWERHOUSE

Part Two

FOR MY PEOPLE

DARK SYMPHONY

FLYING HOME

BOOKER T. AND W.E.B.

NAME IN PRINT

THE WHITE NEGRO

JESSE

MY NEGRO PROBLEM—AND OURS

THE ONLY MAN ON LIBERTY STREET

Nat Turner
"The Confessions" (as reported by Thomas R. Gray)

Agreeable to his own appointment, on the evening he was committed to prison, with permission of the jailer, I visited NAT on Tuesday the 1st November, when, without being questioned at all, he commenced his narrative in the following words:—

SIR,—You have asked me to give a history of the motives which induced me to undertake the late insurrection, as you call it—To do so I must go back to the days of my infancy, and even before I was born. I was thirty-one years of age the 2nd of October last, and born the property of Benj. Turner, of this county. In my childhood a circumstance occurred which made an indelible impression on my mind, and laid the ground work of that enthusiasm, which has terminated so fatally to, both white and black, and for which I am about to atone at the gallows. It is here necessary to relate this circumstance—trifling as it may seem, it was the commencement of that belief which has grown with time, and even now, sir, in this dungeon, helpless and forsaken as I am, I cannot divest myself of. Being at play with other children, when theee or four years old, I was telling them something, which my mother overhearing, said it had happened before I was born —I stuck to my story, however, and related somethings which went, in her opinion, to confirm it—others being called on were greatly astonished, knowing that these things had happened, and caused them to say in my hearing, I surely would be a prophet, as the Lord had shewn me things that had happened before my birth. And my father and mother strengthened me in this my first impression, saying in my presence, I was intended for some great purpose, which they had always thought from certain marks on my head and breast—[a parcel of excrescences which I believe are not at all uncommon, particularly among negroes, as I have seen several with the same. In this case he has either cut them off of they have nearly disappeared]— My grandmother, who was very religious, and to whom I was much attached—my master, who belonged to the church, and other religious persons who visited the house, and whom I often saw at prayers, noticing the singularity of my manners, I suppose, and my uncommon intelligence for a child, remarked I had too much sense to be raised, and if I was, I would never be of any service to any one as a slave —To a mind like mine, restless, inquisitive and observant of every thing that was passing, it is easy to suppose that religion was the subject to which it would be directed, and although this subject principally occupied my thoughts—there was nothing that I saw or heard of to which my attention was not directed—The manner in which I learned to read and write, not only had great influence on my own mind, as I acquired it with the most perfect ease, so much so, that I have no recollection whatever of learning the alphabet—but to the astonishment of the family, one day, when a book was shewn to me to keep me from crying, I began spelling the names of different objects—this was a source of wonder to all in the neighborhood, particularly the blacks—and this learning was constantly improved at all opportunities—when I got large enough to go to work, while employed, I was reflecting on many things that would present themselves to my imagination, and whenever an opportunity occurred of looking at a book, when the school children were getting their lessons, I would find many things that the fertility of my own imagination had depicted to me before; all my time, not devoted to my master's service, was spent either in prayer, or in making experiments in casting different things in moulds made of earth, in attempting to make paper, gun-powder, and many other experiments, that although I could not perfect, yet convinced me of its practicability if I had the means.* I was not addicted to stealing in my youth, nor have ever been —Yet such was the confidence of the negroes in the neighborhood, even at this early period of my life, in my superior judgment, that they would often carry me with them when they were going on any roguery, to plan for them. Growing up among them, with this confidence in my superior judgment, and when this, in their opinions, was perfected by Divine inspiration, from the circumstances already alluded to in my infancy, and which belief was ever afterwards zealously inculcated by the austerity of my life and manners, which became the subject of remark by white and black.—Having soon discovered to be great, I must appear so, and therefore studiously avoided mixing in society, and wrapped myself in mystery, devoting my time to fasting and prayer—By this time, having arrived to man's estate, and hearing the scriptures commented on at meetings, I was struck with that particular passage which says: "Seek ye the kingdom of Heaven and all things shall be added unto you." I reflected much on this passage, and prayed daily for light on this subject—As I was praying one day at my plough, the spirit spoke to me, saying "Seek ye the kingdom of Heaven and all things shall be added unto you." *Question*—what do you mean by the Spirit. *Ans.* The Spirit that spoke to the prophets in former days—and I was greatly astonished, and for two years prayed continually, whenever my duty would permit—and then again I had the same revelation, which fully confirmed me in the impression that I was ordained for some great purpose in the hands of the Almighty. Several years rolled round, in which many events occurred to strengthen me in this my belief. At this time I reverted in my mind to the remarks made of me in my childhood, and the things that had been shewn me—and as it had been said of me in my childhood by those by whom I had been taught to pray, both white and black, and in whom I had the greatest confidence, that I had too much sense to be raised, and if I was, I would never be of any use to any one as a slave. Now finding I had arrived to man's estate, and was a slave, and these revelations being made known to me, I began to direct my attention to this great object, to fulfil the purpose for which, by this time, I felt assured I was intended. Knowing the influence I had obtained over the minds of my fellow servants, (not by the means of conjuring and such like tricks— for to them I always spoke of such things with contempt; but by the communion of the Spirit whose revelations I often communicated to them, and they believed and said my wisdom came from God. I now

* When questioned as to the manner of manufacturing those different articles, he was found well informed on the subject. (Gray's note)

began to prepare them for my purpose, by telling them something was about to happen that would terminate in fulfilling the great promise that had been made to me—About this time I was placed under an overseer, from whom I ran away—and after remaining in the woods thirty days, I returned, to the astonishment of the negroes on the plantation, who thought I had made my escape to some other part of the country, as my father had done before. But the reason of my return was, that the Spirit appeared to me and said I had my wishes directed to the things of this world, and not to the kingdom of Heaven, and that I should return to the service of my earthly master—"For he who knoweth his Master's will, and doeth it not, shall be beaten with many stripes, and thus have I chastened you." And the negroes found fault, and murmured against me, saying that if they had my sense they would not serve any master in the world. And about this time I had a vision—and I saw white spirits and black spirits engaged in battle, and the sun was darkened—the thunder rolled in the Heavens, and blood flowed in streams—and I heard a voice saying, "Such is your luck, such you are called to see, and let it come rough or smooth, you must surely bare it." I now withdrew myself as much as my situation would permit, from the intercourse of my fellow servants, for the avowed purpose of serving the Spirit more fully—and it appeared to me, and reminded me of the things it had already shown me, and that it would then reveal to me the knowledge of the elements, the revolution of the planets, the operation of tides, and changes of the seasons. After this revelation in the year of 1825, and the knowledge of the elements being made known to me, I sought more than ever to obtain true holiness before the great day of judgment should appear, and then I began to receive the true knowledge of faith. And from the first steps of righteousness until the last, was I made perfect; and the Holy Ghost was with me, and said, "Behold me as I stand in the Heavens" —and I looked and saw the forms of men in different attitudes—and there were lights in the sky to which the children of darkness gave other names than what they really were—for they were the lights of the Savior's hands, stretched forth from east to west, even as they were extended on the cross on Calvary for the redemption of sinners. And I wondered greatly at these miracles, and prayed to be informed of a certainty of the meaning thereof—and shortly afterwards, while laboring in the field, I discovered drops of blood on the corn as though it were dew from heaven—and I communicated it to many, both white and black, in the neighborhood—and I then found on the leaves in the woods hieroglyphic characters, and numbers, with the forms of men in different attitudes, portrayed in blood, and representing the figures I had seen before in the heavens. And now the Holy Ghost had revealed itself to me, and made plain the miracles it had shown me— For as the blood of Christ had been shed on this earth, and had ascended to heaven for the salvation of sinners, and was now returning to earth again in the form of dew—and as the leaves on the trees bore the impression of the figures I had seen in the heavens, it was plain to me that the Savior was about to lay down the yoke he had borne for the sins of men, and the great day of judgment was at hand. About this time I told these things to a white man, (Etheldred T. Brantley) on whom it had a wonderful effect—and he ceased from his wickedness, and was attacked immediately with a cutaneous eruption, and blood oozed from the pores of his skin, and after praying and fasting nine days, he was healed, and the Spirit appeared to me again, and said, as the Savior had been baptised so should we be also—and when the white people would not let us be baptised by the church, we went down into the water together, in the sight of many who reviled us, and were baptised by the Spirit—After this I rejoiced greatly, and gave thanks to God. And on the 12th of May, 1828, I heard a loud noise in the heavens, and the Spirit instantly appeared to me and said the Serpent was loosened, and Christ had laid down the yoke he had borne for the sins of men, and that I should take it on and fight against the Serpent, for the time was fast approaching when the first should be last and the last should be first. *Ques.* Do you not find yourself mistaken now? *Ans.* Was not Christ crucified? And by signs in the heavens that it would make known to me when I should commence the great work—and until the first sign appeared, I should conceal it from the knowledge of men—And on the appearance of the sign, (the eclipse of the sun last February) I should arise and prepare myself, and slay my enemies with their own weapons. And immediately on the sign appearing in the heavens, the seal was removed from my lips, and I communicated the great work laid out for me to do, to four in whom I had the greatest confidence, (Henry, Hark, Nelson, and Sam) —It was intended by us to have begun the work of death on the 4th July last—Many were the plans formed and rejected by us, and it affected my mind to such a degree, that I fell sick, and the time passed without our coming to any determination how to commence—Still forming new schemes and rejecting them, when the sign appeared again, which determined me not to wait longer.

Since the commencement of 1830, I had been living with Mr. Joseph Travis, who was to me a kind master, and placed the greatest confidence in me; in fact, I had no cause to complain of his treatment to me. On Saturday evening, the 20th of August, it was agreed between Henry, Hark and myself, to prepare a dinner the next day for the men we expected, and then to concert a plan, as we had not yet determined on any. Hark, on the following morning, brought a pig, and Henry brandy, and being joined by Sam, Nelson, Will and Jack, they prepared in the woods a dinner, where, about three o'clock, I joined them.

Q. Why were you so backward in joining them.

A. The same reason that had caused me not to mix with them for years before.

I saluted them on coming up, and asked Will how came he there, he answered, his life was worth no more than others, and his liberty as dear to him. I asked him if he thought to obtain it? He said he would, or lose his life. This was enough to put him in full confidence. Jack, I knew, was only a tool in the hands of Hark, it was quickly agreed we should commence at home (Mr. J. Travis') on that night, and until we had armed and equipped ourselves, and gathered sufficient force, neither age nor sex was to be spared, (which was invariably adhered to). We remained at the feast, until about two hours in the night, when we went to the house and found Austin; they all went to the cider press and drank, except myself. On returning to the house, Hark went to the door with an axe, for the purpose of breaking it open, as we knew we were strong enough to murder the family, if they were awaked by the noise; but reflecting that it might create an alarm in the neighborhood, we determined to enter the house secretly, and murder them whilst sleeping. Hark got a ladder and set it against the chimney, on which I ascended, and hoisting a window, entered and came down stairs, unbarred the door, and removed the guns from their places. It was then observed that I must spill the first blood. On which, armed with a hatchet, and accompanied by Will, I entered my master's chamber, it being dark, I could not give a death blow, the hatchet glanced from his head, he sprang from the bed and called his wife, it was his last word, Will laid him dead, with a blow of his axe, and Mrs. Travis shared the same fate, as she lay in bed. The murder of this family, five in number, was the work of a moment, not one of them awoke; there was a little infant sleeping in a cradle, that was forgotten, until we had left the house and gone some distance, when Henry and Will returned and killed it; we got here, four guns that would shoot, and several old muskets, with a pound or two of powder. We remained some time at the barn, where we paraded; I formed them in a line as soldiers, and after carrying them through all the manoeuvres I was master of marched them off to Mr. Salathul Francis', about six hundred yards distant. Sam and Will went to the door and knocked. Mr. Francis asked who was there, Sam replied it was him, and he had a letter for him, on which he got up and came to the door; they immediately seized him, and dragging him out a little from the door, he was dispatched by repeated blows on the head; there was no other white person in the family. We started from there for Mrs. Reese's, maintaining the most perfect silence on our march, where finding the door unlocked, we entered, and murdered Mrs. Reese in her bed, while sleeping; her son awoke, but it was only to sleep the sleep of death, he had only time to say who is that, and he was no more. From Mrs. Reese's we went to Mrs. Turner's, a mile distant, which we reached about sunrise, on Monday morning. Henry, Austin, and Sam, went to the still, where, finding Mr. Peebles, Austin shot him, and the rest of us went to the house; as we approached, the family discovered us, and shut the door. Vain hope! Will, with one stroke of his axe, opened it, and we entered and found Mrs. Turner and Mrs. Newsome in the middle of a room, almost frightened to death. Will immediately killed Mrs. Turner, with one blow of his axe. I took Mrs. Newsome by the hand, and with the sword I had when I was apprehended, I struck her several blows over the head, but not being able to kill her, as the sword was dull. Will turning around and discovering it, despatched her also. A general destruction of property and search for money and ammunition, always succeeded the murders. By this time my company amounted to fifteen, and nine men mounted, who started for Mrs. Whitehead's, (the other six were to go through a by way to Mr. Bryant's, and rejoin us at Mrs. Whitehead's,) as we approached the house we discovered Mr. Richard Whitehead standing in the cotton patch, near the lane fence; we called him over into the lane, and Will, the executioner, was near at hand, with his fatal axe, to send him to an untimely grave. As we pushed on to the house, I discovered some one run round the garden, and thinking it was some of the white family, I pursued them, but finding it was a servant girl belonging to the house, I returned to commence the work of death, but they whom I left, had not been idle; all the family were already murdered, but Mrs. Whitehead and her daughter Margaret. As I came round to the door I saw Will pulling Mrs. Whitehead out of the house, and at the step he nearly severed her head from her body, with his broad axe. Miss Margaret, when I discovered her, had concealed herself in the corner, formed by the projection of cellar cap from the house; on my approach she fled, but was soon overtaken, and after repeated blows with a sword, I killed her by a blow on the head, with a fence rail. By this time, the six who had gone by Mr. Bryant's, rejoined us, and informed me they had done the work of death assigned them. We again divided, part going to Mr. Richard Porter's, and from thence to Nathaniel Francis', the others to Mr. Howell Harris', and Mr. T. Doyles. On my reaching Mr. Porter's, he had escaped with his family. I understood there, that the alarm had already spread, and I immediately returned to bring up those sent to Mr. Doyles, and Mr. Howell Harris'; the party I left going on to Mr. Francis', having told them I would join them in that neighborhood. I met these sent to Mr. Doyles' and Mr. Harris' returning, having met Mr. Doyle on the road and killed him; and learning from some who joined them, that Mr. Harris was from home. I immediately pursued the course taken by the party gone on before; but knowing they would complete the work of death and pillage, at Mr. Francis' before I could get there, I went to Mr. Peter Edwards', expecting to find them there, but they had been here also. I then went to Mr. John T. Barrow's, they had been here and murdered him. I pursued on their track to Capt. Newit Harris', where I found the greater part mounted, and ready to start; the men now amounting to about forty, shouted and hurraed as I rode up, some were in the yard, loading their guns, others drinking. They said Captain Harris and his family had escaped, the property in the house they destroyed, robbing him of money and other valuables. I ordered them to mount and march instantly, this was about nine or ten o'clock, Monday morning. I proceeded to Mr. Levi Waller's, two or three miles distant. I took my station in the rear, and as it was my object to carry terror and devastation wherever we went, I placed fifteen or twenty of the best armed and most relied on, in front, who generally approached the houses as fast as their horses could run; this was for two purposes, to prevent escape and strike terror to the inhabitants—on this account I never got to the houses, after leaving Mrs. Whitehead's, until the murders were committed, except in one case. I sometimes got in sight in time to see the work of death completed, viewed the mangled bodies as they lay, in silent satisfaction, and immediately started in quest of other victims—Having murdered Mrs. Waller and ten children, we started for Mr. William Williams'—having killed him and two little boys that were there; while engaged in this, Mrs. Williams fled and got some distance from the house, but she was pursued, overtaken, and compelled to get up behind one of the company, who brought her back, and after showing her the mangled body of her lifeless husband, she was told to get down and lay by his side, where she was shot dead. I then started for Mr. Jacob Williams, where the family were murdered—Here he found a young man named Drury, who had come on business with Mr. Williams—he was pursued, overtaken and shot. Mrs. Vaughan was the next place we visited—and after murdering the family here, I determined on starting for Jerusalem—Our number amounted now to fifty or sixty, all mounted and armed with guns, axes, and swords and clubs—On reaching Mr. James W. Parker's gate, immediately on the road leading to Jerusalem, and about three miles distant, it was proposed to me to call there, but I objected, as I knew he was gone to Jerusalem, and my object was to reach there as soon as possible; but some of the men having relations at Mr. Parker's it was agreed that they might call and get his people. I remained at the gate on the road, with seven or eight; the others going across the field to the house, about half a mile off. After waiting some time for them, I became impatient, and started to the house for them, and on our return we were met by a party of white when, who had pursued our blood-stained track, and who had fired on those at the gate, and dispersed them, which I knew nothing of, not having been at that time rejoined by any of them—Immediately on discovering the whites, I ordered my men to halt and form, as they appeared to be alarmed—The white men, eighteen in number, approached us in about one hundred yards, when one of them fired, (this was against the positive orders of Captain Alexander P. Peete, who commanded, and who had directed the men to reserve their fire until within thirty paces)—And I discovered about half of them retreating, I then ordered my men to fire and rush on them; the few remaining stood their ground until we approached within fifty yards, when they fired and retreated. We pursued and overtook some of them who we thought we left dead; (they were not killed) after pursuing them about two hundred yards, and rising a little hill, I discovered they were met by another party, and had halted, and were reloading their guns, (this was a small party from Jerusalem who knew the negroes were in the field, and had just tied their horses to await their return to the road, knowing that Mr. Parker and family were in Jerusalem, but knew nothing of the party that had gone in with Captain Peete; on hearing the firing they immediately rushed to the spot and arrived just in time to arrest the progress of these barbarous villians, and save the lives of their friends and fellow citizens). Thinking that those who retreated first, and the party who fired on us at fifty or sixty yards distant, had all fallen back to meet others with ammunition. As I saw them reloading their guns, and more coming up than I saw at first, and several of my bravest men being wounded, the others became panick struck and squandered over the field; the white men pursued and fired on us several times. Hark had his horse shot under him, and I caught another for him as it was running by me; five or six of my men were wounded, but none left on the field, finding myself defeated here I instantly determined to go through a private way, and cross the Nottoway river at the Cypress Bridge, three miles below Jerusalem, and attack that place in the rear, as I expected they would look for me on the other road, and I had a great desire to get there to procure arms and ammunition. After going a short distance in this private way, accompanied by about twenty men, I overtook two or three who told me the others were dispersed in every direction. After trying in vain to collect a sufficient force to proceed to Jerusalem, I determined to return, as I was sure they would make back to their old neighborhood, where they would rejoin me, make new recruits, and come down again. On my way back, I called at Mrs. Thomas's, Mrs. Spencer's, and several others places, the white families having fled, we found no more victims to gratify our thirst for blood, we stopped at Maj. Ridley's quarter for the night, and being joined by four of his men, with the recruits made since my defeat, we mustered now about forty strong. After placing out sentinels, I laid down to sleep, but was quickly roused by a great racket; starting up, I found some mounted, and others in great confusion; one of the sentinels having given the alarm that we were about to be attacked, I ordered some to ride round and reconnoitre, and on their return the others being more alarmed, not knowing who they were, fled in different ways, so that I was reduced to about twenty again; with this I determined to attempt to recruit, and proceed on to rally in the neighborhood, I had left. Dr. Blunt's was the nearest house, which we reached just before day; on riding up the yard, Hark fired a gun. We expected Dr. Blunt and his family were at Maj. Ridley's, as I knew there was a company of men there; the gun was fired to ascertain if any of the family were at home; we immediately fired upon and retreated, leaving several of my men. I do not know what became of them, as I never saw them afterwards. Pursuing our course back and coming in sight of Captain Harris', where we had been the day before, we discovered a party of white men at the house, on which all deserted me but two, (Jacob and Nat), we concealed ourselves in the woods until near night, when I sent them in search of Henry, Sam, Nelson, and Hark, and directed them to rally all they could, at the place we had had our dinner the Sunday before, where they would find me, and I accordingly returned there as soon as it was dark and remained until Wednesday evening, when discovering white men riding around the place as though they were looking for some one, and none of my men joining me, I concluded Jacob and Nat had been taken, and compelled to betray me. On this I gave up all hope for the present; and on Thursday night after having supplied myself with provisions from Mr. Travis's, I scratched a hole under a pile of fence rails in a field, where I concealed myself for six weeks, never leaving my hiding place but for a few minutes in the dead of night to get water which was very near; thinking by this time I could venture out, I began to go about in the night and eaves drop the houses in the neighborhood; pursuing this course for about a fortnight and gathering little or no intelligence, afraid of speaking to any human being, and returning every morning to my cave before the dawn of day. I know not how long I might have led this life, if accident had not betrayed me, a dog in the neighborhood passing by my hiding place one night while I was out, was attracted by some meat I had in my cave, and crawled in and stole it, and was coming out just as I returned. A few nights after, two negroes having started to go hunting with the same dog, and passed that way, the dog came again to the place, and having just gone out to walk about, discovered me and barked, on which thinking myself discovered, I spoke to them to beg concealment. On making myself known they fled from me. Knowing then they would betray me, I immediately left my hiding place, and was pursued almost incessantly until I was taken a fortnight afterwards by Mr. Benjamin Phipps, in a little hole I had dug out with my sword, for the purpose of concealment, under the top of a fallen tree. On Mr. Phipps' discovering the place of my concealment, he cocked his gun and aimed at me. I requested him not to shoot and I would give up, upon which he demanded my sword. I delivered it to him, and he brought me to prison. During the time I was pursued, I had many hair breadth escapes, which your time will not permit you to relate. I am here loaded with chains, and willing to suffer the fate that awaits me.

I here proceeded to make some inquiries of him, after assuring him of the certain death that awaited him, and that concealment would only bring destruction on the innocent as well as guilty, of his own color, if he knew of any extensive or concerted plan. His answer was, I do not. When I questioned him as to the insurrection in North Carolina happening about the same time, he denied any knowledge of it; and when I looked him in the face as though I would search his inmost thoughts, he replied, "I see sir, you doubt my word; but can you not think the same ideas, and strange appearances about this time in the heaven's might prompt others, as well as myself, to this undertaking." I now had much conversation with and asked him many questions, having forborne to do so previously, except in the cases noted in parenthesis; but during his statement, I had, unnoticed by him, taken notes as to some particular circumstances, and having the advantage of his statement before me in writing, on the evening of the third day that I had been with him, I began a cross examination, and found his statement corroborated by every circumstance coming within my own knowledge or the confessions of others who had been either killed or executed, and whom he had not seen nor had any knowledge since 22d of August last, he expressed himself fully satisfied as to the impracticability of his attempt. It has been said he was ignorant and cowardly, and that his object was to murder and rob for the purpose of obtaining money to make his escape. It is notorious, that he was never known to have a dollar in his life; to swear an oath, or drink a drop of spirits. As to his ignorance, he certainly never had the advantages of education, but he can read and write, (it was taught him by his parents,) and for natural intelligence and quickness of apprehension, is surpassed by few men I have ever seen. As to his being a coward, his reason as given for not resisting Mr. Phipps, shows the decision of his character. When he saw Mr. Phipps present his gun, he said he knew it was impossible for him to escape as the woods were full of men; he therefore thought it was better to surrender, and trust to fortune for his escape. He is a complete fanatic, or plays his part most admirably. On other subjects he possesses an uncommon share of intelligence, with a mind capable of attaining any thing; but warped and perverted by the influence of early impressions. He is below the ordinary stature, though strong and active, having the true negro face, every feature of which is strongly marked. I shall not attempt to describe the effect of his narrative, as told and commented on by himself, in the condemned hole of the prison. The calm, deliberate composure with which he spoke of his late deeds and intentions, the expression of his fiend-like face when excited by enthusiasm, still bearing the stains of the blood of helpless innocence about him; clothed with rags and covered with chains; yet daring to raise his manacled hands to heaven, with a spirit soaring above the attributes of man; I looked on him and my blood curdled in my veins.

I will not shock the feelings of humanity, nor wound afresh the bosoms of the disconsolate sufferers in this unparalleled and inhuman massacre, by detailing the deeds of their fiend-like barbarity. There were two or three who were in the power of these wretches, had they known it, and who escaped in the most providential manner. There were two whom they thought they left dead on the field at Mr. Parker's, but who were only stunned by the blows of their guns, as they did not take time to re-load when they charged on them. The escape of a little girl who went to school at Mr. Waller's, and where the children were collecting for that purpose, excited general sympathy. As their teacher had not arrived, they were at play in the yard, and seeing the negroes approach, she ran up on a dirt chimney, (such as are common to log houses,) and remained there unnoticed during the massacre of the eleven that were killed at this place. She remained on her hiding place till just before the arrival of a party, who were in pursuit of the murderers, when she came down and fled to a swamp, where, a mere child as she was, with the horrors of the late scene before her, she lay concealed until the next day, when seeing a party go up to the house, she came up, and on being asked how she escaped, replied with the utmost simplicity, "The Lord helped her." She was taken up behind a gentleman of the party, and returned to the arms of her weeping mother. Miss Whitehead concealed herself between the bed and the mat that supported it, while they murdered her sister in the same room, without discovering her. She was afterwards carried off, and concealed for protection by a slave of the family, who gave evidence against several of them on their trial. Mrs. Nathaniel Francis, while concealed in a closet heard their blows, and the shrieks of the victims of these ruthless savages; they then entered the closet, where she was concealed, and went out without discovering her. While in this hiding place, she heard two of her women in a quarrel about the division of her clothes. Mr. John T. Baron, discovering them approaching his house, told his wife to make her escape, and scorning to fly fell fighting on his own threshold. After firing his rifle, he discharged his gun at them, and then broke it over the villain who first approached him, but he was overpowered, and slain. His bravery, however, saved from the hands of these monsters his lovely and amiable wife, who will long lament a husband so deserving of her love. As directed by him, she attempted to escape through the garden, when she was caught and held by one of her servant girls, but another coming to her rescue, she fled to the woods, and concealed herself. Few indeed, were those who escaped their work of death. But fortunate for society, the hand of retributive justice has overtaken them; and not one that was known to be concerned has escaped.

1831

W. E. B. DuBois
"Of Mr. Booker T. Washington and Others" from *The Souls of Black Folk*

From birth till death enslaved; in word, in deed, unmanned!
. . . .
Hereditary bondsmen! Know ye not
Who would be free themselves must strike the blow?

BYRON.

Easily the most striking thing in the history of the American Negro since 1876 is the ascendancy of Mr. Booker T. Washington. It began at the time when war memories and ideals were rapidly passing; a day of astonishing commercial development was dawning; a sense of doubt and hesitation overtook the freedmen's sons,—then it was that his leading began. Mr. Washington came, with a single definite programme, at the psychological moment when the nation was a little ashamed of having bestowed so much sentiment on Negroes, and was concentrating its energies on Dollars. His programme of industrial education, conciliation of the South, and submission and silence as to civil and political rights, was not wholly original; the Free Negroes from 1830 up to war-time had striven to build industrial schools, and the American Missionary Association had from the first taught various trades; and Price and others had sought a way of honorable alliance with the best of the Southerners. But Mr. Washington first indissolubly linked these things; he put enthusiasm, unlimited energy, and perfect faith into this programme, and changed it from a by-path into a veritable Way of Life. And the tale of the methods by which he did this is a fascinating study of human life.

It startled the nation to hear a Negro advocating such a programme after many decades of bitter complaint; it startled and won the applause of the South, it interested and won the admiration of the North; and after a confused murmur of protest, it silenced if it did not convert the Negroes themselves.

To gain the sympathy and coöperation of the various elements comprising the white South was Mr. Washington's first task; and this, at the time Tuskegee was founded, seemed, for a black man, well-nigh impossible. And yet ten years later it was done in the word spoken at Atlanta: "In all things purely social we can be as separate as the five fingers, and yet one as the hand in all things essential to mutual progress." This "Atlanta Compromise" is by all odds the most notable thing in Mr. Washington's career. The South interpreted it in different ways: the radicals received it as a complete surrender of the demand for civil and political equality; the conservatives, as a generously conceived working basis for mutual understanding. So both approved it, and to-day its author is certainly the most distinguished Southerner since Jefferson Davis, and the one with the largest personal following.

Next to this achievement comes Mr. Washington's work in gaining place and consideration in the North. Others less shrewd and tactful had formerly essayed to sit on these two stools and had fallen between them; but as Mr. Washington knew the heart of the South from birth and training, so by singular insight he intuitively grasped the spirit of the age which was dominating the North. And so thoroughly did he learn the speech and thought of triumphant commercialism, and the ideals of material prosperity, that the picture of a lone black boy poring over a French grammar amid the weeds and dirt of a neglected home soon seemed to him the acme of absurdities. One wonders what Socrates and St. Francis of Assisi would say to this.

And yet this very singleness of vision and thorough oneness with his age is a mark of the successful man. It is as though Nature must needs make men narrow in order to give them force. So Mr. Washington's cult has gained unquestioning followers, his work has wonderfully prospered, his friends are legion, and his enemies are confounded. To-day he stands as the one recognized spokesman of his ten million fellows, and one of the most notable figures in a nation of seventy millions. One hesitates, therefore, to criticise a life which, beginning with so little, has done so much. And yet the time is come when one may speak in all sincerity and utter courtesy of the mistakes and shortcomings of Mr. Washington's career, as well as of his triumphs, without being thought captious or envious, and without forgetting that it is easier to do ill than well in the world.

The criticism that has hitherto met Mr. Washington has not always been of this broad character. In the South especially has he had to walk warily to avoid the harshest judgments,—and naturally so, for he is dealing with the one subject of deepest sensitiveness to that section. Twice—once when at the Chicago celebration of the Spanish-American War he alluded to the color-prejudice that is "eating away the vitals of the South," and once when he dined with President Roosevelt—has the resulting Southern criticism been violent enough to threaten seriously his popularity. In the North the feeling has several times forced itself into words, that Mr. Washington's counsels of submission overlooked certain elements of true manhood, and that his educational programme was unnecessarily narrow. Usually, however, such criticism has not found open expression, although, too, the spiritual sons of the Abolitionists have not been prepared to acknowledge that the schools founded before Tuskegee, by men of broad ideals and self-sacrificing spirit, were wholly failures or worthy of ridicule. While, then, criticism has not failed to follow Mr. Washington, yet the prevailing public opinion of the land has been but too willing to deliver the solution of a wearisome problem into his hands, and say, "If that is all you and your race ask, take it."

Among his own people, however, Mr. Washington has encountered the strongest and most lasting opposition, amounting at times to bitterness, and even to-day continuing strong and insistent even though largely silenced in outward expression by the public opinion of the nation. Some of this opposition is, of course, mere envy; the disappointment of displaced demagogues and the spite of narrow minds. But aside from this, there is among educated and thoughtful colored men in all parts of the land a feeling of deep regret, sorrow, and apprehension at the wide currency and ascendancy which some of Mr. Washington's theories have gained. These same men admire his sincerity of purpose, and are willing to forgive much to honest endeavor which is doing something worth the doing. They coöperate with Mr. Washington as far as they conscientiously can; and, indeed, it is no ordinary tribute to this man's tact and power that, steering as he must between so many diverse interests and opinions, he so largely retains the respect of all.

But the hushing of the criticism of honest opponents is a dangerous thing. It leads some of the best of the critics to unfortunate silence and paralysis of effort, and others to burst into speech so passionately and intemperately as to lose listeners. Honest and earnest criticism from those whose interests are most nearly touched,—criticism of writers by readers, of government by those governed, of leaders by those led,—this is the soul of democracy and the safeguard of modern society. If the best of the American Negroes receive by outer pressure a leader whom they had not recognized before, manifestly there is here a certain palpable gain. Yet there is also irreparable loss,—a loss of that peculiarly valuable education which a group receives when by search and criticism it finds and commissions its own leaders. The way in which this is done is at once the most elementary and the nicest problem of social growth. History is but the record of such group-leadership; and yet how infinitely changeful is its type and character! And of all types and kinds, what can be more instructive than the leadership of a group within a group?—that curious double movement where real progress may be negative and actual advance be relative retrogression. All this is the social student's inspiration and despair.

Now in the past the American Negro has had instructive experience in the choosing of group leaders, founding thus a peculiar dynasty which in the light of present conditions is worth while studying. When sticks and stones and beasts form the sole environment of a people, their attitude is largely one of determined opposition to and conquest of natural forces. But when to earth and brute is added an environment of men and ideas, then the attitude of the imprisoned group may take three main forms,—a feeling of revolt and revenge; an attempt to adjust all thought and action to the will of the greater group; or, finally, a determined effort at self-realization and self-development despite environing opinion. The influence of all of these attitudes at various times can be traced in the history of the American Negro, and in the evolution of his successive leaders.

Before 1750, while the fire of African freedom still burned in the veins of the slaves, there was in all leadership or attempted leadership but the one motive of revolt and revenge,—typified in the terrible Maroons, the Danish blacks, and Cato of Stono, and veiling all the Americas in fear of insurrrection. The liberalizing tendencies of the latter half of the eighteenth century brought, along with kindlier relations between black and white, thoughts of ultimate adjustment and assimilation. Such aspiration was especially voiced in the earnest songs of Phyllis, in the martyrdom of Attucks, the fighting of Salem and Poor, the intellectual accomplishments of Banneker and Derham, and the political demands of the Cuffes.

Stern financial and social stress after the war cooled much of the previous humanitarian ardor. The disappointment and impatience of the Negroes at the persistence of slavery and serfdom voiced itself in two movements. The slaves in the South, aroused undoubtedly by vague rumors of the Haitian revolt, made three fierce attempts at insurrection,—in 1800 under Gabriel in Virginia, in 1822 under Vesey in Carolina, and in 1831 again in Virgina under the terrible Nat Turner. In the Free States, on the other hand, a new and curious attempt at self-development was made. In Philadelphia and New York color-prescription led to a withdrawal of Negro communicants from white churches and the formation of a peculiar socio-religious institution among the Negroes known as the African Church,—an organization still living and controlling in its various branches over a million of men.

Walker's wild appeal against the trend of the times showed how the world was changing after the coming of the cotton-gin. By 1830 slavery seemed hopelessly fastened on the South, and the slaves thoroughly cowed into submission. The free Negroes of the North inspired by the mulatto immigrants from the West Indies, began to change the basis of their demands; they recognized the slavery of slaves, but insisted that they themselves were freemen, and sought assimilation and amalgamation with the nation on the same terms with other men. Thus, Forten and Purvis of Philadelphia, Shad of Wilmington, Du Bois of New Haven, Barbadoes of Boston, and others, strove singly and together as men, they said, not as slaves; as "people of color," not as "Negroes." The trend of the times, however, refused them recognition save in individual and exceptional cases, considered them as one with all the despised blacks, and they soon found themselves striving to keep even the rights they formerly had of voting and working and moving as freemen. Schemers of migration and colonization arose among them; but these they refused to entertain, and they eventually turned to the Abolition movement as a final refuge.

Here, led by Remond, Nell, Wells-Brown, and Douglass, a new period of self-assertion and self-development dawned. To be sure, ultimate freedom and assimilation was the ideal before the leaders, but the assertion of the manhood rights of the Negro by himself was the main reliance, and John Brown's raid was the extreme of its logic. After the war and emancipation, the great form of Frederick Douglass, the greatest of American Negro leaders, still led the host. Self-assertion, especially in political lines, was the main programme, and behind Douglass came Elliot, Bruce, and Langston, and the Reconstruction politicians, and, less conspicuous but of greater social significance Alexander Crummell and Bishop Daniel Payne.

Then came the Revolution of 1876, the suppression of the Negro votes, the changing and shifting of ideals, and the seeking of new lights in the great night. Douglass, in his old age, still bravely stood for the ideals of his early manhood,—ultimate assimilation *through* self-assertion, and on no other terms. For a time Price arose as a new leader, destined, it seemed, not to give up, but to re-state the old ideals in a form less repugnant to the white South. But he passed away in his prime. Then came the new leader. Nearly all the former ones had become leaders by the silent suffrage of their fellows, had sought to lead their own people alone, and were usually, save Douglass, little known outside their race. But Booker T. Washington arose as essentially the leader not of one race but of two,—a compromiser between the South, the North, and the Negro. Naturally the Negroes resented, at first bitterly, signs of compromise which surrendered their civil and political rights, even though this was to be exchanged for larger chances of economic development. The rich and dominating North, however, was not only weary of the race problem, but was investing largely in Southern enterprises, and welcomed any method of peaceful coöperation. Thus, by national opinion, the Negroes began to recognize Mr. Washington's leadership; and the voice of criticism was hushed.

Mr. Washington represents in Negro thought the old attitude of adjustment and submission; but adjustment at such a peculiar time as to make his programme unique. This is an age of unusual economic development, and Mr. Washington's programme naturally takes an economic cast, becoming a gospel of Work and Money to such an extent as apparently almost completely to over-shadow the higher aims of life. Moreover, this is an age when the more advanced races are coming in closer contact with the less developed races, and the race-feeling is therefore intensified; and Mr. Washington's programme practically accepts the alleged inferiority of the Negro races. Again, in our own land, the reaction from the sentiment of war time has given impetus to race-prejudice against Negroes, and Mr. Washington withdraws many of the high demands of Negroes as men and American citizens. In other periods of intensified prejudice all the Negro's tendency to self-assertion has been called forth; at this period a policy of submission is advocated. In the history of nearly all other races and peoples the doctrine preached at such crises has been that manly self-respect is worth more than lands and houses, and that a people who voluntarily surrender such respect, or cease striving for it, are not worth civilizing.

In answer to this, it has been claimed that the Negro can survive only through submission. Mr. Washington distinctly asks that black people give up, at least for the present, three things,—

First, political power,

Second, insistence on civil rights,

Third, higher education of Negro youth,—

and concentrate all their energies on industrial education, the accumulation of wealth, and the conciliation of the South. This policy has been courageously and insistently advocated for over fifteen years, and has been triumphant for perhaps ten years. As a result of this tender the palm-branch, what has been the return? In these years there have occurred:

1. The disfranchisement of the Negro.

2. The legal creation of a distinct status of civil inferiority for the Negro.

3. The steady withdrawal of aid from institutions for the higher training of the Negro.

These movements are not, to be sure, direct results of Mr. Washington's teachings; but his propaganda has, without a shadow of doubt, helped their speedier accomplishment. The question then comes: Is it possible, and probable, that nine millions of men can make effective progress in economic lines if they are deprived of political rights, made a servile caste, and allowed only the most meagre chance for developing their exceptional men? If history and reason give any distinct answer to these questions, it is an emphatic *No.* And Mr. Washington thus faces the triple paradox of his career:

1. He is striving nobly to make Negro artisans business men and property-owners; but it is utterly impossible, under modern competitive methods, for workingmen and property-owners to defend their rights and exist without the right of suffrage.

2. He insists on thrift and self-respect, but at the same time counsels a silent submission to civic inferiority such as is bound to sap the manhood of any race in the long run.

3. He advocates common-school and industrial training, and depreciates institutions of higher learning; but neither the Negro common-schools, nor Tuskegee itself, could remain open a day were it not for teachers trained in Negro colleges, or trained by their graduates.

This triple paradox in Mr. Washington's position is the object of criticism by two classes of colored Americans. One class is spiritually descended from Toussaint the Savior, through Gabriel, Vesey, and Turner, and they represent the attitude of revolt and revenge; they hate the white South blindly and distrust the white race generally, and so far as they agree on definite action, think that the Negro's only hope lies in emigration beyond the borders of the United States. And yet, by the irony of fate, nothing has more effectually made this programme seem hopeless than the recent course of the United States toward weaker and darker peoples in the West Indies, Hawaii, and the Philippines,—for where in the world may we go and be safe from lying and brute force?

The other class of Negroes who cannot agree with Mr. Washington has hitherto said little aloud. They deprecate the sight of scattered counsels, of internal disagreement; and especially they dislike making their just criticism of a useful and earnest man an excuse for a general discharge of venom from small-minded opponents. Nevertheless, the questions involved are so fundamental and serious that it is difficult to see how men like the Grimkes, Kelly Miller, J. W. E. Bowen, and other representatives of this group, can much longer be silent. Such men feel in conscience bound to ask of this nation three things:

1. The right to vote.
2. Civic equality.
3. The education of youth according to ability.

They acknowledge Mr. Washington's invaluable service in counselling patience and courtesy in such demands; they do not ask that ignorant black men vote when ignorant whites are debarred, or that any reasonable restrictions in the suffrage should not be applied; they know that the low social level of the mass of the race is responsible for much discrimination against it, but they also know, and the nation knows, that relentless color-prejudice is more often a cause than a result of the Negro's degradation; they seek the abatement of this relic of barbarism, and not its systematic encouragement and pampering by all agencies of social power from the Associated Press to the Church of Christ. They advocate, with Mr. Washington, a broad system of Negro common schools supplemented by thorough industrial training; but they are surprised that a man of Mr. Washington's insight cannot see that no such educational system ever has rested or can rest on any other basis than that of the well-equipped college and university, and they insist that there is a demand for a few such institutions throughout the South to train the best of the Negro youth as teachers, professional men, and leaders.

This group of men honor Mr. Washington for his attitude of conciliation toward the white South; they accept the "Atlanta Compromise" in its broadest interpretation; they recognize, with him, many signs of promise, many men of high purpose and fair judgment, in this section; they know that no easy task has been laid upon a region already tottering under heavy burdens. But, nevertheless, they insist that the way to truth and right lies in straightforward honesty, not in indiscriminate flattery; in praising those of the South who do well and criticising uncompromisingly those who do ill; in taking advantage of the opportunities at hand and urging their fellows to do the same, but at the same time in remembering that only a firm adherence to their higher ideals and aspirations will ever keep those ideals within the realm of possibility. They do not expect that the free right to vote, to enjoy civic rights, and to be educated, will come in a moment; they do not expect to see the bias and prejudices of years disappear at the blast of a trumpet; but they are absolutely certain that the way for a people to gain their reasonable rights is not by voluntarily throwing them away and insisting that they do not want them; that the way for a people to gain respect is not by continually belittling and ridiculing themselves; that, on the contrary, Negroes must insist continually, in season and out of season, that voting is necessary to modern manhood, that color discrimination is barbarism, and that black boys need education as well as white boys.

In failing thus to state plainly and unequivocally the legitimate demands of their people, even at the cost of opposing an honored leader, the thinking classes of American Negroes would shirk a heavy responsibility,—a responsibility to themselves, a responsibility to the struggling masses, a responsibility to the darker races of men whose future depends so largely on this American experiment, but especially a responsibility to this nation,—this common Fatherland. It is wrong to encourage a man or a people in evil-doing; it is wrong to aid and abet a national crime simply because it is unpopular not to do so. The growing spirit of kindliness and reconciliation between the North and South after the frightful difference of a generation ago ought to be a source of deep congratulation to all, and especially to those whose mistreatment caused the war; but if that reconciliation is to be marked by the industrial slavery and civic death of those same black men, with permanent legislation into a position of inferiority, then those black men, if they are really men, are called upon by every consideration of patriotism and loyalty to oppose such a course by all civilized methods, even though such opposition involves disagreement with Mr. Booker T. Washington. We have no right to sit silently by while the inevitable seeds are sown for a harvest of disaster to our children, black and white.

First, it is the duty of black men to judge the South discriminatingly. The present generation of Southerners are not responsible for the past, and they should not be blindly hated or blamed for it. Furthermore, to no class is the indiscriminate endorsement of the recent course of the South toward Negroes more nauseating than to the best thought of the South. The South is not "solid"; it is a land in the ferment of social change, wherein forces of all kinds are fighting for supremacy; and to praise the ill the South is to-day perpetrating is just as wrong as to condemn the good. Discriminating and broad-minded criticism is what the South needs,—needs it for the sake of her own white sons and daughters, and for the insurance of robust, healthy mental and moral development.

To-day even the attitude of the Southern whites toward the blacks is not, as so many assume, in all cases the same; the ignorant Southerner hates the Negro, the workingmen fear his competition, the money-makers wish to use him as a laborer, some of the educated see a menace in his upward development, while others—usually the sons of the masters—wish to help him to rise. National opinion has enabled this last class to maintain the Negro common schools, and to protect the Negro partially in property, life, and limb. Through the pressure of the money-makers, the Negro is in danger of being reduced to semi-slavery, especially in the country districts; the workingmen, and those of the educated who fear the Negro, have united to disfranchise him, and some have urged his deportation; while the passions of the ignorant are easily aroused to lynch and abuse any black man. To praise this intricate whirl of thought and prejudice is nonsense; to inveigh indiscriminately against "the South" is unjust; but to use the same breath in praising Governor Aycock, exposing Senator Morgan, arguing with Mr. Thomas Nelson Page, and denouncing Senator Ben Tillman, is not only sane, but the imperative duty of thinking black men.

It would be unjust to Mr. Washington not to acknowledge that in several instances he has opposed movements in the South which were unjust to the Negro; he sent memorials to the Louisiana and Alabama constitutional conventions, he has spoken against lynching, and in other ways has openly or silently set his influence against sinister schemes and unfortunate happenings. Notwithstanding this, it is equally true to assert that on the whole the distinct impression left by Mr. Washington's propaganda is, first, that the South is justified in its present attitude toward the Negro because of the Negro's degradation; secondly, that the prime cause of the Negro's failure to rise more quickly is his wrong education in the past; and, thirdly, that his future rise depends primarily on his own efforts. Each of these propositions is a dangerous half-truth. The supplementary truths must never be lost sight of: first, slavery and race-prejudice are potent if not sufficient causes of the Negro's position; second, industrial and common-school training were necessarily slow in planting because they had to await the black teachers trained by higher institutions,—it being extremely doubtful if any essentially different development was possible, and certainly a Tuskegee was unthinkable before 1880; and, third, while it is a great truth to say that the Negro must strive and strive mightily to help himself, it is equally true that unless his striving be not simply seconded, but rather aroused and encouraged, by the initiative of the richer and wiser environing group, he cannot hope for great success.

In his failure to realize and impress this last point, Mr. Washington is especially to be criticised. His doctrine has tended to make the whites, North and South, shift the burden of the Negro problem to the Negro's shoulders and stand aside as critical and rather pessimistic spectators; when in fact the burden belongs to the nation, and the hands of none of us are clean if we bend not our energies to righting these great wrongs.

The South ought to be led, by candid and honest criticism, to assert her better self and do her full duty to the race she has cruelly wronged and is still wronging. The North—her co-partner in guilt—cannot salve her conscience by plastering it with gold. We cannot settle this problem by diplomacy and suaveness, by "policy" alone. If worse comes to worst, can the moral fibre of this country survive the slow throttling and murder of nine millions of men?

The black men of America have a duty to perform, a duty stern and delicate,—a forward movement to oppose a part of the work of their greatest leader. So far as Mr. Washington preaches Thrift, Patience, and Industrial Training for the masses, we must hold up his hands and strive with him, rejoicing in his honors and glorying in the strength of this Joshua called of God and of man to lead the headless host. But so far as Mr. Washington apologizes for injustice, North or South, does not rightly value the privilege and duty of voting, belittles the emasculating effects of caste distinctions, and opposes the higher training and ambition of our brighter minds,—so far as he, the South, or the Nation, does this,—we must unceasingly and firmly oppose them. By every civilized and peaceful method we must strive for the rights which the world accords to men, clinging unwaveringly to those great words which the sons of the Fathers would fain forget: "We hold these truths to be self-evident: That all men are created equal; that they are endowed by their Creator with certain unalienable rights; that among these are life, liberty, and the pursuit of happiness."

1903

James Weldon Johnson
O Black and Unknown Bards

O black and unknown bards of long ago,
How came your lips to touch the sacred fire?
How, in your darkness, did you come to know
The power and beauty of the minstrel's lyre?
Who first from midst his bonds lifted his eyes?   5
Who first from out the still watch, lone and long,
Feeling the ancient faith of prophets rise
Within his dark-kept soul, burst into song?

Heart of what slave poured out such melody
As "Steal away to Jesus"? On its strains   10
His spirit must have nightly floated free,
Though still about his hands he felt his chains.
Who heard great "Jordan roll"? Whose starward eye
Saw chariot "swing low"? And who was he

That breathed that comforting, melodic sigh,   15
"Nobody knows de trouble I see"?

What merely living clod, what captive thing,
Could up toward God through all its darkness grope,
And find within its deadened heart to sing
These songs of sorrow, love and faith, and hope?   20
How did it catch that subtle undertone,
That note in music heard not with the ears?
How sound the elusive reed so seldom blown,
Which stirs the soul or melts the heart to tears.

Not that great German master in his dream   25
Of harmonies that thundered amongst the stars
At the creation, ever heard a theme
Nobler than "Go down, Moses." Mark its bars
How like a mighty trumpet-call they stir
The blood. Such are the notes that men have sung   30
Going to valorous deeds; such tones there were
That helped make history when Time was young.

There is a wide, wide wonder in it all,
That from degraded rest and servile toil
The fiery spirit of the seer should call   35
These simple children of the sun and soil.
O black slave singers, gone, forgot, unfamed,
You—you alone, of all the long, long line
Of those who've sung untaught, unknown, unnamed,
Have stretched out upward, seeking the divine.   40

You sang not deeds of heroes or of kings;
No chant of bloody war, no exulting paean
Of arms-won triumphs; but your humble strings
You touched in chord with music empyrean.
You sang far better than you knew; the songs   45
That for your listeners' hungry hearts sufficed
Still live,—but more than this to you belongs:
You sang a race from wood and stone to Christ.

1917

Countee Cullen
Yet Do I Marvel

I doubt not God is good, well-meaning, kind,
And did He stoop to quibble could tell why
The little buried mole continues blind,
Why flesh that mirrors Him must someday die,
Make plain the reason tortured Tantalus   5
Is baited by the fickle fruit, declare
If merely brute caprice dooms Sisyphus
To struggle up a never-ending stair.
Inscrutable His ways are, and immune
To catechism by a mind too strewn   10
With petty cares to slightly understand
What awful brain compels His awful hand.
Yet do I marvel at this curious thing:
To make a poet black, and bid him sing!

1925

Simon the Cyrenian Speaks

He never spoke a word to me,
And yet He called my name;
He never gave a sign to me,
And yet I knew and came.

At first I said, "I will not bear   5
His cross upon my back;
He only seeks to place it there
Because my skin is black."

But He was dying for a dream,
And He was very meek,   10
And in His eyes there shone a gleam
Men journey far to seek.

It was Himself my pity bought;
I did for Christ alone
What all of Rome could not have wrought   15
With bruise of lash or stone.

1925

Mood

I think an impulse stronger than my mind
May some day grasp a knife, unloose a vial,
Or with a little leaden ball unbind
The cords that tie me to the rank and file.
My hands grow quarrelsome with bitterness,
And darkly bent upon the final fray;
Night with its stars upon a grave seems less
Indecent than the too complacent day.

God knows I would be kind, let live, speak fair,
Requite an honest debt with more than just,
And love for Christ's dear sake these shapes that wear
A pride that had its genesis in dust,—
The meek are promised much in a book I know
But one grows weary turning cheek to blow.

1927

Arna Bontemps
A Black Man Talks of Reaping

I have sown beside all waters in my day.
I planted deep, within my heart the fear
that wind or fowl would take the grain away.
I planted safe against this stark, lean year.

I scattered seed enough to plant the land   5
in rows from Canada to Mexico
but for my reaping only what the hand
can hold at once is all that I can show.

Yet what I sowed and what the orchard yields
my brother's sons are gathering stalk and root;   10
small wonder then my children glean in fields
they have not sown, and feed on bitter fruit.

1927

Richard Wright
The Ethics of Living Jim Crow

AN AUTOBIOGRAPHICAL SKETCH

I

My first lesson in how to live as a Negro came when I was quite small.
We were living in Arkansas. Our house stood behind the railroad
tracks. Its skimpy yard was paved with black cinders. Nothing green
ever grew in that yard. The only touch of green we could see was far
away, beyond the tracks, over where the white folks lived. But cinders were good enough for me and I never missed the green growing
things. And anyhow cinders were fine weapons. You could always
have a nice hot war with huge black cinders. All you had to do was
crouch behind the brick pillars of a house with your hands full of gritty
ammunition. And the first woolly black head you saw pop out from
behind another row of pillars was your target. You tried your very
best to knock it off. It was great fun.

I never fully realized the appalling disadvantages of a cinder environment till one day the gang to which I belonged found itself engaged in a war with the white boys who lived beyond the tracks. As usual we laid down our cinder barrage, thinking that this would wipe the white boys out. But they replied with a steady bombardment of broken bottles. We doubled our cinder barrage, but they hid behind trees, hedges, and the sloping embankments of their lawns. Having no such fortifications, we retreated to the brick pillars of our homes. During the retreat a broken milk bottle caught me behind the ear, opening a deep gash which bled profusely. The sight of blood pouring over my face completely demoralized our ranks. My fellow-combatants left me standing paralyzed in the center of the yard, and scurried for their homes. A kind neighbor saw me, and rushed me to a doctor, who took three stitches in my neck.

I sat brooding on my front steps, nursing my wound and waiting for my mother to come from work. I felt that a grave injustice had been done me. It was all right to throw cinders. The greatest harm a cinder could do was leave a bruise. But broken bottles were dangerous; they left you cut, bleeding, and helpless.

When night fell, my mother came from the white folks' kitchen. I raced down the street to meet her. I could just feel in my bones that she would understand. I knew she would tell me exactly what to do next time. I grabbed her hand and babbled out the whole story. She examined my wound, then slapped me.

"How come yuh didn't hide?" she asked me. "How come yuh aways fightin'?"

I was outraged, and bawled. Between sobs I told her that I didn't have any trees or hedges to hide behind. There wasn't a thing I could have used as a trench. And you couldn't throw very far when you were hiding behind the brick pillars of a house. She grabbed a barrel stave, dragged me home, stripped me naked, and beat me till I had a fever of one hundred and two. She would smack my rump with the stave, and, while the skin was still smarting impart to me gems of Jim Crow wisdom. I was never to throw cinders any more. I was never to fight any more wars. I was never, never, under any conditions, to fight *white* folks again. And they were absolutely right in clouting me with the broken milk bottle. Didn't I know she was working hard every day in the hot kitchens of the white folks to make money to take care of me? When was I ever going to learn to be a good boy? She couldn't be bothered with my fights. She finished by telling me that I ought to be thankful to God as long as I lived that they didn't kill me.

All that night I was delirious and could not sleep. Each time I closed my eyes I saw monstrous white faces suspended from the ceiling, leering at me.

From that time on, the charm of my cinder yard was gone. The green trees, the trimmed hedges, the cropped lawns grew very meaningful, became a symbol. Even today when I think of white folks, the hard, sharp outlines of white houses surrounded by trees, lawns, and hedges are present somewhere in the background of my mind. Through the years they grew into an overreaching symbol of fear.

It was a long time before I came in close contact with white folks again. We moved from Arkansas to Mississippi. Here we had the good fortune not to live behind the railroad tracks, or close to white neighborhoods. We lived in the very heart of the local Black Belt. There were black churches and black preachers; there were black schools and black teachers; black groceries and black clerks. In fact, everything was so solidly black that for a long time I did not even think of white folks, save in remote and vague terms. But this could not last forever. As one grows older one eats more. One's clothing cost more. When I finished grammar school I had to go to work. My mother could no longer feed and clothe me on her cooking job.

There is but one place where a black boy who knows no trade can get a job, and that's where the houses and faces are white, where the trees, lawns, and hedges are green. My first job was with an optical company in Jackson, Mississippi. The morning I applied I stood straight and neat before the boss, answering all his questions with sharp yessirs and nosirs. I was very careful to pronounce my *sirs* distinctly, in order that he might know that I was polite, that I knew where I was, and that I knew he was a *white* man. I wanted that job badly.

He looked me over as though he were examining a prize poodle. He questioned me closely about my schooling, being particularly insistent about how much mathematics I had had. He seemed very pleased when I told him I had had two years of algebra.

"Boy, how would you like to try to learn something around here?" he asked me.

"I'd like it fine, sir," I said, happy. I had visions of "working my way up." Even Negroes have those visions.

"All right," he said. "Come on."

I followed him to the small factory.

"Pease," he said to a white man of about thirty-five, "this is Richard. He's going to work for us."

I was then taken to a white boy of about seventeen.

"Morrie, this is Richard, who's going to work for us."

"Whut yuh sayin' there, boy!" Morrie boomed at me.

"Fine!" I answered.

The boss instructed these two to help me, teach me, give me jobs to do, and let me learn what I could in my spare time.

My wages were five dollars a week.

I worked hard, trying to please. For the first month I got along O.K. Both Pease and Morrie seemed to like me. But one thing was missing. And I kept thinking about it. I was not learning anything and nobody was volunteering to help me. Thinking they had forgotten that I was to learn something about the mechanics of grinding lenses, I asked Morrie one day to tell me about the work. He grew red.

"Whut yuh tryin' t' do, nigger, get smart?" he asked.

"Naw; I ain't tryin' t' git smart," I said.

"Well, don't, if yuh know whut's good for yuh!"

I was puzzled. Maybe he just doesn't want to help me, I thought. I went to Pease.

"Say, are yuh crazy, you black bastard?" Pease asked me, his gray eyes growing hard.

I spoke out, reminding him that the boss had said I was to be given a chance to learn something.

"Nigger, you think you're *white*, don't you?"

"Naw, sir!"

"Well, you're acting mighty like it!"

"But Mr. Pease, the boss said . . ."

Pease shook his fist in my face.

"This is a *white* man's work around here, and you better watch yourself!"

From then on they changed toward me. They said good-morning no more. When I was just a bit slow in performing some duty, I was called a lazy black son-of-a-bitch.

Once I thought of reporting all this to the boss. But the mere idea of what would happen to me if Pease and Morrie should learn that I had "snitched" stopped me. And after all the boss was a white man, too. What was the use?

The climax came at noon one summer day. Peace called me to his workbench. To get to him I had to go between two narrow benches and stand with my back against a wall.

"Yes, sir," I said.

"Richard, I want to ask you something," Pease began pleasantly, not looking up from his work.

"Yes, sir," I said again.

Morrie came over, blocking the narrow passage between the benches. He folded his arms, staring at me solemnly.

I looked from one to the other, sensing that something was coming.

"Yes, sir," I said for the third time.

Pease looked up and spoke very slowly.

"Richard, *Mr. Morrie* here tells me you called me *Pease*."

I stiffened. A void seemed to open up in me. I knew this was the show-down.

He meant that I had failed to call him Mr. Pease. I looked at Morrie. He was gripping a steel bar in his hands. I opened my mouth to speak, to protest, to assure Pease that I had never called him simply *Pease*, and that I had never had any intentions of doing so, when Morrie grabbed me by the collar, ramming my head against the wall.

"Now, be careful, nigger!" snarled Morrie, baring his teeth. "I heard yuh call 'im *Pease*! 'N' if yuh say yuh didn't, yuh're callin' me a *lie*, see?" He waved the steel bar threateningly.

If I had said: No, sir, Mr. Pease, I never called you *Pease*, I would have been automatically calling Morrie a liar. And if I had said: Yes, sir, Mr. Pease, I called you *Pease*, I would have been pleading guilty to having uttered the worst insult that a Negro can utter to a southern white man. I stood hesitating, trying to frame a neutral reply.

"Richard, I asked you a question!" said Pease. Anger was creeping into his voice.

"I don't remember calling you *Pease*, Mr. Pease," I said cautiously. "And if I did, I sure didn't mean . . ."

"You black son-of-a-bitch! You called me *Pease*, then!" he spat, slapping me till I bent sideways over a bench. Morrie was on top of me, demanding:

"Didn't yuh call 'im *Pease*? If yuh say yuh didn't, I'll rip yo' gut string loose with this bar, yuh black granny dodger! Yuh can't call a white man a lie 'n' git erway with it, you black son-of-a-bitch!"

I wilted. I begged them not to bother me. I knew what they wanted. They wanted me to leave.

"I'll leave," I promised. "I'll leave right *now*."

They gave me a minute to get out of the factory. I was warned not to show up again, or tell the boss.

I went.

When I told the folks at home what had happened, they called me a fool. They told me that I must never again attempt to exceed my boundaries. When you are working for white folks, they said, you got to "stay in your place" if you want to keep working.

II

My Jim Crow education continued on my next job, which was portering in a clothing store. One morning, while polishing brass out front, the boss and his twenty-year-old son got out of their car and half dragged and half kicked a Negro woman into the store. A policeman standing at the corner looked on, twirling his nightstick. I watched out of the corner of my eye, never slackening the strokes of my chamois upon the brass. After a few minutes, I heard shrill screams coming from the rear of the store. Later the woman stumbled out, bleeding, crying, and holding her stomach. When she reached the end of the block, the policeman grabbed her and accused her of being drunk. Silently, I watched him throw her into a patrol wagon.

When I went to the rear of the store, the boss and his son were washing their hands at the sink. They were chuckling. The floor was bloody and stewn with wisps of hair and clothing. No doubt I must have appeared pretty shocked, for the boss slapped me reassuringly on the back.

"Boy, that's what we do to niggers when they don't want to pay their bills," he said, laughing.

His son looked at me and grinned.

"Here, hava cigarette," he said.

Not knowing what to do, I took it. He lit his and held the match for me. This was a gesture of kindness, indicating that even if they had beaten the poor old woman, they would not beat me if I knew enough to keep my mouth shut.

"Yes, sir," I said, and asked no questions.

After they had gone, I sat on the edge of a packing box and stared at the bloody floor till the cigarette went out.

That day at noon, while eating in a hamburger joint, I told my fellow Negro porters what had happened. No one seemed surprised. One fellow, after swallowing a huge bite, turned to me and asked:

"Huh! Is tha' all they did t' her?"

"Yeah. Wasn't tha' enough?" I asked.

"Shucks! Man, she's a lucky bitch!" he said, burying his lips deep into a juicy hamburger. "Hell, it's a wonder they didn't lay her when they got through."

III

I was learning fast, but not quite fast enough. One day, while I was delivering packages in the suburbs, my bicycle tire was punctured. I walked along the hot, dusty road, sweating and leading my bicycle by the handle-bars.

A car slowed at my side.

"What's the matter, boy?" a white man called.

I told him my bicycle was broken and I was walking back to town.

"That's too bad," he said. "Hop on the running board."

He stopped the car. I clutched hard at my bicycle with one hand and clung to the side of the car with the other.

"All set?"

"Yes, sir," I answered. The car started.

It was full of young white men. They were drinking. I watched the flask pass from mouth to mouth.

"Wanna drink, boy?" one asked.

I laughed as the wind whipped my face. Instinctively obeying the freshly planted precepts of my mother, I said:

"Oh, no!"

The words were hardly out of my mouth before I felt something hard and cold smash me between the eyes. It was an empty whisky bottle. I saw stars, and fell backwards from the speeding car into the dust of the road, my feet becoming entangled in the steel spokes of my bicycle. The white men piled out and stood over me.

"Nigger, ain't yuh learned no better sense'n tha' yet?" asked the man who hit me. "Ain' yuh learned t' say *sir* t' a white man yet?"

Dazed, I pulled to my feet. My elbows and legs were bleeding. Fists doubled, the white man advanced, kicking my bicycle out of the way.

"Aw, leave the bastard alone. He's got enough," said one.

They stood looking at me. I rubbed my shins, trying to stop the flow of blood. No doubt they felt a sort of contemptuous pity, for one asked:

"Yuh wanna ride t' town now, nigger? Yuh reckon yuh know enough t' ride now?"

"I wanna walk," I said, simply.

Maybe it sounded funny. They laughed.

"Well, walk, you black son-of-a-bitch!"

When they left they comforted me with:

"Nigger, yuh sho better be damn glad it wuz us yuh talked t' tha' way. Yuh're a lucky bastard, 'cause if yuh'd said tha' t' somebody else, yuh might've been a dead nigger now."

IV

Negroes who have lived South know the dread of being caught alone upon the streets in white neighborhoods after the sun has set. In such a simple situation as this the plight of the Negro in America is graphically symbolized. While white strangers may be in these neighborhoods trying to get home, they can pass unmolested. But the color of a Negro's skin makes him easily recognizable, makes him suspect, converts him into a defenseless target.

Late one Saturday night I made some deliveries in a white neighborhood. I was pedaling my bicycle back to the store as fast as I could, when a police car, swerving toward me, jammed me into the curbing.

"Get down and put up your hands!" the policemen ordered.

I did. They climbed out of the car, guns drawn, faces set, and advanced slowly.

"Keep still!" they ordered.

I reached my hands higher. They searched my pockets and packages. They seemed dissatisfied when they could find nothing incriminating. Finally, one of them said:

"Boy, tell your boss not to send you out in white neighborhoods after sundown."

As usual, I said:

"Yes, sir."

V

My next job was as hall-boy in a hotel. Here my Jim Crow education broadened and deepened. When the bell-boys were busy, I was often called to assist them. As many of the rooms in the hotel were occupied by prostitutes, I was constantly called to carry them liquor and cigarettes. These women were nude most of the time. They did not bother about clothing, even for bell-boys. When you went into their rooms, you were supposed to take their nakedness for granted, as though it startled you no more than a blue vase or a red rug. Your presence awoke in them no sense of shame, for you were not regarded as human. If they were alone, you could steal sidelong glimpses at them. But if they were receiving men, not a flicker of your eyelids could show. I remember one incident vividly. A new woman, a huge, snowy-skinned blonde, took a room on my floor. I was sent to wait upon her. She was in bed with a thick-set man; both were nude and uncovered. She said she wanted some liquor and slid out of bed and waddled across the floor to get her money from a dresser drawer. I watched her.

"Nigger, what in hell you looking at?" the white man asked me, raising himself upon his elbows.

"Nothing," I answered, looking miles deep into the blank wall of the room.

"Keep your eyes where they belong, if you want to be healthy!" he said.

"Yes, sir."

VI

One of the bell-boys I knew in this hotel was keeping steady company with one of the Negro maids. Out of a clear sky the police descended upon his home and arrested him, accusing him of bastardy. The poor boy swore he had had no intimate relations with the girl. Nevertheless, they forced him to marry her. When the child arrived, it was found to be much lighter in complexion than either of the two supposedly legal parents. The white men around the hotel made a great joke of it. They spread the rumor that some white cow must have scared the poor girl while she was carrying the baby. If you were in their presence when this explanation was offered, you were supposed to laugh.

VII

One of the bell-boys was caught in bed with a white prostitute. He was castrated and run out of town. Immediately after this all the bell-boys and hall-boys were called together and warned. We were given to understand that the boy who had been castrated was a "mighty, mighty lucky bastard." We were impressed with the fact that next time the management of the hotel would not be responsible for the lives of "trouble-makin' niggers." We were silent.

VIII

One night, just as I was about to go home, I met one of the Negro maids. She lived in my direction, and we fell in to walk part of the way home together. As we passed the white night-watchman, he slapped the maid on her buttock. I turned around, amazed. The watchman looked at me with a long, hard, fixed-under stare. Suddenly he pulled his gun and asked:

"Nigger, don't yuh like it?"

I hesitated.

"I asked yuh don't yuh like it?" he asked again, stepping forward.

"Yes, sir," I mumbled.

"Talk like it, then!"

"Oh, yes, sir!" I said with as much heartiness as I could muster.

Outside, I walked ahead of the girl, ashamed to face her. She caught up with me and said:

"Don't be a fool! Yuh couldn't help it!"

This watchman boasted of having killed two Negroes in self-defense.

Yet, in spite of all this, the life of the hotel ran with an amazing smoothness. It would have been impossible for a stranger to detect anything. The maids, the hall-boys, and the bell-boys were all smiles. They had to be.

IX

I had learned my Jim Crow lessons so thoroughly that I kept the hotel job till I left Jackson for Memphis. It so happened that while in Memphis, I applied for a job at a branch of the optical company. I was hired. And for some reason, as long as I worked there, they never brought my past against me.

Here my Jim Crow education assumed quite a different form. It was no longer brutally cruel, but subtly cruel. Here I learned to lie, to steal, to dissemble. I learned to play that dual role which every Negro must play if he wants to eat and live.

For example, it was almost impossible to get a book to read. It was assumed that after a Negro had imbibed what scanty schooling the state furnished he had no further need for books. I was always borrowing books from men on the job. One day I mustered enough courage to ask one of the men to let me get books from the library in his name. Surprisingly, he consented. I cannot help but think that he consented because he was a Roman Catholic and felt a vague sympathy for Negroes, being himself an object of hatred. Armed with a library card, I obtained books in the following manner: I would write a note to the librarian, saying: "Please let this nigger boy have the following books." I would then sign it with the white man's name.

When I went to the library, I would stand at the desk, hat in hand,

looking as unbookish as possible. When I received the books desired
I would take them home. If the books listed in the note happened to be
out, I would sneak into the lobby and forge a new one. I never took
any chances guessing with the white librarian about what the ficti-
tious white man would want to read. No doubt if any of the white
patrons had suspected that some of the volumes they enjoyed had been
in the home of a Negro, they would not have tolerated it for an instant.

The factory force of the optical company in Memphis was much
larger than that in Jackson, and more urbanized. At least they liked
to talk, and would engage the Negro help in conversation whenever
possible. By this means I found that many subjects were taboo from
the white man's point of view. Among the topics they did not like to
discuss with Negroes were the following: American white women; the
Ku Klux Klan; France, and how Negro soldiers fared while there;
French women; Jack Johnson; the entire northern part of the United
States; the Civil War; Abraham Lincoln; U. S. Grant; General Sherman;
Catholics; the Pope; Jews; the Republican Party; slavery; social equality;
Communism; Socialism; the 13th and 14th Amendments to the Con-
stitution; or any topic calling for positive knowledge or manly self-
assertion on the part of the Negro. The most accepted topics were sex
and religion.

There were many times when I had to exercise a great deal of in-
genuity to keep out of trouble. It is a southern custom that all men
must take off their hats when they enter an elevator. And especially
did this apply to us blacks with rigid force. One day I stepped into an
elevator with my arms full of packages. I was forced to ride with my
hat on. Two white men stared at me coldly. Then one of them very
kindly lifted my hat and placed it upon my armful of packages. Now
the most accepted response for a Negro to make under such circumstances is to look at the white man out of the corner of his eye and grin.
To have said: "Thank you!" would have made the white man *think*
that you *thought* you were receiving from him a personal service. For
such an act I have seen Negroes take a blow in the mouth. Finding the
first alternative distasteful, and the second dangerous, I hit upon an
acceptable course of action which fell safely between these two poles.
I immediately—no sooner than my hat was lifted—pretended that my
packages were about to spill, and appeared deeply distressed with keeping them in my arms. In this fashion I evaded having to acknowledge
his service, and, in spite of adverse circumstances, salvaged a slender
shred of personal pride.

How do Negroes feel about the way they have to live? How do they discuss it when alone among themselves? I think this question can be answered in a single sentence. A friend of mine who ran an elevator once told me:

"Lawd, man! Ef it wuzn't fer them polices 'n' them ol' lynch-mobs, there wouldn't be nothin' but uproar down here!"

1937

Eudora Welty
Powerhouse

Powerhouse is playing!

He's here on tour from the city—"Powerhouse and His Keyboard"—"Powerhouse and His Tasmanians"—think of the things he calls himself! There's no one in the world like him. You can't tell what he is. "Nigger man"?—he looks more Asiatic, monkey, Jewish, Babylonian, Peruvian, fanatic, devil. He has pale gray eyes, heavy lids, maybe horny like a lizard's, but big glowing eyes when they're open. He has African feet of the greatest size, stomping, both together, on each side of the pedals. He's not coal black—beverage colored—looks like a preacher when his mouth is shut, but then it opens—vast and obscene. And his mouth is going every minute: like a monkey's when it looks for something. Improvising, coming on a light and childish melody—*smooch*—he loves it with his mouth.

Is it possible that he could be this! When you have him there performing for you, that's what you feel. You know people on a stage—and people of a darker race—so likely to be marvelous, frightening.

This is a white dance. Powerhouse is not a show-off like the Harlem boys, not drunk, not crazy—he's in a trance; he's a person of joy, a fanatic. He listens as much as he performs, a look of hideous, powerful rapture on his face. Big arched eyebrows that never stop traveling, like a Jew's—wandering-Jew eyebrows. When he plays he beats down piano and seat and wears them away. He is in motion every moment —what could be more obscene? There he is with his great head, fat stomach, and little round piston legs, and long yellow-sectioned strong big fingers, at rest about the size of bananas. Of course you know how he sounds—you've heard him on records—but still you need to see him. He's going all the time, like skating around the skating rink or rowing a boat. It makes everybody crowd around, here in this shadowless steel-trussed hall with the rose-like posters of Nelson Eddy and the testimonial for the mind-reading horse in handwriting magnified five hundred times. Then all quietly he lays his finger on a key with the promise and serenity of a sibyl touching the book.

Powerhouse is so monstrous he sends everybody into oblivion. When any group, any performers, come to town, don't people always come out and hover near, leaning inward, about them, to learn what it is? What is it? Listen. Remember how it was with the acrobats. Watch them carefully, hear the least word, especially what they say to one another, in another language—don't let them escape you; it's the only time for hallucination, the last time. They can't stay. They'll be somewhere else this time tomorrow.

Powerhouse has as much as possible done by signals. Everybody, laughing as if to hide a weakness, will sooner or later hand him up a written request. Powerhouse reads each one, studying with a secret face: that is the face which looks like a mask—anybody's; there is a moment when he makes a decision. Then a light slides under his eyelids, and he says, "92!" or some combination of figures—never a name. Before a number the band is all frantic, misbehaving, pushing, like children in a schoolroom, and he is the teacher getting silence. His hands over the keys, then says sternly, "You-all ready? You-all ready to do some serious walking?"—waits—then, STAMP. Quiet. STAMP, for the second time. This is absolute. Then a set of rhythmic kicks against the floor to communicate the tempo. Then, O Lord! say the distended eyes from beyond the boundary of the trumpets, Hello and good-bye, and they are all down the first note like a waterfall.

This note marks the end of any known discipline. Powerhouse seems to abandon them all—he himself seems lost—down in the song, yelling up like somebody in a whirlpool—not guiding them—hailing them only. But he knows, really. He cries out, but he must know exactly. "Mercy! . . . What I say! . . . Yeah!" And then drifting, listening—"Where that skin beater?"—wanting drums, and starting up and pouring it out in the greatest delight and brutality. On the sweet pieces such a leer for everybody! He looks down so benevolently upon all our faces and whispers the lyrics to us. And if you could hear him at this moment on "Marie, the Dawn is Breaking"! He's going up the keyboard with a few fingers in some very derogatory triplet-routine, he gets higher and higher, and then he looks over the end of the piano, as if over a cliff. But not in a show-off way—the song makes him do it.

He loves the way they all play, too—all those next to him. The far section of the band is all studious, wearing glasses, every one—they don't count. Only those playing around Powerhouse are the real ones. He has a bass fiddler from Vicksburg, black as pitch, named Valentine, who plays with his eyes shut and talking to himself, very young: Powerhouse has to keep encouraging him. "Go on, go on, give it up, bring it on out there!" When you heard him like that on records, did you know he was really pleading?

He calls Valentine out to take a solo.

"What you going to play?" Powerhouse looks out kindly from behind the piano; he opens his mouth and shows his tongue, listening.

Valentine looks down, drawing against his instrument, and says without a lip movement, " 'Honeysuckle Rose.' "

He has a clarinet player named Little Brother, and loves to listen to anything he does. He'll smile and say, "Beautiful!" Little Brother takes a step forward when he plays and stands at the very front, with the whites of his eyes like fishes swimming. Once when he played a low note, Powerhouse muttered in dirty praise, "He went clear downstairs to get that one!"

After a long time, he holds up the number of fingers to tell the band how many choruses still to go—usually five. He keeps his directions down to signals.

It's a bad night outside. It's a white dance, and nobody dances, except a few straggling jitterbugs and two elderly couples. Everybody just stands around the band and watches Powerhouse. Sometimes they steal glances at one another, as if to say, Of course, you know how it is with *them*—Negroes—band leaders—they would play the same way, giving all they've got, for an audience of one. . . . When somebody, no matter who, gives everything, it makes people feel ashamed for him.

Late at night they play the one waltz they will ever consent to play—by request, "Pagan Love Song." Powerhouse's head rolls and sinks like a weight between his waving shoulders. He groans, and his fingers drag into the keys heavily, holding on to the notes, retrieving. It is a sad song.

"You know what happened to me?" says Powerhouse.

Valentine hums a response, dreaming at the bass.

"I got a telegram my wife is dead," says Powerhouse, with wandering fingers.

"Uh-huh?"

His mouth gathers and forms a barbarous O while his fingers walk up straight, unwillingly, three octaves.

"Gypsy? Why how come her to die, didn't you just phone her up in the night last night long distance?"

"Telegram says—here the words: Your wife is dead." He puts 4/4 over the 3/4.

"Not but four words?" This is the drummer, an unpopular boy named Scoot, a disbelieving maniac.

Powerhouse is shaking his vast cheeks. "What the hell was she trying to do? What was she up to?"

"What name has it got signed, if you got a telegram?" Scoot is spitting away with those wire brushes.

Little Brother, the clarinet player, who cannot now speak, glares and tilts back.

"Uranus Knockwood is the name signed." Powerhouse lifts his eyes open. "Ever heard of him?" A bubble shoots out on his lip like a plate on a counter.

Valentine is beating slowly on with his palm and scratching the strings with his long blue nails. He is fond of a waltz, Powerhouse interrupts him.

"I don't know him. Don't know who he is." Valentine shakes his head with the closed eyes.

"Say it agin."

"Uranus Knockwood."

"That ain't Lenox Avenue."

"It ain't Broadway."

"Ain't ever seen it wrote out in any print, even for horse racing."

"Hell, that's on a star, boy, ain't it?" Crash of the cymbals.

"What the hell was she up to?" Powerhouse shudders. "Tell me, tell me, tell me." He makes triplets, and begins a new chorus. He holds three fingers up.

"You say you got a telegram." This is Valentine, patient and sleepy, beginning again.

Powerhouse is elaborate. "Yas, the time I go out, go way downstairs along a long cor-ri-dor to where they puts us: coming back along the cor-ri-dor: steps out and hands me a telegram: Your wife is dead."

"Gypsy?" The drummer like a spider over his drums.

"Aaaaaaaaa!" shouts Powerhouse, flinging out both powerful arms for three whole beats to flex his muscles, then kneading a dough of bass notes. His eyes glitter. He plays the piano like a drum some- times—why not?

"Gypsy? Such a dancer?"

"Why you don't hear it straight from your agent? Why it ain't come from headquarters? What you been doing, getting telegrams in the *corridor*, signed nobody?"

They all laugh. End of that chorus.

"What time is it?" Powerhouse calls. "What the hell place is this? Where is my watch and chain?"

"I hang it on you," whimpers Valentine. "It still there."

There it rides on Powerhouse's great stomach, down where he can never see it.

"Sure did hear some clock striking twelve while ago. Must be *mid- night*."

"It going to be intermission," Powerhouse declares, lifting up his finger with the signet ring.

He draws the chorus to an end. He pulls a big Northern hotel towel out of the deep pocket in his vast, special-cut tux pants and pushes his forehead into it.

"If she went and killed herself!" he says with a hidden face. "If she up and jumped out that window!" He gets to his feet, turning vaguely, wearing the towel on his head.

"Ha, ha!"

"Sheik, sheik!"

"She wouldn't do that." Little Brother sets down his clarinet like a precious vase, and speaks. He still looks like an East Indian queen, implacable, divine, and full of snakes. "You ain't going to expect people doing what they says over long distance."

"Come on!" roars Powerhouse. He is already at the back door, he has pulled it wide open, and with a wild, gathered-up face is smelling the terrible night.

Powerhouse, Valentine, Scoot and Little Brother step outside into the drenching rain.

"Well, they emptying buckets," says Powerhouse in a mollified voice. On the street he holds his hands out and turns up the blanched palms like sieves.

A hundred dark, ragged, silent, delighted Negroes have come around from under the eaves of the hall, and follow wherever they go.

"Watch out Little Brother don't shrink," says Powerhouse. "You just the right size now, clarinet don't suck you in. You got a dry throat, Little Brother, you in the desert?" He reaches into the pocket and pulls out a paper of mints. "Now hold 'em in your mouth—don't chew 'em. I don't carry around nothing without limit."

"Go in that joint and have beer," says Scoot, who walks ahead.

"Beer? Beer? You know what beer is? What do they say is beer? What's beer? Where I been?"

"Down yonder where it say World Café—that do?" They are in Negrotown now.

Valentine patters over and holds open a screen door warped like a sea shell, bitter in the wet, and they walk in, stained darker with the rain and leaving footprints. Inside, sheltered dry smells stand like screens around a table covered with a red-checkered cloth, in the center of which flies hang onto an obelisk-shaped ketchup bottle. The midnight walls are checkered again with admonishing "Not Responsible" signs and black-figured, smoky calendars. It is a waiting, silent, limp room. There is a burned-out-looking nickelodeon and right beside it a long-necked wall instrument labeled "Business Phone, Don't Keep Talking." Circled phone numbers are written up everywhere. There is a worn-out peacock feather hanging by a thread to an old, thin, pink, exposed light bulb, where it slowly turns around and around, whoever breathes.

A waitress watches.

"Come here, living statue, and get all this big order of beer we fixing to give."

"Never seen you before anywhere." The waitress moves and comes forward and slowly shows little gold leaves and tendrils over her teeth. She shoves up her shoulders and breasts. "How I going to know who you might be? Robbers? Coming in out of the black of night right at midnight, setting down so big at my table?"

"Boogers," says Powerhouse, his eyes opening lazily as in a cave.

The girl screams delicately with pleasure. O Lord, she likes talk and scares.

"Where you going to find enough beer to put out on this here table?" She runs to the kitchen with bent elbows and sliding steps.

"Here's a million nickels," says Powerhouse, pulling his hand out of his pocket and sprinkling coins out, all but the last one, which he makes vanish like a magician.

Valentine and Scoot take the money over to the nickelodeon, which looks as battered as a slot machine, and read all the names of the records out loud.

"Whose 'Tuxedo Junction'?" asks Powerhouse.

"You know whose."

"Nickelodeon, I request you please to play 'Empty Red Blues' and let Bessie Smith sing."

Silence: they hold it like a measure.

"Bring me all those nickels on back here," says Powerhouse. "Look at that! What you tell me the name of this place?"

"White dance, week night, raining, Alligator, Mississippi, long ways from home."

"Uh-huh."

"Sent for You Yesterday and Here You Come Today" plays.

The waitress, setting the tray of beer down on a back table, comes up taut and apprehensive as a hen. "Says in the kitchen, back there putting their eyes to little hole peeping out, that you is Mr. Powerhouse. . . . They knows from a picture they seen."

"They seeing right tonight, that is him," says Little Brother.

"You him?"

"That is him in the flesh," says Scoot.

"Does you wish to touch him?" asks Valentine. "Because he don't bite."

"You passing through?"

"Now you got everything right."

She waits like a drop, hands languishing together in front.

"Little-Bit, ain't you going to bring the beer?"

She brings it, and goes behind the cash register and smiles, turning different ways. The little fillet of gold in her mouth is gleaming.

"The Mississippi River's here," she says once.

Now all the watching Negroes press in gently and bright-eyed through the door, as many as can get in. One is a little boy in a straw sombrero which has been coated with aluminum paint all over.

Powerhouse, Valentine, Scoot and Little Brother drink beer, and their eyelids come together like curtains. The wall and the rain and the humble beautiful waitress waiting on them and the other Negroes watching enclose them.

"Listen!" whispers Powerhouse, looking into the ketchup bottle and slowly spreading his performer's hands over the damp, wrinkling cloth with the red squares. "Listen how it is. My wife gets missing me. Gypsy. She goes to the window. She looks out and sees you know what. Street. Sign saying Hotel. People walking. Somebody looks up. Old man. She looks down, out the window. Well? . . . *Sssst- Plooey!* What she do? Jump out and bust her brains all over the world."

He opens his eyes.

"That's it," agrees Valentine. "You gets a telegram."

"Sure she misses you," Little Brother adds.

"No, it's night time." How softly he tells them! "Sure. It's the night time. She say, What do I hear? Footsteps walking up the hall? That him? Footsteps go on off. It's not me. I'm in Alligator, Mississippi, she's crazy. Shaking all over. Listens till her ears and all grow out like old music-box horns but still she can't hear a thing. She says, All right! I'll jump out the window then. Got on her nightgown. I know that nightgown, and her thinking there. Says, Ho hum, all right, and jumps out the window. Is she mad at me! Is she crazy! She don't leave *nothing* behind her!"

"Ya! Ha!"

"Brains and insides everywhere, Lord, Lord."

All the watching Negroes stir in their delight, and to their higher delight he says affectionately, "Listen! Rats in here."

"That must be the way, boss."

"Only, naw, Powerhouse, that ain't true. That sounds too *bad.*"

"Does? I even know who finds her," cries Powerhouse. "That no-good pussyfooted crooning creeper, that creeper that follow around after me, coming up like weeds behind me, following around after me everything I do and messing around on the trail I leave. Bets my numbers, sings my songs, gets close to my agent like a Betsy-bug; when I going out he just coming in. I got him now! I got my eye on him."

"Know who he is?"

"Why, it's that old Uranus Knockwood!"

"Ya! Ha!"

"Yeah, and he coming now, he going to find Gypsy. There he is, coming around that corner, and Gypsy kadoodling down, oh-oh, watch out! *Sssssst! Plooey!* See, there she is in her little old nightgown, and her insides and brains all scattered round."

A sigh fills the room.

"Hush about her brains. Hush about her insides."

"Ya! Ha! You talking about her brains and insides—old Uranus Knockwood," says Powerhouse, "look down and say Jesus! He say, Look here what I'm walking round in!"

They all burst into halloos of laughter. Powerhouse's face looks like a big hot iron stove.

"Why he picks her up and carries her off!" he says.

"Ya! Ha!"

"Carries her *back* around the corner. . . ."

"Oh, Powerhouse!"

"You know him."

"Uranus Knockwood!"

"Yeahhh!"

"He take our wives when we gone!"

"He come in when we goes out!"

"Uh-huh!"

"He go out when we comes in!"

"Yeahhh!"

"He standing behind the door!"

"Old Uranus Knockwood."

"You know him."

"Middle-size man."

"Wears a hat."

"That's him."

Everybody in the room moans with pleasure. The little boy in the fine silver hat opens a paper and divides out a jelly roll among his followers.

And out of the breathless ring somebody moves forward like a slave, leading a great logy Negro with bursting eyes, and says, "This here is Sugar-Stick Thompson, that dove down to the bottom of July Creek and pulled up all those drowned white people fall out of a boat. Last summer, pulled up fourteen."

"Hello," says Powerhouse, turning and looking around at them all with his great daring face until they nearly suffoate.

Sugar-Stick, their instrument, cannot speak; he can only look back at the others.

"Can't even swim. Done it by holding his breath," says the fellow with the hero.

Powerhouse looks at him seekingly.

"I his half brother," the fellow puts in.

They step back.

"Gypsy say," Powerhouse rumbles gently again, looking at *them*, " 'What is the use? I'm gonna jump out so for—so far. . . .' *Ssssst—!*"

"Don't, boss, don't do it again," says Little Brother.

"It's awful," says the waitress. "I hates that Mr. Knockwoods. All that the truth?"

"Want to see the telegram I got from him?" Powerhouse's hand goes to the vast pocket.

"Now wait, now wait, boss." They all watch him.

"It must be the real truth," says the waitress, sucking in her lower lip, her luminous eyes turning sadly, seeking the windows.

"No, babe, it ain't the truth." His eyebrows fly up, and he begins to whisper to her out of his vast oven mouth. His hand stays in his pocket. "Truth is something worse, I ain't said what, yet. It's something hasn't come to me, but I ain't saying it won't. And when it does, then want me to tell you?" He sniffs all at once, his eyes come open and turn up, almost too far. He is dreamily smiling.

"Don't, boss, don't, Powerhouse!"

"Oh!" the waitress screams.

"Go on git out of here!" bellows Powerhouse, taking his hand out of his pocket and clapping after her red dress.

The ring of watchers breaks and falls away.

"*Look* at that! Intermission is up," says Powerhouse.

He folds money under a glass, and after they go out, Valentine leans back in and drops a nickel in the nickelodeon behind them, and it lights up and begins to play "The Goona Goo." The feather dangles still.

"Take a telegram!" Powerhouse shouts suddenly up into the rain over the street. "Take a answer. Now what was that name?"

They get a little tired.

"Uranus Knockwood."

"You ought to know."

"Yas? Spell it to me."

They spell it all the ways it could be spelled. It puts them in a wonderful humor.

"Here's the answer. I got it right here. 'What in the hell you talking about? Don't make any difference: I gotcha.' Name signed: Powerhouse."

"That going to reach him, Powerhouse?" Valentine speaks in a maternal voice.

"Yas, yas."

All hushing, following him up the dark street at a distance, like old rained-on black ghosts, the Negroes are afraid they will die laughing.

Powerhouse throws back his vast head into the steaming rain, and a look of hopeful desire seems to blow somehow like a vapor from his own dilated nostrils over his face and bring a mist to his eyes.

"Reach him and come out the other side."

"That's it, Powerhouse, that's it. You got him now."

Powerhouse lets out a long sigh.

"But ain't you going back there to call up Gypsy long distance, the way you did last night in that other place? I seen a telephone. . . . Just to see if she there at home?"

There is a measure of silence. That is one crazy drummer that's going to get his neck broken some day.

"No," growls Powerhouse. "No! How many thousand times tonight I got to say No?"

He holds up his arm in the rain.

"You sure-enough unroll your voice some night, it about reach up yonder to her," says Little Brother, dismayed.

They go on up the street, shaking the rain off and on them like birds.

Back in the dance hall, they play "San" (99). The jitterbugs start up like windmills stationed over the floor, and in their orbits—one circle, another, a long stretch and a zigzag—dance the elderly couple with old smoothness, undisturbed and stately.

When Powerhouse first came back from intermission, no doubt full of beer, they said, he got the band tuned up again in his own way. He didn't strike the piano keys for pitch—he simply opened his mouth and gave falsetto howls—in A, D and so on—they tuned by him. Then he took hold of the piano, as if he saw it for the first time in his life, and tested it for strength, hit it down in the bass, played an octave with his elbow, lifted the top, looked inside, and leaned against it with all his might. He sat down and played it for a few minutes with outrageous force and got it under his power—a bass deep and coarse as a sea net—then produced something glimmering and fragile, and smiled. And who could ever remember any of the things he says? They are just inspired remarks that roll out of his mouth like smoke.

They've requested "Somebody Loves Me," and he's already done twelve or fourteen choruses, piling them up nobody knows how, and it will be a wonder if he ever gets through. Now and then he calls and

shouts, " 'Somebody loves me! Somebody loves me, I wonder who!' "
His mouth gets to be nothing but a volcano. "I wonder who!"

"Maybe . . ." He uses all his right hand on a trill.

"Maybe . . ." He pulls back his spread fingers, and looks out upon
the place where he is. A vast, impersonal and yet furious grimace
transfigures his wet face.

". . . Maybe it's you!"

1941

Margaret Walker
For My People

For my people everywhere singing their slave songs repeatedly:
    their dirges and their ditties and their blues and jubilees,
    praying their prayers nightly to an unknown god, bend-
    ing their knees humbly to an unseen power;
For my people lending their strength to the years: to the gone
    years and the now years and the maybe years, washing
    ironing cooking scrubbing sewing mending hoeing plow-
    ing digging planting pruning patching dragging alone
    never gaining never reaping never knowing and never
    understanding;
For my playmates in the clay and dust and sand of Alabama
    backyards playing baptizing and preaching, and doctor
    and jail and soldier and school and mama and cooking
    and playhouse and concert and store and Miss Choomby
    and hair and company;
For the cramped bewildered years we went to school to learn
    to know the reasons why and the answers to and the

people who and the places where and the days when, in
memory of the bitter hours when we discovered we were
black and poor and small and different and nobody wondered and nobody understood;

For the boys and girls who grew in spite of these things to
be Man and Woman, to laugh and dance and sing and
play and drink their wine and religion and success, to
marry their playmates and bear children and then die of
consumption and anemia and lynching;

For my people thronging 47th Street in Chicago and Lenox
Avenue in New York and Rampart Street in New Orleans,
lost disinherited dispossessed and HAPPY people filling
the cabarets and taverns and other people's pockets need-
ing bread and shoes and milk and land and money and
Something—Something all our own;

For my people walking blindly, spreading joy, losing time
being lazy, sleeping when hungry, shouting when bur-
dened, drinking when hopeless, tied and shackled and
tangled among ourselves by the unseen creatures who
tower over us omnisciently and laugh;

For my people blundering and groping and floundering in the
dark of churches and schools and clubs and societies,
associations and councils and committees and conventions, distressed and disturbed and deceived and devoured
by money-hungry glory-craving leeches, preyed on by
facile force of state and fad and novelty by false prophet
and holy believer;

For my people standing staring trying to fashion a better way
from confusion from hypocrisy and misunderstanding,
trying to fashion a world that will hold all the people all
the faces all the adams and eves and their countless
generations;

Let a new earth rise. Let another world be born. Let a bloody
peace be written in the sky. Let a second generation full
of courage issue forth, let a people loving freedom come
to growth, let a beauty full of healing and a strength of
final clenching be the pulsing in our spirits and our
blood. Let the martial songs be written, let the dirges
disappear. Let a race of men now rise and take control!

1942

Melvin B. Tolson
Dark Symphony

I ALLEGRO MODERATO

Black Crispus Attucks taught
       Us how to die
Before white Patrick Henry's bugle breath
Uttered the vertical
       Transmitting cry: 5
"Yea, give me liberty, or give me death."
And from that day to this
       Men black and strong
For Justice and Democracy have stood,
Steeled in the faith that Right   10
       Will conquer Wrong
And Time will usher in one brotherhood.
No Banquo's ghost can rise
       Against us now
And say we crushed men with a tyrant's boot   15

Reprinted by permission of Dodd, Mead & Company, Inc. from *Rendezvous with America* by Melvin B. Tolson. Copyright 1944 by Dodd, Mead & Company, Inc.

Or pressed the crown of thorns
    On Labor's brow,
Or ravaged lands and carted off the loot.

II   LENTO GRAVE

The centuries-old pathos in our voices
Saddens the great white world,   20
And the wizardry of our dusky rhythms
Conjures up shadow-shapes of ante-bellum years:

Black slaves singing *One More River to Cross*
In the torture tombs of slave ships,
Black slaves singing *Steal Away to Jesus*   25
In jungle swamps,
Black slaves singing *The Crucifixion*
In slave pens at midnight,
Black slaves singing *Swing Low, Sweet Chariot*
In cabins of death,   30
Black slaves singing *Go Down, Moses*
In the canebrakes of the Southern Pharaohs.

III   ANDANTE SOSTENUTO

They tell us to forget
The Golgotha we tread . . .
We who are scourged with hate,   35
A price upon our head.
They who have shackled us
Require of us a song,
They who have wasted us
Bid us o'erlook the wrong.   40

They tell us to forget
Democracy is spurned.
They tell us to forget
The Bill of Rights is burned.
Three hundred years we slaved,   45
We slave and suffer yet:
Though flesh and bone rebel,
They tell us to forget!

Oh, how can we forget
Our human rights denied?   50

Oh, how can we forget
Our manhood crucified?
When Justice is profaned
And plea with curse is met,
When Freedom's gates are barred,   55
Oh, how can we forget?

IV TEMPO PRIMO

The New Negro strides upon the continent
In seven league boots . . .
The New Negro
Who sprang from the vigor-stout loins   60
Of Nat Turner, gallows-martyr for Freedom,
Of Joseph Cinquez, Black Moses of the Amistad Mutiny,
Of Frederick Douglass, oracle of the Catholic Man,
Of Sojourner Truth, eye and ear of Lincoln's legions,
Of Harriet Tubman, St. Bernard of the Underground
        Railroad.   65

V LARGHETTO

None in the Land can say
To us black men Today:
You send the tractors on their bloody path,
And create Oakies for *The Grapes of Wrath.*
You breed the slum that breeds a *Native Son* 70
To damn the good earth Pilgrim Fathers won.

None in the Land can say
To us black men Today:
You dupe the poor with rags-to-riches tales,
And leave the workers empty dinner pails.   75
You stuff the ballot box, and honest men
Are muzzled by your demogogic din.

None in the Land can say
To us black men Today:
You smash stock markets with your coined blitzkriegs 80
And make a hundred million guinea pigs.
You counterfeit our Christianity,
And bring contempt upon Democracy.

None in the Land can say
To us black men Today: 85
You prowl when citizens are fast asleep,
And hatch Fifth Column plots to blast the deep
Foundations of the State and leave the Land
A vast Sahara with a Fascist brand.

None in the Land can say   90
To us black men Today:
You send flame-gutting tanks, like swarms of flies,
And plump a hell from dynamiting skies.
You fill machine-gunned towns with rotting dead—
A No Man's Land where children cry for bread.   95

VI TEMPO DI MARCIA

Out of abysses of Illiteracy,
Through labyrinths of Lies,
Across wastelands of Disease . . .
We advance!

Out of dead-ends of Poverty,   100
Through wildernesses of Superstition,
Across barricades of Jim Crowism . . .
We advance!

With the People of the World . . .
We advance!   105

1944

Ralph Ellison
Flying Home

When Todd came to, he saw two faces suspended above him in a sun so hot and blinding that he could not tell if they were black or white. He stirred, feeling a pain that burned as though his whole body had been laid open to the sun which glared into his eyes. For a moment an old fear of being touched by white hands seized him. Then the very sharpness of the pain began slowly to clear his head. Sounds came to him dimly. He done come to. Who are they? he thought. Naw he ain't, I coulda sworn he was white. Then he heard clearly:

"You hurt bad?"

Something within him uncoiled. It was a Negro sound.

"He still out," he heard.

"Give 'im time. . . . Say, son, you hurt bad?"

Was he? There was that awful pain. He lay rigid, hearing their breathing and trying to weave a meaning between them and his being stretched painfully upon the ground. He watched them warily, his mind traveling back over a painful distance. Jagged scenes, swiftly unfolding as in a movie trailer, reeled through his mind, and he saw himself piloting a tailspinning plane and landing and landing and falling from the cockpit and trying to stand. Then, as in a great silence, he remembered the sounds of crunching bone, and now, looking up into the anxious faces of an old Negro man and a boy from where he lay in the same field, the memory sickened him and he wanted to remember no more.

"How you feel, son?"

Todd hesitated, as though to answer would be to admit an inacceptable weakness. Then, "It's my ankle," he said.

"Which one?"

"The left."

With a sense of remoteness he watched the old man bend and remove his boot, feeling the pressure ease.

"That any better?"

"A lot. Thank you."

He had the sensation of discussing someone else, that his concern was with some far more important thing, which for some reason escaped him.

"You done broke it bad," the old man said. "We have to get you to a doctor."

He felt that he had been thrown into a tailspin. He looked at his watch; how long had he been here? He knew there was but one important thing in the world, to get the plane back to the field before his officers were displeased.

"Help me up," he said. "Into the ship."

"But it's broke too bad. . . ."

"Give me your arm!"

"But, son . . ."

Clutching the old man's arm he pulled himself up, keeping his left leg clear, thinking, "I'd never make him understand," as the leather-smooth face came parallel with his own.

"Now, let's see."

He pushed the old man back, hearing a bird's insistent shrill. He swayed giddily. Blackness washed over him, like infinity.

"You best sit down."

"No, I'm O.K."

"But, son. You jus' gonna make it worse. . . ."

It was a fact that everything in him cried out to deny, even against the flaming pain in his ankle. He would have to try again.

"You mess with that ankle they have to cut your foot off," he heard.

Holding his breath, he started up again. It pained so badly that he had to bite his lips to keep from crying out and he allowed them to help him down with a pang of despair.

"It's best you take it easy. We gon' git you a doctor."

Of all the luck, he thought. Of all the rotten luck, now I have done it. The fumes of high-octane gasoline clung in the heat, taunting him.

"We kin ride him into town on old Ned," the boy said.

Ned? He turned, seeing the boy point toward an ox team browsing where the buried blade of a plow marked the end of a furrow. Thoughts of himself riding an ox through the town, past streets full of white faces, down the concrete runways of the airfield made swift images of humiliation in his mind. With a pang he remembered his girl's last letter. "Todd," she had written, "I don't need the papers to tell me you had the intelligence to fly. And I have always known you to be as brave as anyone else. The papers annoy me. Don't you be contented to prove over and over again that you're brave or skillful just because you're black, Todd. I think they keep beating that dead horse because they don't want to say why you boys are not yet fighting. I'm really disappointed, Todd. Anyone with brains can learn to fly, but then what? What about using it, and who will you use it for? I wish, dear, you'd write about this. I sometimes think they're playing a trick on us. It's very humiliating. . . ." He wiped cold sweat from his face, thinking, What does she know of humiliation? She's never been down South. Now the humiliation would come. When you must have them judge you, knowing that they never accept your mistakes as your own, but hold it against your whole race—that was humiliation. Yes, and humiliation was when you could never be simply yourself, when you were always a part of this old black ignorant man. Sure, he's all right. Nice and kind and helpful. But he's not you. Well, there's one humiliation I can spare myself.

"No," he said, "I have orders not to leave the ship. . . ."

"Aw," the old man said. Then turning to the boy, "Teddy, then you better hustle down to Mister Graves and get him to come. . . ."

"No, wait!" he protested before he was fully aware. Graves might be white. "Just have him get word to the field, please. They'll take care of the rest."

He saw the boy leave, running.

"How far does he have to go?"

"Might' nigh a mile."

He rested back, looking at the dusty face of his watch. But now they know something has happened, he thought. In the ship there was a perfectly good radio, but it was useless. The old fellow would never operate it. That buzzard knocked me back a hundred years, he thought. Irony danced within him like the gnats circling the old man's head. With all I've learned I'm dependent upon this "peasant's" sense of time and space. His leg throbbed. In the plane, instead of time being measured by the rhythms of pain and a kid's legs, the instruments would have told him at a glance. Twisting upon his elbows he saw where dust had powdered the plane's fuselage, feeling the lump form in his throat that was always there when he thought of flight. It's crouched there, he thought, like the abandoned shell of a locust. I'm naked without it. Not a machine, a suit of clothes you wear. And with a sudden embarrassment and wonder he whispered, "It's the only dignity I have. . . ."

He saw the old man watching, his torn overalls clinging limply to him in the heat. He felt a sharp need to tell the old man what he felt. But that would be meaningless. If I tried to explain why I need to fly back, he'd think I was simply afraid of white officers. But it's more than fear . . . a sense of anguish clung to him like the veil of sweat that hugged his face. He watched the old man, hearing him humming snatches of a tune as he admired the plane. He felt a furtive sense of resentment. Such old men often came to the field to watch the pilots with childish eyes. At first it had made him proud; they had been a meaningful part of a new experience. But soon he realized they did not understand his accomplishments and they came to shame and embarrass him, like the distasteful praise of an idiot. A part of the meaning of flying had gone then, and he had not been able to regain if. If I were a prizefighter I would be more human, he thought. Not a monkey doing tricks, but a man. They were pleased simply that he was a Negro who could fly, and that was not enough. He felt cut off from them by age, by understanding, by sensibility, by technology and by his need to measure himself against the mirror of other men's appreciation. Somehow he felt betrayed, as he had when as a child he grew to discover that his father was dead. Now for him any real appreciation lay with his white officers; and with them he could never be sure. Between ignorant black men and condescending whites, his course of flight seemed mapped by the nature of things away from all needed and natural landmarks. Under some sealed orders, couched in ever more technical and mysterious terms, his path curved swiftly away from both the shame the old man symbolized and the cloudy terrain of white men's regard. Flying blind, he knew but one point of landing and there he would receive his wings. After that the enemy would appreciate his skill and he would assume his deepest meaning, he thought sadly, neither from those who condescended nor from those who praised without understanding, but from the enemy who would recognize his manhood and skill in terms of hate. . . .

He sighed, seeing the oxen making queer, prehistoric shadows against the dry brown earth.

"You just take it easy, son," the old man soothed. "That boy won't take long. Crazy as he is about airplanes."

"I can wait," he said.

"What kinda airplane you call this here'n?"

"An Advanced Trainer," he said, seeing the old man smile. His fingers were like gnarled dark wood against the metal as he touched the low-slung wing.

" 'Bout how fast can she fly?"

"Over two hundred an hour."

"Lawd! That's so fast I bet it don't seem like you moving!"

Holding himself rigid, Todd opened his flying suit. The shade had gone and he lay in a ball of fire.

"You mind if I take a look inside? I was always curious to see. . . ."

"Help yourself. Just don't touch anything."

He heard him climb upon the metal wing, grunting. Now the questions would start. Well, so you don't have to think to answer. . . .

He saw the old man looking over into the cockpit, his eyes bright as a child's.

"You must have to know a lot to work all these here things."

He was silent, seeing him step down and kneel beside him.

"Son, how come you want to fly way up there in the air?"

Because it's the most meaningful act in the world . . . because it makes me less like you, he thought.

But he said: "Because I like it, I guess. It's as good a way to fight and die as I know."

"Yeah? I guess you right," the old man said. "But how long you think before they gonna let you all fight?"

He tensed. This was the question all Negroes asked, put with the same timid hopefulness and longing that always opened a greater void within him than that he had felt beneath the plane the first time he had flown. He felt light-headed. It came to him suddenly that there was something sinister about the conversation, that he was flying unwillingly into unsafe and uncharted regions. If he could only be insulting and tell this old man who was trying to help him to shut up!

"I bet you one thing . . ."

"Yes?"

"That you was plenty scared coming down."

He did not answer. Like a dog on a trail the old man seemed to smell out his fears, and he felt anger bubble within him.

"You sho' scared me. When I seen you coming down in that thing with it a-rollin' and a-jumping' like a pitchin' hoss, I thought sho' you was a goner. I almost had me a stroke!"

He saw the old man grinning, "Ever'thin's been happening round here this morning, come to think of it."

"Like what?" he asked.

"Well, first thing I know, here come two white fellers looking for Mister Rudolph, that's Mister Graves's cousin. That got me worked up right away. . . ."

"Why?"

"Why? 'Cause he done broke outta the crazy house, that's why. He liable to kill somebody," he said. "They oughta have him by now though. Then here you come. First I think it's one of them white boys. Then doggone if you don't fall outta there. Lawd, I'd done heard about you boys but I haven't never seen one o' you-all. Cain't tell you how it felt to see somebody what look like me in a airplane!"

The old man talked on, the sound streaming around Todd's thoughts like air flowing over the fuselage of a flying plane. You were a fool, he thought, remembering how before the spin the sun had blazed right against the billboard signs beyond the town, and how a boy's blue kite had bloomed beneath him, tugging gently in the wind like a strange, odd-shaped flower. He had once flown such kites himself and tried to find the boy at the end of the invisible cord. But he had been flying too high and too fast. He had climbed steeply away in exultation. Too steeply, he thought. And one of the first rules you learn is that if the angle of thrust is too steep the plane goes into a spin. And then, instead of pulling out of it and going into a dive you let a buzzard panic you. A lousy buzzard!

"Son, what made all that blood on the glass?"

"A buzzard," he said, remembering how the blood and feathers had sprayed back against the hatch. It had been as though he had flown into a storm of blood and blackness.

"Well, I declare! They's lots of 'em around here. They after dead things. Don't eat nothing what's alive."

"A little bit more and he would have made a meal out of me," Todd said grimly.

"They bad luck all right. Teddy's got a name for 'em, calls 'em jim-crows," the old man laughed.

"It's a damned good name."

"They the damnedest birds. Once I seen a hoss all stretched out like he was sick, you know. So I hollers, 'Gid up from there, suh!' Just to make sho! An' doggone, son, if I don't see two ole jimcrows come flying right up outa that hoss's insides! Yessuh! The sun was shinin' on 'em and they couldn't a been no greasier if they'd been eating barbecue."

Todd thought he would vomit, his stomach quivered.

"You made that up," he said.

"Nawsuh! Saw him just like I see you."

"Well, I'm glad it was you."

"You see lots a funny things down here, son."

"No, I'll let you see them," he said.

"No."

"By the way, the white folks round here don't like to see you boys up there in the sky. They ever bother you?"

"No."

"Well, they'd like to."

"Someone always wants to bother someone else," Todd said. "How do you know?"

"I just know."

"Well," he said defensively, "no one has bothered us."

Blood pounded in his ears as he looked away into space. He tensed, seeing a black spot in the sky, and strained to confirm what he could not clearly see.

"What does that look like to you?" he asked excitedly.

"Just another bad luck, son."

Then he saw the movement of wings with disappointment. It was gliding smoothly down, wings outspread, tail feathers gripping the air, down swiftly—gone behind the green screen of trees. It was like a bird, he had imagined there, only the sloping branches of the pines remained, sharp against the pale stretch of sky. He lay barely breathing and stared at the point where it had disappeared, caught in a spell of loathing and admiration. Why did they make them so disgusting and yet teach them to fly so well? It's like when I was up in heaven, he heard, starting.

The old man was chuckling, rubbing his stubbled chin.

"What did you say?"

"Sho', I died and went to heaven . . . maybe by time I tell you about it they be done come after you."

"I hope so," he said wearily.

"You boys ever sit around and swap lies?"

"Not often. Is this going to be one?"

"Well, I ain't so sho', on account of it took place when I was dead."
The old man paused. "That wasn't no lie 'bout the buzzards, though.

"All right," he said.

"Sho' you want to hear 'bout heaven?"

"Please," he answered, resting his head upon his arm.

"Well, I went to heaven and right away started to sproutin' me some
wings. Six good ones, they was. Just like them the white angels had.
I couldn't hardly believe it. I was so glad that I went off on some
clouds by myself and tried 'em out. You know, 'cause I didn't want to
make a fool outta myself the first thing. . . ."

It's an old tale, Todd thought. Told me years ago. Had forgotten.
But at least it will keep him from talking about buzzards.

He closed his eyes, listening.

". . . First thing I done was to git up on a low cloud and jump off.
And doggone, boy, if them wings didn't work! First I tried the right;
then I tried the left; then I tried 'em both together. Then Lawd, I
started to move on out among the folks. I let 'em see me. . . ."

He saw the old man gesturing flight with his arms, his face full of
mock pride as he indicated an imaginary crowd, thinking, It'll be in
the newspapers, as he heard, ". . . so I went and found me some colored
angels—somehow I didn't believe I was an angel till I seen a real black
one, ha, yes! Then I was sho'—but they tole me I better come down
'cause us colored folks had to wear a special kin' a harness when we
flew. That was how come they wasn't flyin'. Oh yes, an' you had to be
extra strong for a black man even, to fly with one of them harnes-
ses. . . ."

This is a new turn, Todd thought, what's he driving at?

"So I said to myself, I ain't gonna be bothered with no harness! Oh
naw! 'Cause if God let you sprout wings you oughta have sense enough
not to let nobody make you wear something what gits in the way of
flyin'. So I starts to flyin'. Heck, son," he chuckled, his eyes twinkling,
"you know I had to let eve'ybody know that old Jefferson could fly
good as anybody else. And I could too, fly smooth as a bird! I could
even loop-the-loop—only I had to make sho' to keep my long white
robe down roun' my ankles. . . . "

Todd felt uneasy. He wanted to laugh at the joke, but his body refused, as of an independent will. He felt as he had as a child when after he had chewed a sugar-coated pill which his mother had given him,
she had laughed at his efforts to remove the terrible taste.

". . . Well," he heard, "I was doing all right 'til I got to speeding.

Found out I could fan up a right strong breeze, I could fly so fast. I could do all kin'sa stunts too. I started flying up to the stars and divin' down and zooming roun' the moon. Man, I like to scare the devil outa some ole white angels. I was raisin' hell. Not that I meant any harm, son. But I was just feeling good. It was so good to know I was free at last. I accidentally knocked the tips offa some stars and they tell me I caused a storm and a coupla lynchings down here in Macon County— though I swear I believe them boys what said that was making up lies on me. . . ."

He's mocking me, Todd thought angrily. He thinks it's a joke. Grinning down at me . . . His throat was dry. He looked at his watch; why the hell didn't they come? Since they had to, why? One day I was flying down one of them heavenly streets. You got yourself into it, Todd thought. Like Jonah in the whale.

"Justa throwin' feathers in everybody's face. An' ole Saint Peter called me in. Said, 'Jefferson, tell me two things, what you doin' flyin' without a harness; an' how come you flyin' so fast?' So I tole him I was flyin' without a harness 'cause it got in my way, but I couldn'ta been flyin' so fast, 'cause I wasn't usin' but one wing. Saint Peter said, 'You wasn't flyin' with but one wing?' 'Yessuh,' I says, scared-like. So he says, 'Well, since you got sucha extra fine pair of wings you can leave off yo' harness awhile. But from now on none of that there one-wing flyin', 'cause you gittin' up too damn much speed!' "

And with one mouth full of bad teeth you're making too damned much talk, thought Todd. Why don't I send him after the boy? His body ached from the hard ground and seeking to shift his position he twisted his ankle and hated himself for crying out.

"It gittin' worse?"

"I . . . I twisted it," he groaned.

"Try not to think about it, son. That's what I do."

He bit his lip, fighting pain with counter-pain as the voice resumed its rhythmical droning. Jefferson seemed caught in his own creation.

". . . After all that trouble I just floated roun' heaven in slow motion. But I forgot, like colored folks will do, and got to flyin' with one wing again. This time I was restin' my old broken arm and got to flyin' fast enough to shame the devil. I was comin' so fast, Lawd, I got myself called befo' ole Saint Peter again. He said, 'Jeff, didn't I warn you 'bout that speedin'?' 'Yessuh,' I says, 'but it was an accident.' He looked at me sad-like and shook his head and I knowed I was gone. He said, 'Jeff, you and that speedin' is a danger to the heavenly community. If I was to let you keep on flyin', heaven wouldn't be nothin' but uproar. Jeff, you got to go!' Son, I argued and pleaded with that old white man, but it didn't do a bit of good. They rushed me straight to them pearly gates and gimme a parachute and a map of the state of Alabama . . ."

Todd heard him laughing so that he could hardly speak, making a screen between them upon which his humiliation glowed like fire.

"Maybe you'd better stop awhile," he said, his voice unreal.

"Ain't much more," Jefferson laughed. "When they gimme the parachute ole Saint Peter ask me if I wanted to say a few words before I went. I felt so bad I couldn't hardly look at him, specially with all them white angels standin' around. Then somebody laughed and made me mad. So I tole him, 'Well, you done took my wings. And you puttin' me out. You got charge of things so's I can't do nothin' about it. But you got to admit just this: While I was up here I was the flyinest son-ofabitch what ever hit heaven!' "

At the burst of laughter Todd felt such an intense humiliation that only great violence would wash it away. The laughter which shook the old man like a boiling purge set up vibrations of guilt within him which not even the intricate machinery of the plane would have been adequate to transform and he heard himself screaming, "Why do you laugh at me this way?"

He hated himself at that moment, but he had lost control. He saw Jefferson's mouth fall open, "What—?"

"Answer me!"

His blood pounded as though it would surely burst his temples and he tried to reach the old man and fell, screaming, "Can I help it because they won't let us actually fly? Maybe we are a bunch of buzzards feeding on a dead horse, but we can hope to be eagles, can't we? Can't we?"

He fell back, exhausted, his ankle pounding. The saliva was like straw in his mouth. If he had the strength he would strangle this old man. This grinning, gray-headed clown who made him feel as he felt when watched by the white officers at the field. And yet this old man had neither power, prestige, rank nor technique. Nothing that could rid him of this terrible feeling. He watched him, seeing his face struggle to express a turmoil of feeling.

"What you mean, son? What you talking 'bout . . .?"

"Go away. Go tell your tales to the white folks."

"But I didn't mean nothing like that. . . . I . . . I wasn't tryin' to hurt your feelings. . . ."

"Please. Get the hell away from me!"

"But I didn't, son. I didn't mean all them things a-tall."

Todd shook as with a chill, searching Jefferson's face for a trace of the mockery he had seen there. But now the face was somber and tired and old. He was confused. He could not be sure that there had ever been laughter there, that Jefferson had ever really laughed in his whole life. He saw Jefferson reach out to touch him and shrank away, wondering if anything except the pain, now causing his vision to waver, was real. Perhaps he had imagined it all.

"Don't let it get you down, son," the voice said pensively.

He heard Jefferson sigh wearily, as though he felt more than he could say. His anger ebbed, leaving only the pain.

"I'm sorry," he mumbled.

"You just wore out with pain, was all. . . ."

He saw him through a blur, smiling. And for a second he felt the embarrassed silence of understanding flutter between them.

"What you was doin' flyin' over this section, son? Wasn't you scared they might shoot you for a cow?"

Todd tensed. Was he being laughed at again? But before he could decide, the pain shook him and a part of him was lying calmly behind the screen of pain that had fallen between them, recalling the first time he had ever seen a plane. It was as though an endless series of hangars had been shaken ajar in the air base of his memory and from each, like a young wasp emerging from its cell, arose the memory of a plane.

The first time I ever saw a plane I was very small and planes were new in the world. I was four-and-a-half and the only plane that I had ever seen was a model suspended from the ceiling of the automobile exhibit at the State Fair. But I did not know that it was only a model. I did not know how large a real plane was, nor how expensive. To me it was a fascinating toy, complete in itself, which my mother said could only be owned by rich little white boys. I stood rigid with admiration, my head straining backwards as I watched the gray little plane describing arcs above the gleaming tops of the automobiles. And I vowed that, rich or poor, someday I would own such a toy. My mother had to drag me out of the exhibit and not even the merry-go-round, the Ferris wheel, or the racing horses could hold my attention for the rest of the Fair. I was too busy imitating the tiny drone of the plane with my lips, and imitating with my hands the motion, swift and circling, that it made in flight.

After that I no longer used the pieces of lumber that lay about our back yard to construct wagons and autos . . . now it was used for airplanes. I built biplanes, using pieces of board for wings, a small box for the fuselage, another piece of wood for the rudder. The trip to the Fair had brought something new into my small world. I asked my mother repeatedly when the Fair would come back again. I'd lie in the grass and watch the sky, and each fighting bird became a soaring plane. I would have been good a year just to have seen a plane again. I became a nuisance to everyone with my questions about airplanes. But planes were new to the old folks, too, and there was little that they could tell me. Only my uncle knew some of the answers. And better still, he could carve propellers from pieces of wood that would whirl rapidly in the wind, wobbling noisily upon oiled nails.

I wanted a plane more than I'd wanted anything; more than I wanted the red wagon with rubber tires, more than the train that ran on a track with its train of cars. I asked my mother over and over again:

"Mamma?"

"What do you want, boy?" she'd say.

"Mamma, will you get mad if I ask you?" I'd say.

"What do you want now? I ain't got time to be answering a lot of fool questions. What you want?"

"Mamma, when you gonna get me one . . .?" I'd ask.

"Get you one what?" she'd say.

"You know, Mamma; what I been asking you. . . ."

"Boy," she'd say, "if you don't want a spanking you better come on an' tell me what you talking about so I can get on with my work."

"Aw, Mamma, you know. . . ."

"What I just tell you?" she'd say.

"I mean when you gonna buy me a airplane."

"Airplane! Boy, is you crazy? How many times I have to tell you to stop that foolishness. I done told you them things cost too much. I bet I'm gon' wham the living daylight out of you if you don't quit worrying me 'bout them things!"

But this did not stop me, and a few days later I'd try all over again.

Then one day a strange thing hapened. It was spring and for some reason I had been hot and irritable all morning. It was a beautiful spring. I could feel it as I played barefoot in the backyard. Blossoms hung from the thorny black locust trees like clusters of fragrant white grapes. Butterflies flickered in the sunlight above the short new dew-wet grass. I had gone in the house for bread and butter and coming out I heard a steady unfamiliar drone. It was unlike anything I had ever heard before. I tried to place the sound. It was no use. It was a sensation like that I had when searching for my father's watch, heard ticking unseen in a room. It made me feel as though I had forgotten to perform some task that my mother had ordered . . . then I located it, overhead. In the sky, flying quite low and about a hundred yards off was a plane! It came so slowly that it seemed barely to move. My mouth hung wide; my bread and butter fell into the dirt. I wanted to jump up and down and cheer. And when the idea struck I trembled with excitement: "Some little white boy's plane's done flew away and all I got to do is stretch out my hands and it'll be mine!" It was a little plane like that at the Fair, flying no higher than the eaves of our roof. Seeing it come steadily forward I felt the world grow warm with promise. I opened the screen and climbed over it and clung there, waiting. I would catch the plane as it came over and swing down fast and run into the house before anyone could see me. Then no one could come to claim the plane. It droned nearer. Then when it hung like a silver cross in the blue directly above me I stretched out my hand and grabbed. It was like sticking my finger through a soap bubble. The plane flew on, as though I had simply blown my breath after it. I grabbed again, frantically, trying to catch the tail. My fingers clutched the air and disappointment surged tight and hard in my throat. Giving one last desperate grasp, I strained forward. My fingers ripped against the screen, I was falling. The ground burst hard against me. I drummed the earth with my heels and when my breath returned, I lay there bawling.

My mother rushed through the door.

"What's the matter, chile! What on earth is wrong with you?"

"It's gone! It's gone!"

"What gone?"

"The airplane . . ."

"Airplane?"

"Yessum, jus' like the one at the Fair. . . . I . . . I tried to stop it an' it kep' right on going. . . ."

"When, boy?"

"Just now," I cried, through my tears.

"Where it go, boy, what way?"

"Yonder, there . . ."

She scanned the sky, her arms akimbo and her checkered apron flapping in the wind as I pointed to the fading plane. Finally she looked down at me, slowly shaking her head.

"It's gone! It's gone!" I cried.

"Boy, is you a fool?" she said. "Don't you see that there's a real airplane 'stead of one of them toy ones?"

"Real . . .?" I forgot to cry. "Real?"

"Yass, real. Don't you know that thing you reaching for is bigger'n a auto? You here trying to reach for it and I bet it's flying 'bout two hundred miles higher'n this roof." She was disgusted with me. "You come on in this house before somebody else sees what a fool you done turned out to be. You must think these here lil ole arms of you'n is mighty long. . . ."

I was carried into the house and undressed for bed and the doctor was called. I cried bitterly, as much from the disappointment of finding the plane so far beyond my reach as from the pain.

When the doctor came I heard my mother telling him about the plane and asking if anything was wrong with my mind. He explained that I had had a fever for several hours. But I was kept in bed for a week and I constantly saw the plane in my sleep, flying just beyond my fingertips, sailing so slowly that it seemed barely to move. And each time I'd reach out to grab it I'd miss and through each dream I'd hear my grandma warning:

> *Young man, young man,*
> *You' arms too short*
> *To box with God. . . .*

"Hey, son!"

At first he did not know where he was and looked at the old man pointing, with blurred eyes.

"Ain't that one of you-all's airplanes coming after you?"

As his vision cleared he saw a small black shape above a distant field, soaring through waves of heat. But he could not be sure and with the pain he feared that somehow a horrible recurring fantasy of being split in twain by the whirling blades of a propeller had come true.

"You think he sees us?" he heard

"See? I hope so."

"He's coming like a bat outa hell!"

Straining, he heard the faint sound of a motor and hoped it would soon be over.

"How you feeling?"

"Like a nightmare," he said.

"Hey, he's done curved back the other way!"

"Maybe he saw us," he said. "Maybe he's gone to send out the ambulance and ground crew." And, he thought with despair, maybe he didn't even see us.

"Where did you send the boy?"

"Down to Mister Graves," Jefferson said. "Man what owns this land."

"Do you think he phoned?"

Jefferson looked at him quickly.

"Aw sho'. Dabney Graves is got a bad name on accounta them killings but he'll call though. . . ."

"What killings?"

"Them five fellers . . . ain't you heard?" he asked with surprise.

"No."

"Everybody knows 'bout Dabney Graves, especially the colored. He done killed enough of us."

Todd had the sensation of being caught in a white neighborhood after dark.

"What did they do?" he asked.

"Thought they was men," Jefferson said. "An' some he owed money, like he do me. . . ."

"But why do you stay here?"

"You black, son."

"I know, but . . ."

"You have to come by the white folks, too."

He turned away from Jefferson's eyes, at once consoled and accused. And I'll have to come by them soon, he thought with despair. Closing his eyes, he heard Jefferson's voice as the sun burned blood-red upon his lips.

"I got nowhere to go," Jefferson said, "an' they'd come after me if I did. But Dabney Graves is a funny fellow. He's all the time making jokes. He can be mean as hell, then he's liable to turn right around and back the colored against the white folks. I seen him do it. But me, I hates him for that more'n anything else. 'Cause just as soon as he gits tired helping a man he don't care what happens to him. He just leaves him stone cold. And then the other white folks is double hard on anybody he done helped. For him, it's just a joke. He don't give a hilla beans for nobody—but hisself. . . ."

Todd listened to the thread of detachment in the old man's voice. It was as though he held his words arm's length before him to avoid their destructive meaning.

"He'd just as soon do you a favor and then turn right around and have you strung up. Me, I stays outa his way 'cause down here that's what you gotta do."

If my ankle would only ease for a while, he thought. The closer I spin toward the earth the blacker I become, flashed through his mind. Sweat ran into his eyes and he was sure that he would never see the plane if his head continued whirling. He tried to see Jefferson, what it was that Jefferson held in his hand? It was a little black man, another Jefferson! A little black Jefferson that shook with fits of belly-laughter while the other Jefferson looked on with detachment. Then Jefferson looked up from the thing in his hand and turned to speak, but Todd was far away, searching the sky for a plane in a hot dry land on a day and age he had long forgotten. He was going mysteriously with his mother through empty streets where black faces peered from behind drawn shades and someone was rapping at a window and he was looking back to see a hand and a frightened face frantically beckoning from a cracked door and his mother was looking down the empty perspective of the street and shaking her head and hurrying him along and at first it was only a flash he saw and a motor was droning as through the sun-glare he saw it gleaming silver as it circled and he was seeing a burst like a puff of white smoke and hearing his mother yell, Come along, boy, I got no time for them fool airplanes, I got no time, and he saw it a second time, the plane flying high, and the burst appeared suddenly and fell slowly, billowing out and sparkling like fireworks and he was watching and being hurried along as the air filled with a flurry of white pinwheeling cards that caught in the wind and scattered over the rooftops and into the gutters and a woman was running and snatching a card and reading it and screaming and he darted into the shower, grabbing as in winter he grabbed for snowflakes and bounding away at his mother's, Come on here, boy! Come on, I say! and he was watching as she took the card away, seeing her face grow puzzled and turning taut as her voice quavered, "Niggers Stay From the Polls," and died to a moan of terror as he saw the eyeless sockets of a white hood staring at him from the card and above he saw the plane spiraling gracefully, agleam in the sun like a fiery sword. And seeing it soar he was caught, transfixed between a terrible horror and a horrible fascination.

The sun was not so high now, and Jefferson was calling, and gradually he saw three figures moving across the curving roll of the field.

"Look like some doctors, all dressed in white," said Jefferson.

They're coming at last, Todd thought. And he felt such a release of tension within him that he thought he would faint. But no sooner did he close his eyes than he was seized and he was struggling with three white men who were forcing his arms into some kind of coat. It was too much for him, his arms were pinned to his sides and as the pain blazed in his eyes, he realized that it was a straitjacket. What filthy joke was this?

"That oughta hold him, Mister Graves," he heard.

His total energies seemed focused in his eyes as he searched their faces. That was Graves; the other two wore hospital uniforms. He was poised between two poles of fear and hate as he heard the one called Graves saying, "He looks kinda purty in that there suit, boys. I'm glad you dropped by."

"This boy ain't crazy, Mister Graves," one of the others said. "He needs a doctor, not us. Don't see how you led us way out here anyway. It might be a joke to you, but your cousin Rudolph liable to kill somebody. White folks or niggers, don't make no difference. . . ."

Todd saw the man turn red with anger. Graves looked down upon him, chuckling.

"This nigguh belongs in a straitjacket, too, boys. I knowed that the minit Jeff's kid said something 'bout a nigguh flyer. You all know you cain't let the nigguh git up that high without his going crazy. The nigguh brain ain't built right for high altitudes. . . ."

Todd watched the drawling red face, feeling that all the unnamed horror and obscenities that he had ever imagined stood materialized before him.

"Let's git outta here," one of the attendants said.

Todd saw the other reach toward him, realizing for the first time that he lay upon a stretcher as he yelled.

"Don't put your hands on me!"

They drew back, surprised.

"What's that you say, nigguh?" asked Graves.

He did not answer and thought that Graves's foot was aimed at his head. It landed on his chest and he could hardly breathe. He coughed helplessly, seeing Graves's lips stretch taut over his yellow teeth, and tried to shift his head. It was as though a half-dead fly was dragging slowly across his face and a bomb seemed to burst within him. Blasts of hot, hysterical laughter tore from his chest, causing his eyes to pop and he felt that the veins in his neck would surely burst. And then a part of him stood behind it all, watching the surprise in Graves's red face and his own hysteria. He thought he would never stop, he would laugh himself to death. It rang in his ears like Jefferson's laughter and he looked for him, centering his eyes desperately upon his face, as though somehow he had become his sole salvation in an insane world of outrage and humiliation. It brought a certain relief. He was suddenly aware that although his body was still contorted it was an echo that no longer rang in his ears. He heard Jefferson's voice with gratitude.

"Mister Graves, the Army done tole him not to leave his airplane."

"Nigguh, Army or no, you gittin' off my land! That airplane can stay 'cause it was paid for by taxpayers' money. But you gittin' off. An' dead or alive, it don't make no difference to me."

Todd was beyond it now, lost in a world of anguish.

"Jeff," Graves said, "you and Teddy come and grab holt. I want you to take this here black eagle over to that nigguh airfield and leave him."

Jefferson and the boy approached him silently. He looked away, realizing and doubting at once that only they could release him from his overpowering sense of isolation.

They bent for the stretcher. One of the attendants moved toward Teddy.

"Think you can manage it, boy?"

"I think I can, suh," Teddy said.

"Well, you better go behind then, and let yo' pa go ahead so's to keep that leg elevated."

He saw the white men walking ahead of Jefferson and the boy carried him along in silence. Then they were pausing and he felt a hand wiping his face; then he was moving again. And it was as though he had been lifted out of his isolation, back into the world of men. A new current of communication flowed between the man and boy and himself. They moved him gently. Far away he heard a mockingbird liquidly calling. He raised his eyes, seeing a buzzard poised unmoving in space. For a moment the whole afternoon seemed suspended and he waited for the horror to seize him again. Then like a song within his head he heard the boy's soft humming and saw the dark bird glide into the sun and glow like a bird of flaming gold.

1944

Dudley Randall
Booker T. and W. E. B.

"It seems to me," said Booker T.,
"It shows a mighty lot of cheek
To study chemistry and Greek
When Mister Charlie needs a hand
To hoe the cotton on his land,   5
And when Miss Ann looks for a cook,
Why stick your nose inside a book?"

"I don't agree," said W.E.B.,
"If I should have the drive to seek
Knowledge of chemistry or Greek,   10
I'll do it. Charles and Miss can look
Another place for hand or cook.
Some men rejoice in skill of hand,
And some in cultivating land,
But there are others who maintain   15
The right to cultivate the brain."

Reprinted from *Poem Counterpoem*, copyright, 1966 by permission of the
author.

"It seems to me," said Booker T.,
"That all you folks have missed the boat
Who shout about the right to vote,
And spend vain days and sleepless nights   20
In uproar over civil rights.
Just keep your mouths shut, do not grouse,
But work, and save, and buy a house."

"I don't agree," said W.E.B.,
"For what can property avail   25
If dignity and justice fail.
Unless you help to make the laws,
They'll steal your house with trumped-up clause.
A rope's as tight, a fire as hot,
No matter how much cash you've got.   30
Speak soft, and try your little plan,
But as for me, I'll be a man."

"It seems to me," said Booker T.—

"I don't agree,"
Said W.E.B.   35

1952

Langston Hughes
Name In Print

"Just look at the front pages of the newspapers," said Simple, spreading his nightly copy of the *Daily News* out on the bar. "There is never hardly any colored names anywhere. Most headlines is all about white folks."

"That is not true today," I said. "Many headlines are about Negroes, Chinese, Indians, and other colored folks like ourselves."

"Most on the inside pages," said Simple, blowing foam from his beer. "But I am talking about front-page news. The only time colored folks is front-page news is when there's been a race riot or a lynching or a boycott and a whole lot of us have been butchered up or arrested. Then they announce it."

"You," I said, "have a race phobia. You see prejudice where there is none, and Jim Crow where it doesn't exist. How can you be constructive front-page news if you don't *make* front-page news?"

"How can I make front-page news in a white paper if I am not white?" asked Simple. "Or else I have to be Ralph Bunche or Eartha

Kitt. That is why I am glad we have got colored papers like the *Afro, Defender, Courier,* and *Sepia,* so I can be news, too."

"I presume that when you say 'I' you mean the racial I—Negroes. You are not talking about yourself."

"Of course I am not talking about myself," said Simple, draining his glass. "I have never been nowhere near news except when I was in the Harlem Riots. Then the papers did not mention me by name. They just said 'mob.' I were a part of the mob. When the Mayor's Committee report come out, they said I were 'frustrated.' Which is true, I were. It is very hard for a Negro like me to get his name in the news, the reason being that white folks do not let us nowhere near news in the first place. For example, take all these graft investigations that's been going on in Brooklyn and New York every other week, unions and docks, cops and bookies, and million-dollar handouts. Do you read about any Negroes being mixed up in them, getting even a hundred dollars of them millions, or being called up before the grand jury? You do not. White folks are just rolling in graft! But where are the Negroes? Nowhere near the news. Irish names, Italian names, Jewish names, all kinds of names in the headlines every time Judge Liebowitz opens his mouth. Do you read any colored names? The grand jury don't even bother to investigate Harlem. There has never been a million dollars' worth of graft in Harlem in all the years since the Indians sold Manhattan for a handful of beads. Indians and Negroes don't get nowhere near graft, neither into much news. Find me some Negro news in tonight's *News.*"

"I would hardly wish to get into the papers if I had to make news by way of graft," I said. "There is nothing about graft of which any race can be proud."

"Our race could do right well with some of that big money, though," said Simple, signaling the barman for another beer. "But it does not have to be graft, in unions or out. I am just using that as an example. Take anything else on the front pages. Take flying saucers in the sky. Everybody but a Negro has seen one. If a Negro did see a flying saucer, I bet the papers wouldn't report it. They probably don't even let flying saucers fly over Harlem, just to keep Negroes from seeing them. This morning in the subway I read where Carl Krubelewski had seen a flying saucer, also Ralph Curio saw one. And way up in Massachusetts a while back, Henry Armpriester seen one. Have you ever read about Roosevelt Johnson or Ralph Butler or Carl Jenkins or anybody that sounded like a Negro seeing one? I did not. Has a flying saucer ever passed over Lenox Avenue? Nary one! Not even Daddy Grace has glimpsed one, neither Mother Horne, nor Adam Powell. Negroes can't get on the front page no kind of way. We can't even see a flying saucer."

"It would probably scare the wits out of you, if you did see one," I said, "so you might not live to read your name in the papers."

"I could read my name from the other world then," said Simple, "and be just as proud. Me, Jesse B. Semple—my name in print for once —killed by looking at a flying saucer."

1953

Norman Mailer
The White Negro: Superficial Reflections on the Hipster

Probably, we will never be able to determine the psychic havoc of the concentration camps and the atom bomb upon the unconscious mind of almost everyone alive in these years. For the first time in civilized history, perhaps for the first time in all of history, we have been forced to live with the suppressed knowledge that the smallest facets of our personality or the most minor projection of our ideas, or indeed the absence of ideas and the absence of personality could mean equally well that we might still be doomed to die as a cipher in some vast statistical operation in which our teeth would be counted, and our hair would be saved, but our death itself would be unknown, unhonored, and unremarked, a death which could not follow with dignity as a possible consequence to serious actions we had chosen, but rather a death by *deus ex machina* in a gas chamber or a radioactive city; and so if in the midst of civilization—that civilization founded upon the Faustian urge to dominate nature by mastering time, mastering the links of social cause and effect—in the middle of an economic civilization founded upon the confidence that time could indeed be subjected to our will, our psyche was subjected itself to the intolerable anxiety that death being causeless, life was causeless as well, and time deprived of cause and effect had come to a stop.

The Second World War presented a mirror to the human condition which blinded anyone who looked into it. For if tens of millions were killed in concentration camps out of the inexorable agonies and contractions of super-states founded upon the always insoluble contradictions of injustice, one was then obliged also to see that no matter how crippled and perverted an image of man was the society he had created, it was nonetheless his creation, his collective creation (at least his collective creation from the past) and if society was so murderous, then who could ignore the most hideous of questions about his own nature?

Worse. One could hardly maintain the courage to be individual, to speak with one's own voice, for the years in which one could complacently accept oneself as part of an elite by being a radical were forever gone. A man knew that when he dissented, he gave a note upon his life which could be called in any year of overt crisis. No wonder then that these have been the years of conformity and depression. A stench of fear has come out of every pore of American life, and we suffer from a collective failure of nerve. The only courage, with rare exceptions, that we have been witness to, has been the isolated courage of isolated people.

2

It is on this bleak scene that a phenomenon has appeared: the American existentialist—the hipster, the man who knows that if our collective condition is to live with instant death by atomic war, relatively quick death by the State as *l'univers concentrationnaire*, or with a slow death by conformity with every creative and rebellious instinct stifled (at what damage to the mind and the heart and the liver and the nerves no research foundation for cancer will discover in a hurry), if the fate of twentieth-century man is to live with death from adolescence to premature senescence, why then the only life-giving answer is to accept the terms of death, to live with death as immediate danger, to divorce oneself from society, to exist without roots, to set out on that uncharted journey into the rebellious imperatives of the self. In short, whether the life is criminal or not, the decision is to encourage the psychopath in oneself, to explore that domain of experience where security is boredom and therefore sickness, and one exists in the present, in that enormous present which is without past or future, memory or planned intention, the life where a man must go until he is beat, where he must gamble with his energies through all those small or large crises of courage and unforeseen situations which beset his day, where he must be with it or doomed not to swing. The unstated essence of Hip, its psychopathic brilliance, quivers with the knowledge that new kinds of victories increase one's power for new kinds of perception; and defeats, the wrong kind of defeats, attack the body and imprison one's energy until one is jailed in the prison air of other people's habits, other people's defeats, boredom, quiet desperation and muted icy self-destroying rage. One is Hip or one is Square (the alternative which each new generation coming into American life is beginning to feel), one is a rebel or one conforms, one is a frontiersman in the Wild West of American night life, or else a Square cell, trapped in the totalitarian tissues of American society, doomed willy-nilly to conform if one is to succeed.

A totalitarian society makes enormous demands on the courage of men, and a partially totalitarian society makes even greater demands, for the general anxiety is greater. Indeed if one is to be a man, almost any kind of unconventional action often takes disproportionate courage. So it is no accident that the source of Hip is the Negro for he has been living on the margin between totalitarianism and democracy for two centuries. But the presence of Hip as a working philosophy in the sub-worlds of American life is probably due to jazz, and its knifelike entrance into culture, its subtle but so penetrating influence on an avant-garde generation—that postwar generation of adventurers who (some consciously, some by osmosis) had absorbed the lessons of disillusionment and disgust of the twenties, the depression, and the war. Sharing a collective disbelief in the words of men who had too much money and controlled too many things, they knew almost as powerful a disbelief in the socially monolithic ideas of the single mate, the solid family and the respectable love life. If the intellectual antecedents of this generation can be traced to such separate influences as D. H. Lawrence, Henry Miller, and Wilhelm Reich, the viable philosophy of Hemingway fit most of their facts: in a bad world, as he was to say over and over again (while taking time out from his parvenu snobbery and dedicated gourmandize), in a bad world there is no love nor mercy nor charity nor justice unless a man can keep his courage, and this indeed fitted some of the facts. What fitted the need of the adventurer even more precisely was Hemingway's categorical imperative that what made him feel good became therefore The Good.

So no wonder that in certain cities of America, in New York of course, and New Orleans, in Chicago and San Francisco and Los Angeles, in such American cities as Paris and Mexico, D.F., this particular part of a generation was attracted to what the Negro had to offer. In such places as Greenwich Village, a ménage-à-trois was completed —the bohemian and the juvenile delinquent came face-to-face with the Negro, and the hipster was a fact in American life. If marijuana was the wedding ring, the child was the language of Hip for its argot gave expression to abstract states of feeling which all could share, at least all who were Hip. And in this wedding of the white and the black it was the Negro who brought the cultural dowry. Any Negro who wishes to live must live with danger from his first day, and no experience can ever be casual to him, no Negro can saunter down a street with any real certainty that violence will not visit him on his walk. The cameos of security for the average white: mother and the home, job and the family, are not even a mockery to millions of Negroes; they are impossible. The Negro has the simplest of alternatives: live a life of constant humility or ever-threatening danger. In such a pass where paranoia is as vital to survival as blood, the Negro had stayed alive and begun to grow by following the need of his body where he could. Knowing in the cells of his existence that life was war, nothing but war, the Negro (all exceptions admitted) could rarely afford the sophisticated inhibitions of civilization, and so he kept for his survival the art of the primitive, he lived in the enormous present, he subsisted for his Saturday night kicks, relinquishing the pleasures of the mind for the more obligatory pleasures of the body, and in his music he gave voice to the character and quality of his existence, to his rage and the infinite variations of joy, lust, languor, growl, cramp, pinch, scream and despair of his orgasm. For jazz is orgasm, it is the music of orgasm, good orgasm and bad, and so it spoke across a nation, it had the communication of art and even where it was watered, perverted, corrupted, and almost killed, it spoke in no matter what laundered popular way of instantaneous existential states to which some whites could respond, it was indeed a communication by art because it said, "I feel this, and now you do too."

So there was a new breed of adventurers, urban adventurers who drifted out at night looking for action with a black man's code to fit their facts. The hipster had absorbed the existentialist synapses of the Negro, and for practical purposes could be considered a white Negro.

To be an existentialist, one must be able to feel oneself—one must know one's desires, one's rages, one's anguish, one must be aware of the character of one's frustration and know what would satisfy it. The overcivilized man can be an existentialist only if it is chic, and deserts it quickly for the next chic. To be a real existentialist (Sartre admittedly to the contrary) one must be religious, one must have one's sense of the "purpose"—whatever the purpose may be—but a life which is directed by one's faith in the necessity of action is a life committed to the notion that the substratum of existence is the search, the end meaningful but mysterious; it is impossible to live such a life unless one's emotions provide their profound conviction. Only the French, alienated beyond alienation from their unconscious could welcome an existential philosophy without ever feeling it at all; indeed only a Frenchman by declaring that the unconscious did not exist could then proceed to explore the delicate involutions of consciousness, the microscopically sensuous and all but ineffable *frissons* of mental becoming, in order finally to create the theology of atheism and so submit that in a world of absurdities the existential absurdity is most coherent.

In the dialogue between the atheist and the mystic, the atheist is on the side of life, rational life, undialectical life—since he conceives of death as emptiness, he can, no matter how weary or despairing, wish for nothing but more life; his pride is that he does not transpose his weakness and spiritual fatigue into a romantic longing for death, for such appreciation of death is then all too capable of being elaborated by his imagination into a universe of meaningful structure and moral orchestration.

Yet this masculine argument can mean very little for the mystic. The mystic can accept the atheist's description of his weakness, he can agree that his mysticism was a response to despair. And yet . . . and yet his argument is that he, the mystic, is the one finally who has chosen to live with death, and so death is his experience and not the atheist's, and the atheist by eschewing the limitless dimensions of profound despair has rendered himself incapable to judge the experience. The real argument which the mystic must always advance is the very intensity of his private vision—his argument depends from the vision precisely because what was felt in the vision is so extraordinary that no rational argument, no hypotheses of "oceanic feelings" and certainly no skeptical reductions can explain away what has become for him the reality

more real than the reality of closely reasoned logic. His inner experience of the possibilities within death is his logic. So, too, for the
existentialist. And the psychopath. And the saint and the bullfighter
and the lover. The common denominator for all of them is their
burning consciousness of the present, exactly that incandescent consciousness which the possibilities within death has opened for them.
There is a depth of desperation to the condition which enables one to
remain in life only by engaging death, but the reward is their knowledge that what is happening at each instant of the electric present is
good or bad for them, good or bad for their cause, their love, their
action, their need.

It is this knowledge which provides the curious community of feeling
in the world of the hipster, a muted cool religious revival to be sure,
but the element which is exciting, disturbing, nightmarish perhaps, is
that incompatibles have come to bed, the inner life and the violent life,
the orgy and the dream of love, the desire to murder and the desire to
create, a dialectical conception of existence with a lust for power, a
dark, romantic, and yet undeniably dynamic view of existence for it
sees every man and woman as moving individually through each
moment of life forward into growth or backward into death.

3

It may be fruitful to consider the hipster a philosophical psychopath, a
man interested not only in the dangerous imperatives of his psychopathy but in codifying, at least for himself, the suppositions on which
his inner universe is constructed. By this premise the hipster is a psychopath, and yet not a psychopath but the negation of the psychopath, for
he possesses the narcissistic detachment of the philosopher, that asborp-
tion in the recessive nuances of one's own motive which is so alien to
the unreasoning drive of the psychopath. In this country where new
millions of psychopaths are developed each year, stamped with the mint
of our contradictory popular culture (where sex is sin and yet sex is
paradise), it is as if there has been room already for the development
of the antithetical psychopath who extrapolates from his own condition, from the inner certainty that his rebellion is just, a radical vision
of the universe which thus separates him from the general ignorance,
reactionary prejudice, and self-doubt of the more conventional psychopath. Having converted his unconscious experience into much conscious
knowledge, the hipster has shifted the focus of his desire from immediate gratification toward that wider passion for future power which is
the mark of civilized man. Yet with an irreducible difference. For Hip

is the sophistication of the wise primitive in a giant jungle, and so its appeal is still beyond the civilized man. If there are ten million Americans who are more or less psychopathic (and the figure is most modest), there are probably not more than one hundred thousand men and women who consciously see themselves as hipsters, but their importance is that they are an elite with the potential ruthlessness of an elite, and a language most adolescents can understand instinctively, for the hipster's intense view of existence matches their experience and their desire to rebel.

Before one can say more about the hipster, there is obviously much to be said about the psychic state of the psychopath—or, clinically, the psychopathic personality. Now, for reasons which may be more curious than the similarity of the words, even many people with a psychoanalytical orientation often confuse the psychopath with the psychotic. Yet the terms are polar. The psychotic is legally insane, the psychopath is not; the psychotic is almost always incapable of discharging in physical acts the rage of his frustration, while the psychopath at his extreme is virtually as incapable of restraining his violence. The psychotic lives in so misty a world that what is happening at each moment of his life is not very real to him whereas the psychopath seldom knows any reality greater than the face, the voice, the being of the particular people among whom he may find himself at any moment. Sheldon and Eleanor Glueck describe him as follows:

> The psychopath . . . can be distinguished from the person sliding into or clambering out of a "true psychotic" state by the long tough persistence of his anti-social attitude and behaviour and the absence of hallucinations, delusions, manic flight of ideas, confusion, disorientation, and other dramatic signs of psychosis.

The late Robert Lindner, one of the few experts on the subject, in his book *Rebel Without a Cause—The Hypnoanalysis of a Criminal Psychopath* presented part of his definition in this way:

> . . . the psychopath is a rebel without a cause, an agitator without a slogan, a revolutionary without a program: in other words, his rebelliousness is aimed to achieve goals satisfactory to himself alone; he is incapable of exertions for the sake of others. All his efforts, hidden under no matter what disguise, represent investments designed to satisfy his immediate wishes and desires. . . . The psychopath, like the child, cannot delay the pleasures of gratification; and this trait is one

of his underlying, universal characteristics. He cannot wait upon erotic gratification which convention demands should be preceded by the chase before the kill: he must rape. He cannot wait upon the development of prestige in society: his egoistic ambitions lead him to leap into headlines by daring performances. Like a red thread the predominance of this mechanism for immediate satisfaction runs through the history of every psychopath. It explains not only his behaviour but also the violent nature of his acts.

Yet even Lindner who was the most imaginative and most sympathetic of the psychoanalysts who have studied the psychopathic personality was not ready to project himself into the essential sympathy—which is that the psychopath may indeed be the perverted and dangerous front-runner of a new kind of personality which could become the central expression of human nature before the twentieth century is over. For the psychopath is better adapted to dominate those mutually contradictory inhibitions upon violence and love which civilization has exacted of us, and if it be remembered that not every psychopath is an extreme case, and that the condition of psychopathy is present in a host of people including many politicians, professional soldiers, newspaper columnists, entertainers, artists, jazz musicians, call-girls, promiscuous homosexuals and half the executives of Hollywood, television, and advertising, it can be seen that there are aspects of psychopathy which already exert considerable cultural influence.

What characterizes almost every psychopath and part-psychopath is that they are trying to create a new nervous system for themselves. Generally we are obliged to act with a nervous system which has been formed from infancy, and which carries in the style of its circuits the very contradictions of our parents and our early milieu. Therefore, we are obliged, most of us, to meet the tempo of the present and the future with reflexes and rhythms which come from the past. It is not only the "dead weight of the institutions of the past" but indeed the inefficient and often antiquated nervous circuits of the past which strangle our potentiality for responding to new possibilities which might be exciting for our individual growth.

Through most of modern history, "sublimation" was possible: at the expense of expressing only a small portion of oneself, that small portion could be expressed intensely. But sublimation depends on a reasonable tempo to history. If the collective life of a generation has moved too quickly, the "past" by which particular men and women of that generation may function is not, let us say, thirty years old, but relatively a hundred or two hundred years old. And so the nervous system is overstressed beyond the possibility of such compromises as sublimation, especially since the stable middle-class values so prerequisite to sublimation have been virtually destroyed in our time, at least as nourishing values free of confusion or doubt. In such a crisis of accelerated historical tempo and deteriorated values, neurosis tends to be replaced by psychopathy, and the success of psychoanalysis (which even ten years ago gave promise of becoming a direct major force) diminishes because of its inbuilt and characteristic incapacity to handle patients more complex, more experienced, or more adventurous than the analyst himself. In practice, psychoanalysis has by now become all too often no more than a psychic blood-letting. The patient is not so much changed as aged, and the infantile fantasies which he is encouraged to express are condemned to exhaust themselves against the analyst's nonresponsive reactions. The result for all too many patients is a diminution, a "tranquilizing" of their most interesting qualities and vices. The patient is indeed not so much altered as worn out—less bad, less good, less bright, less willful, less destructive, less creative. He is thus able to conform to that contradictory and unbearable society which first created his neurosis. He can conform to what he loathes because he no longer has the passion to feel loathing so intensely.

The psychopath is notoriously difficult to analyze because the fundamental decision of his nature is to try to live the infantile fantasy, and in this decision (given the dreary alternative of psychoanalysis) there may be a certain instinctive wisdom. For there is a dialectic to changing one's nature, the dialectic which underlies all psychoanalytic method: it is the knowledge that if one is to change one's habits, one must go back to the source of their creation, and so the psychopath exploring backward along the road of the homosexual, the orgiast, the drug-addict, the rapist, the robber and the murderer seeks to find those violent parallels to the violent and often hopeless contradictions he knew as an infant and as a child. For if he has the courage to meet the parallel situation at the moment when he is ready, then he has a chance to act as he has never acted before, and in satisfying the frustration— if he can succeed—he may then pass by symbolic substitute through the locks of incest. In thus giving expression to the buried infant in himself, he can lessen the tension of those infantile desires and so free himself to remake a bit of his nervous system. Like the neurotic he is looking for the opportunity to grow up a second time, but the psychopath knows instinctively that to express a forbidden impulse actively is far more beneficial to him than merely to confess the desire in the safety of a doctor's room. The psychopath is ordinately ambitious, too ambitious ever to trade his warped brilliant conception of his possible victories in life for the grim if peaceful attrition of the analyst's couch. So his associational journey into the past is lived out in the theatre of the present, and he exists for those charged situations where his senses are so alive that he can be aware actively (as the analysand is aware passively) of what his habits are, and how he can change them. The strength of the psychopath is that he knows (where most of us can only guess) what is good for him and what is bad for him at exactly those instants when an old crippling habit has become so attacked by experience that the potentiality exists to change it, to replace a negative and empty fear with an outward action, even if—and here I obey the logic of the extreme psychopath—even if the fear is of himself, and the action is to murder. The psychopath murders—if he has the courage—out of the necessity to purge his violence, for if he cannot empty his hatred then he cannot love, his being is frozen with implacable self-hatred for his cowardice. (It can of course be suggested that it take little courage for two strong eighteen-year-old hoodlums, let us say, to beat in the brains of a candy-store keeper, and indeed the act—even by the logic of the psychopath—is not likely to prove very therapeutic, for the victim is not an immediate equal. Still, courage of a sort is necessary, for one murders not only a weak fifty-year-old man but an institution as well, one violates private property, one enters into a new relation with the police and introduces a dangerous element into one's life. The hoodlum is therefore daring the unknown, and so no matter how brutal the act, it is not altogether cowardly.)

At bottom, the drama of the psychopath is that he seeks love. Not love as the search for a mate, but love as the search for an orgasm more apocalyptic than the one which preceded it. Orgasm is his therapy—he knows at the seed of his being that good orgasm opens his possibilities and bad orgasm imprisons him. But in this search, the psychopath becomes an embodiment of the extreme contradictions of the society which formed his character, and the apocalyptic orgasm often remains as remote as the Holy Grail, for there are clusters and nests and ambushes of violence in his own necessities and in the imperatives and retaliations of the men and women among whom he lives his life, so that even as he drains his hatred in one act or another, so the conditions of his life create it anew in him until the drama of his movements bears a sardonic resemblance to the frog who climbed a few feet in the well only to drop back again.

Yet there is this to be said for the search after the good orgasm:

when one lives in a civilized world, and still can enjoy none of the
cultural nectar of such a world because the paradoxes on which
civilization is built demand that there remain a cultureless and alienated
bottom of exploitable human material, then the logic of becoming a
sexual outlaw (if one's psychological roots are bedded in the bottom)
is that one has at least a running competitive chance to be physically
healthy so long as one stays alive. It is therefore no accident that
psychopathy is most prevalent with the Negro. Hated from outside and
therefore hating himself, the Negro was forced into the position of
exploring all those moral wildernesses of civilized life which the Square
automatically condemns as delinquent or evil or immature or morbid
or self-destructive or corrupt. (Actually the terms have equal weight.
Depending on the telescope of the cultural clique from which the
Square surveys the universe, "evil" or "immature" are equally strong
terms of condemnation.) But the Negro, not being privileged to gratify
his self-esteem with the heady satisfactions of categorical condemnation, chose to move instead in that other direction where all situations
are equally valid, and in the worst of perversion, promiscuity, pimpery,
drug addiction, rape, razor-slash, bottle-break, what-have-you, the
Negro discovered and elaborated a morality of the bottom, an ethical
differentiation between the good and the bad in every human activity
from the go-getter pimp (as opposed to the lazy one) to the relatively
dependable pusher or prostitute. Add to this, the cunning of their language, the abstract ambiguous alternatives in which from the danger
of their oppression they learned to speak ("Well, now, man, like I'm
looking for a cat to turn me on . . ."), add even more the profound
sensitivity of the Negro jazzman who was the cultural mentor of a
people, and it is not too difficult to believe that the language of Hip
which evolved was an artful language, tested and shaped by an intense
experience and therefore different in kind from white slang, as different
as the special obscenity of the soldier, which in its emphasis upon "ass"
as the soul and "shit" as circumstance, was able to express the existential states of the enlisted man. What makes Hip a special language
is that it cannot really be taught—if one shares none of the experiences
of elation and exhaustion which it is equipped to describe, then it
seems merely arch or vulgar or irritating. It is a pictorial language, but
pictorial like nonobjective art, imbued with the dialectic of small but
intense change, a language for the microcosm, in this case, man, for it
takes the immediate experiences of any passing man and magnifies the
dynamic of his movements, not specifically but abstractly so that he is
seen more as a vector in a network of forces than as a static character

in a crystallized field. (Which latter is the practical view of the snob.)
For example, there is real difficulty in trying to find a Hip substitute
for "stubborn." The best possibility I can come up with is: "That cat
will never come off his groove, dad." But groove implies movement,
narrow movement but motion nonetheless. There is really no way to
describe someone who does not move at all. Even a creep does move—
if at a pace exasperatingly more slow than the pace of the cool cats.

4

Like children, hipsters are fighting for the sweet, and their language
is a set of subtle indications of their success or failure in the competition for pleasure. Unstated but obvious is the social sense that there is
not nearly enough sweet for everyone. And so the sweet goes only to
the victor, the best, the most, the man who knows the most about how
to find his energy and how not to lose it. The emphasis is on energy
because the psychopath and the hipster are nothing without it since
they do not have the protection of a position or a class to rely on
when they have overextended themselves. So the language of Hip is a
language of energy, how it is found, how it is lost.

But let us see. I have jotted down perhaps a dozen words, the Hip
perhaps most in use and most likely to last with the minimum of varia-
tion. The words are man, go, put down, make, beat, cool, swing, with it,
crazy, dig, flip, creep, hip, square. They serve a variety of purposes
and the nuance of the voice uses the nuance of the situation to convey
the subtle contextual difference. If the hipster moves through his life on
a constant search with glimpses of Mecca in many a turn of his
experience (Mecca being the apocalyptic orgasm) and if everyone in
the civilized world is at least in some small degree a sexual cripple, the
hipster lives with the knowledge of how he is sexually crippled and
where he is sexually alive, and the faces of experience which life
presents to him each day are engaged, dismissed or avoided as his
need directs and his lifemanship makes possible. For life is a contest
between people in which the victor generally recuperates quickly and
the loser takes long to mend, a perpetual competition of colliding
explorers in which one must grow or else pay more for remaining the
same (pay in sickness, or depression, or anguish for the lost opportunity), but pay or grow.

Therefore one finds words like go, and make it, and with it, and
swing: "Go" with its sense that after hours or days or months or
years of monotony, boredom, and depression one has finally had one's
chance, one has amassed enough energy to meet an exciting opportu-

nity with all one's present talents for the flip (up or down) and so one is ready to go, ready to gamble. Movement is always to be preferred to inaction. In motion a man has a chance, his body is warm, his instincts are quick, and when the crisis comes, whether of love or violence, he can make it, he can win, he can release a little more energy for himself since he hates himself a little less, he can make a little better nervous system, make it a little more possible to go again, to go faster next time and so make more and thus find more people with whom he can swing. For to swing is to communicate, is to convey the rhythms of one's own being to a lover, a friend, or an audience, and—equally necessary—be able to feel the rhythms of their response. To swing with the rhythms of another is to enrich oneself—the conception of the learning process as dug by Hip is that one cannot really learn until one contains within oneself the implicit rhythm of the subject or the person. As an example, I remember once hearing a Negro friend have an intellectual discussion at a party for half an hour with a white girl who was a few years out of college. The Negro literally could not read or write, but he had an extraordinary ear and a fine sense of mimicry. So as the girl spoke, he would detect the particular formal uncertainties in her argument, and in a pleasant (if slightly Southern) English accent, he would respond to another facet of her doubts. When she would finish what she felt was a particularly well-articulated idea, he would smile privately and say, "Other-direction . . . do you really believe in that?"

"Well . . . No," the girl would stammer, "now that you get down to it, there is something disgusting about it to me," and she would be off again for five more minutes.

Of course the Negro was not learning anything about the merits and demerits of the argument, but he was learning a great deal about a type of girl he had never met before, and that was what he wanted. Being unable to read or write, he could hardly be interested in ideas nearly as much as in lifemanship, and so he eschewed any attempt to obey the precision or lack of precision in the girl's language, and instead sensed her character (and the values of her social type) by swinging with the nuances of her voice.

So to swing is to be able to learn, and by learning take a step toward making it, toward creating. What is to be created is not nearly so important as the hipster's belief that when he really makes it, he will be able to turn his hand to anything, even to self-discipline. What he must do before that is find his courage at the moment of violence, or equally make it in the act of love, find a little more between his woman and himself, or indeed between his mate and himself (since many hipsters are bisexual), but paramount, imperative, is the necessity to make it because in making it, one is making the new habit, unearthing the new talent which the old frustration denied.

Whereas if you goof (the ugliest word in Hip), if you lapse back into being a frightened stupid child, or if you flip, if you lose your control, reveal the buried weaker more feminine part of your nature, then it is more difficult to swing the next time, your ear is less alive, your bad and energy-wasting habits are further confirmed, you are farther away from being with it. But to be with it is to have grace, is to be closer to the secrets of that inner unconscious life which will nourish you if you can hear it, for you are then nearer to that God which every hipster believes is located in the senses of his body, that trapped, mutilated and nonetheless megalomaniacal God who is It, who is energy, life, sex, force, the Yoga's *prana*, the Reichian's orgone, Lawrence's "blood," Hemingway's "good," the Shavian life-force; "It"; God; not the God of the churches but the unachievable whisper of mystery within the sex, the paradise of limitless energy and perception just beyond the next wave of the next orgasm.

To which a cool cat might reply, "Crazy, man!"

Because, after all, what I have offered above is an hypothesis, no more, and there is not the hipster alive who is not absorbed in his own tumultuous hypotheses. Mine is interesting, mine is way out (on the avenue of the mystery along the road to "It") but still I am just one cat in a world of cool cats, and everything interesting is crazy, or at least so the Squares who do not know how to swing would say.

(And yet crazy is also the self-protective irony of the hipster. Living with questions and not with answers, he is so different in his isolation and in the far reach of his imagination from almost everyone with whom he deals in the outer world of the Square, and meets generally so much enmity, competition, and hatred in the world of Hip, that his isolation is always in danger of turning upon itself, and leaving him indeed just that, crazy.)

If, however, you agree with my hypothesis, if you as a cat are way out too, and we are in the same groove (the universe now being glimpsed as a series of ever-extending radii from the center), why then you say simply, "I dig," because neither knowledge nor imagination comes easily, it is buried in the pain of one's forgotten experience, and so one must work to find it, one must occasionally exhaust oneself by digging into the self in order to perceive the outside. And indeed it is essential to dig the most, for if you do not dig you lose your superiority over the Square, and so you are less likely to be cool (to be in control of a situation because you have swung where the Square has not, or because you have allowed to come to consciousness a pain, a guilt, a shame or a desire which the other has not had the courage to face). To be cool is to be equipped, and if you are equipped it is more difficult for the next cat who comes along to put you down. And of course one can hardly afford to be put down too often, or one is beat, one has lost one's confidence, one has lost one's will, one is impotent in the world of action and so closer to the demeaning flip of becoming a queer, or indeed closer to dying, and therefore it is even more difficult to recover enough energy to try to make it again, because once a cat is beat he has nothing to give, and no one is interested any longer in making it with him. This is the terror of the hipster—to be beat—because once the sweet of sex has deserted him, he still cannot give up the search. It is not granted to the hipster to grow old gracefully—he has been captured too early by the oldest dream of power, the gold fountain of Ponce de Leon, the fountain of youth where the gold is in the orgasm.

To be beat is therefore a flip, it is a situation beyond one's experience, impossible to anticipate—which indeed in the circular vocabulary of Hip is still another meaning for flip, but then I have given just a few of the connotations of these words. Like most primitive vocabularies each word is a prime symbol and serves a dozen or a hundred functions of communication in the instinctive dialectic through which the hipster perceives his experience, that dialectic of the instantaneous differentials of existence in which one is forever moving forward into more or retreating into less.

5

It is impossible to conceive a new philosophy until one creates a new language, but a new popular language (while it must implicitly contain a new philosophy) does not necessarily present its philosophy overtly. It can be asked then what really is unique in the life-view of Hip which raises its argot above the passing verbal whimsies of the bohemian or the lumpenproletariat.

The answer would be in the psychopathic element of Hip which has almost no interest in viewing human nature, or better, in judging human nature, from a set of standards conceived a priori to the experience, standards inherited from the past. Since Hip sees every answer as posing immediately a new alternative, a new question, its emphasis is on complexity rather than simplicity (such complexity that its language without the illumination of the voice and the articulation of the face and body remains hopelessly incommunicative). Given its emphasis on complexity, Hip abdicates from any conventional moral responsibility because it would argue that the result of our actions are unforeseeable, and so we cannot know if we do good or bad, we cannot even know (in the Joycean sense of the good and the bad) whether we have given energy to another, and indeed if we could, there would still be no idea of what ultimately the other would do with it.

Therefore, men are not seen as good or bad (that they are good-and-bad is taken for granted) but rather each man is glimpsed as a collection of possibilities, some more possible than others (the view of character implicit in Hip) and some humans are considered more capable than others of reaching more possibilities within themselves in less time, provided, and this is the dynamic, provided the particular character can swing at the right time. And here arises the sense of context which differentiates Hip from a Square view of character. Hip sees the context as generally dominating the man, dominating him because his character is less significant than the context in which he must function. Since it is arbitrarily five times more demanding of one's energy to accomplish even an inconsequential action in an unfavorable context than a favorable one, man is then not only his character but his context, since the success or failure of an action in a given context reacts upon the character and therefore affects what the character will be in the next context. What dominates both character and context is the energy available at the moment of intense context.

Character being thus seen as perpetually ambivalent and dynamic enters then into an absolute relativity where there are no truths other than the isolated truths of what each observer feels at each instant of his existence. To take a perhaps unjustified metaphysical extrapolation, it is as if the universe which has usually existed conceptually as a Fact (even if the Fact were Berkeley's God) but a Fact which it was the aim of all science and philosophy to reveal, becomes instead a changing reality whose laws are remade at each instant by everything living, but most particularly man, man raised to a neo-medieval summit where the truth is not what one has felt yesterday or what one expects to feel tomorrow but rather truth is no more nor less than what one feels at each instant in the perpetual climax of the present.

What is consequent therefore is the divorce of man from his values, the liberation of the self from the Super-Ego of society. The only Hip morality (but of course it is an ever-present morality) is to do what one feels whenever and wherever it is possible, and—this is how the war of the Hip and the Square begins—to be engaged in one primal battle: to open the limits of the possible for oneself, for oneself alone, because that is one's need. Yet in widening the arena of the possible, one widens it reciprocally for others as well, so that the nihilistic fulfillment of each man's desire contains its antithesis of human co-operation.

If the ethic reduces to Know Thyself and Be Thyself, what makes it radically different from Socratic moderation with its stern conservative respect for the experience of the past is that the Hip ethic is immoderation, childlike in its adoration of the present (and indeed to respect the past means that one must also respect such ugly consequences of the past as the collective murders of the State). It is this adoration of the present which contains the affirmation of Hip, because its ultimate logic surpasses even the unforgetable solution of the Marquis de Sade to sex, private property, and the family, that all men and women have absolute but temporary rights over the bodies of all other men and women—the nihilism of Hip proposes as its final tendency that every social restraint and category be removed, and the affirmation implicit in the proposal is that man would then prove to be more creative than murderous and so would not destroy himself. Which is exactly what separates Hip from the authoritarian philosophies which now appeal to the conservative and liberal temper—what haunts the middle of the twentieth century is that faith in man has been lost, and the appeal of authority has been that it would restrain us from ourselves. Hip, which would return us to ourselves, at no matter what price in individual violence, is the affirmation of the barbarian, for it requires a primitive passion about human nature to believe that individual acts of violence are always to be preferred to the collective violence of the State; it takes literal faith in the creative possibilities of the human being to envisage acts of violence as the catharsis which prepares growth.

Whether the hipster's desire for absolute sexual freedom contains any genuinely radical conception of a different world is of course another matter, and it is possible, since the hipster lives with his hatred, that many of them are the material for an elite of storm troopers ready to follow the first truly magnetic leader whose view of mass murder is phrased in a language which reaches their emotions. But given the desperation of his condition as a psychic outlaw, the hipster is equally a candidate for the most reactionary and most radical of movements, and so it is just as possible that many hipsters will come —if the crisis deepens—to a radical comprehension of the horror of society, for even as the radical has had his incommunicable dissent confirmed in his experience by precisely the frustration, the denied opportunities, and the bitter years which his ideas have cost him, so the sexual adventurer deflected from his goal by the implacable animosity of a society constructed to deny the sexual radical as well, may yet come to an equally bitter comprehension of the slow relentless inhumanity of the conservative power which controls him from without and from within. And in being so controlled, denied, and starved into the attrition of conformity, indeed the hipster may come to see that his condition is no more than an exaggeration of the human condition, and if he would be free, then everyone must be free. Yes, this is possible too, for the heart of Hip is its emphasis upon courage at the moment of crisis, and it is pleasant to think that courage contains within itself (as the explanation of its existence) some glimpse of the necessity of life to become more than it has been.

It is obviously not very possible to speculate with sharp focus on the future of the hipster. Certain possibilities must be evident, however, and the most central is that the organic growth of Hip depends on whether the Negro emerges as a dominating force in American life. Since the Negro knows more about the ugliness and danger of life than the white, it is probable that if the Negro can win his equality, he will possess a potential superiority, a superiority so feared that the fear itself has become the underground drama of domestic politics. Like all conservative political fear it is the fear of unforeseeable consequences, for the Negro's equality would tear a profound shift into the psychology, the sexuality, and the moral imagination of every white alive.

With this possible emergence of the Negro, Hip may erupt as a psychically armed rebellion whose sexual impetus may rebound against the antisexual foundation of every organized power in America, and bring into the air such animosities, antipathies, and new conflicts of interest that the mean empty hypocrisies of mass conformity will no longer work. A time of violence, new hysteria, confusion and rebellion will then be likely to replace the time of conformity. At that time, if the liberal should prove realistic in his belief that there is peaceful room for every tendency in American life, then Hip would end by being absorbed as a colorful figure in the tapestry. But if this is not the reality, and the economic, the social, the psychological, and finally the moral crises accompanying the rise of the Negro should prove insupportable, then a time is coming when every political guidepost will be gone, and millions of liberals will be faced with political dilemmas they have so far succeeded in evading, and with a view of human nature they do not wish to accept. To take the desegregation of the schools in the South as an example, it is quite likely that the reactionary sees the reality more closely than the liberal when he argues that the deeper issue is not desegregation but miscegenation. (As a radical I am of course facing in the opposite direction from the White Citizen's Councils—obviously I believe it is the absolute human right of the Negro to mate with the white, and matings there will undoubtedly be, for there will be Negro high school boys brave enough to chance their lives.) But for the average liberal whose mind has been dulled by the committee-ish cant of the professional liberal, miscegenation is not an issue because he has been told that the Negro does not desire it. So, when it comes, miscegenation will be a terror, comparable perhaps to the derangement of the American Communists when the icons to Stalin came tumbling down. The average American Communist held to the myth of Stalin for reasons which had little to do with the political evidence and everything to do with their psychic necessities. In this sense it is equally a psychic necessity for the liberal to believe that the Negro and even the reactionary Southern white are eventually and fundamentally people like himself, capable of becoming good liberals too if only they can be reached by good liberal reason. What the liberal cannot bear to admit is the hatred beneath the skin of a society so unjust that the amount of collective violence buried in the people is perhaps incapable of being contained, and therefore, if one wants a better world one does well to hold one's breath, for a worse world is bound to come first, and the dilemma may well be this: given such hatred, it must either vent itself nihilistically or become turned into the cold murderous liquidations of the totalitarian state.

6

No matter what its horrors the twentieth century is a vastly exciting century for its tendency is to reduce all of life to its ultimate alternatives. One can well wonder if the last war of them all will be between the blacks and the whites, or between the women and the men, or between the beautiful and ugly, the pillagers and managers, or the rebels and the regulators. Which of course is carrying speculation beyond the point where speculation is still serious, and yet despair at the monotony and bleakness of the future have become so engrained in the radical temper that the radical is in danger of abdicating from all imagination. What a man feels is the impulse for his creative effort, and if an alien but nonetheless passionate instinct about the meaning of life has come so unexpectedly from a virtually illiterate people, come out of the most intense conditions of exploitation, cruelty, violence, frustration, and lust, and yet has succeeded as an instinct in keeping this tortured people alive, then it is perhaps possible that the Negro holds more of the tail of the expanding elephant of truth than the radical, and if this is so, the radical humanist could do worse than to brood upon the phenomenon. For if a revolutionary time should come again, there would be a crucial difference if someone had already delineated a neo-Marxian calculus aimed at comprehending every circuit and process of society from ukase to kiss as the communications of human energy—a calculus capable of translating the economic relations of man into his psychological relations and then back again, his productive relations thereby embracing his sexual relations as well, until the crises of capitalism in the twentieth century would yet be understood as the unconscious adaptations of a society to solve its economic imbalance at the expense of a new mass psychological imbalance. It is almost beyond the imagination to conceive of a work in which the drama of human energy is engaged, and a theory of its social currents and dissipations, its imprisonments, expressions, and tragic wastes are fitted into some gigantic synthesis of human action where the body of Marxist thought, and particularly the epic grandeur of *Das Kapital* (that first of the major *psychologies* to approach the mystery of social cruelty so simply and practically as to say that we are a collective body of humans whose life-energy is wasted, displaced, and procedurally stolen as it passes from one of us to another)—where particularly the epic grandeur of *Das Kapital* would find its place in an even more God-like view of human justice and injustice, in some more excruciating vision of those intimate and institutional processes which lead to our creations and disasters, our growth, our attrition, and our rebellion.

1957

Ellen Douglas
Jesse

When we knew him, Jesse Daniels was already an old man. He had been draft age during the first World War, and had gone to France.

"I couldn't take my fiddle to the war with me," he told me, when we were talking about his travels one day, "but I took my Jew's harp and my sweet potato. I was already a good fiddler at that time, and a good drummer, too. Music come easy to me. I played with Louis Armstrong in New Orleans, 1915, 1916." He paused and looked at me as if to see if I was impressed.

"Louis Armstrong!" I said. "Did you really?"

He nodded. "Then I got drafted," he went on, "and when I come back to New Orleans after the war, all that old gang was busted up, kind of, some gone one way and some another. I played here and there—Vicksburg, Natchez, out to Texas, up to Chicago. I never liked Chicago and all them places much. Too cold. And no fishing to speak of. I'd play up there in the spring and summer some years and then come back here to Philippi in the winter. A man can make out in Philippi. Plant him a patch of greens, fish, get him up a little band. I always got two or three boys here willing to go in on a band with me, and we could make enough to live. Nowadays, though, it's even better. You get your unemployment every year a long time—some years I got it twenty or more weeks; and then when you get up my age you got your Social Security. So now I don't have to play nowhere if I don't want to. I had a job out to Minnesota two, three years before my Social Security come in, playing concerts at a—a—you know what I'm talking about, Miss, one of them old peoples. . . ."

"An old people's home?" I asked.

"That's it," he said. "Nothing but old peoples. And they treat 'em so nice. They got the best of all kinds of food, and they got radios and TV's, everything. And they kept us on a long time just to play for 'em every night. They got beards."

"What?"

"Beards. Everyone of 'em, Miss. The men, I mean. Everyone of 'em got long beards. They don't let 'em cut 'em off. They some kind of special peoples. You know what I mean? They belongs to something or other special. Some kind of a house they calls it."

"Oh," I said. "Is it the House of David?"

"That's it, Miss. That's where they keeps they old folks. It was a good job—easy hours, steady work, good pay. But I'm glad to be home. I never did catch on to the fishing up there, and it seems to me the fishing down here gets better every year. I caught me around a hundred or more breams in Calloway's Blue Hole yesterday."

"Better not let the game warden hear about it," I said.

"No indeed, Miss. I sold half of 'em before I ever went home."

The first time I saw Jesse was the day I drove down to his house to interview him about teaching my son Ralph to play the guitar. We had heard of him from friends who had hired his little band to play at a party, and who knew that he gave guitar lessons. I had telephoned him to expect me, and following his directions had driven slowly along Pearl Street until I found his house. A neat, three-room shotgun house with a small vine-covered porch, it was one of only two recently painted buildings in the block; the others were weathered to a uniform soft gray.

Very few respectable Negroes live on Pearl Street, particularly if they have children. It's a noisy neighborhood, the red-light houses sandwiched in between night clubs like the *Casablanca* and the *Live and Let Live*; tumble-down fish markets, Chinese grocery stores, cafes and second-hand clothing and furniture stores crowded into a ten-block

Negro slum. But it was an appropriate neighborhood for an old time jazz musician, and I thought nothing of Jesse's living there.

His house was a block from the *Casablanca*, a huge rickety old dance hall with an unsavory reputation, and two blocks from what was rumored to be an integrated house of prostitution. But it was a sturdy house, the small porch clean, the yard, unlike the cluttered yards of neighboring houses, broom-marked where it had been recently swept. An old washtub by the front steps was full of white petunias.

Jesse was waiting for me on the front porch when I arrived. As he stood up and came toward the car, my heart sank. I didn't think he could possibly teach anyone anything. He was a scarecrow of a man, a great, tall, loose bundle of sticks with a shambling walk. His long arms and legs seemed to have a will of their own, moving somehow in unexpected directions; his gestures were outlandish, extravagant, as if his arms and hands didn't know what he was talking about and always thought he was telling a wild story. He looked, too, as if he had deliberately dressed himself as ridiculously as possible. He had on an old, battered felt hat turned inside out, the upside-down brim tilted at a dashing angle, and a pair of jeans six inches too short. The black sticks of his legs showed above his shoes, so thin at the ankles I could have put my thumb and forefinger around them. I got out of the car and introduced myself to him, while he took off his hat and bowed and wagged his head self-consciously.

But when he began to tell me about himself and to discuss the lessons, he relaxed, and his face had a certain amount of sober dignity and self-possession that were reassuring. His eyes were small and alert, his high, sloping forehead merged into a shining bald dome fringed with stiff, short black hair, he had a long jaw, deeply lined from nostrils to chin, and a wide, kind mouth. He apologized for the way he was dressed, saying he had just come in from fishing, and we made sensible arrangements about hours and prices.

"I got to see if the boy's got talent before I know can I teach him," he said. "I come the first time free."

The arrangement we made was for me to pick him up every Monday and Thursday afternoon and bring him to my house, and then to take him home afterward. He charged a dollar and a half a lesson. When he came out to get into the car the following week, the day of the first lesson, he wore a sensible, dark suit, and a respectable if ancient hat.

Jesse lived almost two miles from our house, and I spent considerable time alone with him that year, driving back and forth. That was how we happened to have so much conversation. When we got to the house, he was all business, going straight with Ralph to his room, closing the door, and setting to work. They laboriously tuned their guitars, and played over and over again three or four boogies, of which Ralph does not even remember the names, and *The St. Louis Blues, Home on the Range*, and *The Red River Valley*. These songs apparently made up Jesse's whole repertoire—if he knew any others, he did not teach them to Ralph. Usually he did not sing the words to the songs, but hummed the tunes in his cracked old voice, interrupting himself now and then to call out the chord changes in the guitar accompaniment. Sometimes, in the course of a lesson, he would send Ralph out to borrow a cigarette from me; two or three times he came out himself, and in that case, at first, if I were having a drink or a can of beer, I would offer him one. But ordinarily, except for the faint sound of the guitars behind Ralph's closed door, I scarcely knew he was in the house.

Driving back and forth, Jesse and I talked a little about fishing or about Ralph's progress on the guitar, but mostly we talked about Jesse's life. Naturally, considering his age and profession, one of the first things I asked him was whether he had known Bud Scott, who was a famous old-time musician in our part of the country. I had heard him play when I was thirteen or fourteen, and had never forgotten it; he was coal black, enormously fat, and, when he sang, opened his huge mouth so that you could see all the cavernous red interior, and shouted out the words in a hoarse, raucous, gravelly voice that could be heard in the next county, even over the deafening, brassy tumult of his band. He died the year I heard him, but he had played for dances from St. Francisville to Greenville in my mother's day, and was one of our monuments, seeming until he died as indestructible as the Confederate soldier on his shaft in the courthouse yard. Jesse said, yes, he had known Bud well, in fact had played with him many times, and with his son, Bud, Jr., who after the old man died had what nowadays they call a "combo." I remembered that Bud, Jr. had played the night of the Natchez fire, and Jesse told me he was in the combo at that time. It was during one of his out-of-work periods, when he had come South to regroup, so to speak.

The Natchez fire was in late Spring 1939, and except for the 1927 flood, it was the worst thing that ever happened in our part of the country. I suppose it has been forgotten everywhere else; so many people have been killed since 1939. But it will be a long time before our Negroes forget it. The dance was in a ramshackle night club in Natchez, and all the colored young people in the county were there. The place was hung with Spanish moss, dry as tinder and flitted with some inflammable insecticide to get rid of the mosquitoes. Someone threw away a lighted match, or perhaps there was a spark of static electricity, no one ever knew exactly how it happened, but the place went off like a firecracker—simply exploded into flame. A few people near the front and back doors got out, but in the panic almost everyone was burned or suffocated or trampled to death—five hundred people. There was scarcely a Negro family in Natchez that didn't lose a child. Even in Philippi, a hundred miles away, we felt it. Everyone had connections with somebody who died in the Natchez fire.

Jesse told me that he just missed playing with Bud Scott, Jr., that night. At the time, he said, he had had a lady friend living in Ferriday, over the river from Natchez, and he was with her that day. She didn't want to go to the dance and persuaded Jesse to drive with her to Lake Providence instead, to visit her brother's family. He didn't even bother to get anyone in his place, he said. He didn't have that on his conscience. He just didn't show up. The next morning, getting up for breakfast, they heard about it on the radio. But Scott, Jr. and almost everyone in the band died in the fire.

Jesse told me he had been lucky like that all his life; even when he was living in Chicago during the twenties and thirties playing in what must have been mostly dives and speakeasies, he had stayed out of trouble.

"How did you manage?" I asked. "Weren't you scared of all those gangsters up there?"

"Yes, *ma'm*, I was scared. You *got* to be scared. And you got to keep your money in your bosom. I know plenty mens up there still sits with they back in a corner in the cafe—you know, where they can see the door and all, so nobody can sneak up on them. I had a friend up there wasn't scared, and he ended up in Lake Michigan with a concrete block to his feet. I warned him, too. I told him, 'You can get along fine up here if you keep your eyes and your mouth shut, and stay scared.' But he wanted to be a big man."

I asked Jesse once if he had ever heard the *Natchez Fire Blues* or the *Philippi Pearl Street Blues*, and he told me he knew them and knew the fellows who had written both of them. They are not good songs, only run-of-the-mill blues, or what we call *race music*, the kind that is played on the local radio stations (or used to be before rock and roll come in) every afternoon from one until five to advertise hair straighteners. Jesse laughed when I asked him about the *Pearl Street Blues*, and asked me if I had ever heard *Greenville Smokin'*, *Leland Burnin'*

Down, written by the same fellow. I said I had never even heard of it, and he shrugged and said, well, they didn't play it on the radio, and he reckoned there were white men in Leland, Greenville, too, who would think nothing of shooting any nigger they heard singing that song. I was curious, and two or three times afterward I tried to get him to play *Greenville Smokin', Leland Burnin' Down* for me on the guitar and sing it, but he never would. I even tried to get him to explain what he meant about the shooting part, and he seemed to try, but somehow he always got confused or got me confused. Once when I asked him about it, he said he didn't think the "bossman" would like it, and then I gave up. I realized that he did not want to assume anything, to take anything for granted. He was afraid of us.

I suppose people will wonder why it mattered to me, and sometimes I wonder myself; but I was troubled, and troubled people will grasp at any straw to vindicate themselves. It doesn't have to be anything that is important to anyone. I suppose, too, that my uneasiness is part of the reason we talked about the Natchez fire. I didn't want him to think I had dismissed it long ago, as so many white people have, as something that happened to a bunch of niggers.

He must have sensed what was going on in my mind, because one day just before we got out of the car in front of my house he said to me abruptly, for no reason that I could discover, "Miss, you such a good Christian, your daddy must be a preacher."

I'm not so foolish that I didn't know he was trying to flatter me, to say what he thought would please, but even if he had been sincere, what could I have said in reply? That the churches are crowded every Sunday with his bitterest enemies? That I might not be what he would call "a Christian" at all?

"No," I said, "he's not a preacher, but he's an elder."

"I knew it," Jesse said. "I knew he was bound to be saved."

One more thing I'll say about wanting to make Jesse Daniels my friend. I have a passion for talking over old times, for hearing from old people how it was at such and such a time in such and such a place; and particularly, if I can bring to bear anything out of my own recollections, can say, "That's right; of course; because I remember, or Gran told me something that fits right in with what you're saying." It gives me intense pleasure to hear my father tell how his father used to wad his old muzzle-loading shotgun with Spanish moss, aim it up into the holly tree in the front yard (Right there—that's the tree) and bring down enough robins to have robin pie for dinner. More than anything I want to hear *how it was*, to gather all the facts, and then to *understand.* For this reason it gave me a queer satisfaction to think of Jesse's driving to Lake Providence with his lady friend the day of the fire, sitting in the warm darkness on the little porch of her brother's house, laughing and drinking and slapping mosquitoes, going to bed and making love, and then getting up the next morning to hear the impersonal voice of the radio announcer describe the horror in which they had so nearly been consumed.

From the beginning my husband did not like Jesse. That is, he didn't dislike him, but he didn't take to him, and as time went on he had a number of things against him. In the first place, Jesse wasn't much of a musician, and Richard thought we were throwing our money away. He was right, too. Jesse came twice a week for more than a year, and I don't believe he taught Ralph a dozen chords. I'll never forget how embarrassed I was for Jesse one afternoon after the lesson when I persuaded him to sit down at the piano in the living room and play and sing for us. Richard had come home early, and I thought I would give him a chance to judge Jesse for himself. Jesse was delighted to play. He put his greasy hat on top of the piano and, drawing up the chair, sat down and banged away at the keys as loudly as if he were playing in a crowded night club, and shouted out the words. But his scarred and knotty old fingers faltered, struck wrong notes, and could not even keep the time. We sat stiff-faced and silent until he finished and then praised him as enthusiastically as we could.

He knew how terrible he had sounded. "I got to have a couple of drinks to get going," he said, "and then, too, folks dancing and hollering, that limbers me up. I can't do no good cold." He got up and bowed and scraped his foot to Richard with exaggerated servility. "I try it for you again one day soon, Bossman," he went on. "I work up a coupla pieces good."

Richard looked as astonished and horrified as if someone had slapped him. "Bossman," indeed! That was a little too much for him. And there was no reason, no excuse either of us could think of for servility. Richard had said nothing that could be interpreted as expecting or requiring it. Jesse just saw a white man and went into his act—like a firehorse at the clang of the alarm.

One reason he didn't see us more clearly and another reason for Richard's disapproval of him was that he was a heavy drinker. At least half the time he came to the house he was a little bit tight. He had to use so much of his energy and intelligence on trying to appear sober that he hadn't much left either for observing us or for teaching guitar. Even Ralph got to the place where he could tell whether Jesse had been drinking, and Ralph's experience with drinkers is negligible. After he told me a couple of times that Jesse hadn't made sense again that afternoon, I had to tell him not to come unless he was sober.

It didn't make much difference to him one way or the other. He made a good living. He taught guitar to half-a-dozen white children and piano to several Negro children. (It is hard to see how he kept his piano students, except that he was probably the only Negro piano teacher in Philippi.) He played almost every Friday and Saturday night at Negro dances and parties. He collected his Social Security, and his wife worked. He also "befriended" old people by helping them fill out forms for getting on the Social Security and the State old age pension, charging twenty-five or fifty cents a person. He told me about this project one afternoon when I was driving him home—said he naturally felt sorry for old folks who didn't have any education, and wanted to do his part to help them. Of course, it is against the law to charge for such a service. I happen to know that the agent at the local Welfare Department threatened several times to have him prosecuted. But she never did anything about it. And Jesse continued to think of himself as a very charitable man. Somehow the fact never penetrated that the social workers at the Welfare Department would fill out the forms for nothing. Oh, he was an old scoundrel, all right. To do him justice, though, I know that many of his "clients" may have been afraid to ask the workers to fill out their forms, or they may not have understood that they could, even if they had been told so when they applied for their pensions. Besides, it is commonly thought among the Negroes here that the Welfare Agent has absolute power over the state's money and that she gives pensions to those she likes and withholds them from those who offend her; the caprices of the state legislature are always taken for her personal caprices, and it may even be that in the interest of prestige she fosters this misapprehension. Jesse's clients and perhaps even Jesse undoubtedly thought that a neatly filled out form would help win the agent's favor.

Before many months of our acquaintance with Jesse had passed, I began to dread Ralph's guitar days. Sometimes it seemed to me that he quite consciously tried to make me uncomfortable. A chance remark, a nervous laugh, an exaggerated gesture, and my afternoon was ruined. One day he told me how when he was a teen-age boy working for a white family in Natchez he had had to play horsey to the child in the house. "Man, that boy never got tired playing horse," he said. "Not 'til he got up practically grown. I can hear his maw now, when he was a boy big as Raff. 'Come on, Jesse. Johnny wants to play horse,' and I'd have to ride him 'til ,my knees shook. I'd ruther of picked a hundred pounds of cotton." There was something in his voice and manner that made me want to say, "But *I* had nothing to do with it."

"He does it deliberately," I told Richard that night. "He knows how to make us squirm. And besides that, it's gotten so I can't have a drink on Monday or Thursday afternoon until he's gone. If he's sober, I don't want to start him drinking, and if he's drinking, I don't want to give him any more."

"You never should have offered him the first can of beer," Richard said. "After all, he's supposed to be working for you, not paying a call. You only gave it to him because he's a Nagro."

"I was trying to be nice to him," I said.

Richard shrugged impatiently. "And get a little free credit for high principles," he said.

We talked half-heartedly that night of firing Jesse, but there was no one else in town to teach Ralph, and we were not spending enough money on the lessons to care much one way or the other. So we went on with them for almost a year and a half, until we found a white teacher, a high school senior who agreed to take Ralph on. Ralph learned more from that boy in a month than he had learned from Jesse in a year and a half.

About a month before we found the high school boy to teach Ralph, Jesse told me the story of his childhood. I was driving him home one hot Thursday afternoon in September, when the subject of where he had lived as a child drifted into the conversation. I don't know why we had never talked of his home before. I suppose I had been more inter-ested in his adult life than in his childhood; and I had assumed, too, that he had been born either in or near Philippi, since it had been his headquarters for so long. But for some reason he mentioned Buchanan County that afternoon, and when I asked him if he had ever lived there, he said, yes, he had been born and raised in Buchanan County, ten miles from Pollock, the county seat.

"You live there any after you were grown?" I asked idly.

"No'm," he said. "I left."

"They say it's rough country over there in the hills," I said. "My father told me one time about a feud they had going when he was a boy, just like the Hatfields and McCoys, and they had to call out the National Guard to make them quit killing each other. Did you ever hear about that?"

"Yes, ma'm," he said. "I didn't live there at the time. I'd been gone from Buchanan County since I was thirteen. But I heard about it from some of my cousins down to Natchez. It didn't surprise me none. Them white folks been shooting each other for thirty years before they called out the Guard. I remember one night when I was a little bitty boy, they had a fight on the road going past the place where we lived. The white man owned the place and my step-daddy was out looking for a mare had got loose, and the white man got hit in the arm by a stray bullet."

"No wonder you left," I said. I was still trying to keep the conversation going.

Jesse did not answer and, when I glanced at him, he seemed to be deep in thought. His long arm, bent at the elbow, was half out the open window of the car. His shabby old hat was on his lap, and in his left hand he was absently rolling a dead cigarette back and forth. He never smoked in the car with me, and if he got into the car with a lighted cigarette, he always carefully put it out and either put it in his pocket or held it in his hand until he got out. He was perfectly sober that afternoon, dressed in his neat dark suit, his long face the picture of quiet dignity.

We drove on for a block, and stopped at the first of several traffic lights on the way to Jesse's house, before he spoke again. Then he repeated himself. "Born and raised in Buchanan County," he said. "Away out in the country from Pollock. I ain't been back there since I left. Thirteen years old when I left, and I been on my own ever since."

"That was pretty young to go on your own," I said.

"I had five brothers and three sisters, and I reckon they all dead but me."

"You must have been the baby, then," I said.

"No, ma'm. I had a baby sister," he said. "Died in my arms. So little I didn't know the difference."

I wasn't sure what he meant, although at first I thought he was saying that she was so small, so frail, he couldn't tell when the life went out of her. And I assumed that he was talking about sometime recently, that his sister had been an old woman when she died.

"What?" I said. I always hopefully asked him to repeat himself when our conversations got confusing, although sometimes the repetition only made them more confusing.

"I was ten years old at the time," he said. "And she was two. I was so little I didn't know she was dead."

"Oh, *Jesse*," I said. "Where was your mama?"

"My mama was dead," he said. "She been dead six months when

the baby died. And so we had nobody but each other. I and her was the two youngest children, and the baby, she was a half to me. Like I told you, I had a step-daddy. *Gret*, big, black nigger, eyes like coals, *hot*; tall, big as a mountain he seemed like to me. I wasn't nothing but a skinny piece of nothing." He smiled and looked down at his thin arm. "I always been skinny," he said. "Food don't put no weight on me."

"But where was he?" I asked. "Who was taking care of you all?"

"*I* taken care of *her*," Jesse said. He nodded his head, as if even now he could say that he was satisfied with the way he had cared for his little sister. "Ain't it hot?" he said.

We had turned now, down a dusty side street between rows of shot-gun houses set on twenty-foot lots. I slowed down to let half-a-dozen little Negro boys who were playing ball in the street get out of our way. We raised a cloud of choking dust as we drove, even going so slowly, and it settled on dusty shrubs and porches, and in a gray film on the children's dark, sweat-streaked bodies.

"I loved that little baby," Jesse said. "She was the prettiest, littlest thing you ever seen. She was light like my mama. I takes my dark color from my daddy. She would follow me around and mind me good as if I was a man; and I had to be mama and daddy both to her, if I was but ten. I always loved children ever since, because she was took from me, I reckon, and I been sorry I had none of my own."

"But where was your step-daddy?" I said. "Weren't there any grown people around?"

"Well," he said, "us two lived together in a cabin on a place belonged to some white people over there in Buchanan County. My step-daddy was no good. Soon as my mama died he went off to work in the next county. Left us. And I was just as glad, I was so scared of him. He had a terrible hot rage on him. Most times I could run, but he would of kilt that baby sooner or later. He would come around maybe once in a month to see how we was getting along, and that was too soon to suit me. If I never saw him, it would of been too much. And like I told you, my other brothers and sisters was all older than me, grown by the time my mama died—twelve years old or more, and all but two out taking care of themselves. Them two left when she died. Oh, Lord, they was scattered over the country. Some I don't even remember seeing in my life. And yet, my mama wasn't so old when she died. She had her first when she was fifteen, so my uncle told me, once. I had this uncle, see, my mama's brother, Will Hobson was his name, lived down the road from us about five miles, and he used to come around regular every week to see how we was doing. He would cut us a stack of wood when we needed it. Yes, he was good to us. But he had plenty children of his own, ten or twelve, and a mean wife. He would of took us in, but she wouldn't have us." He hesitated and then corrected himself. "I don't blame her. I did wrong to say she was mean. She had more than she could feed already. And like I say, he come around regular to see after us. The white people where we stayed was good to us, too. They could just as easy have took the house from us after my mama died and my step went off, but they didn't. I used to go up to their house every so often and they'd give me a sack of meal, and meat and molasses. I could cook pretty good. They give us blankets, too, because my step, he took all the covers when he went. And the white man come down and turned a garden for me to plant greens and such that Spring, but after all we didn't stay long enough to eat them. I fished, too. I will say for myself, I could catch plenty fish even then."

He paused, and I said nothing, already so heartsick at the story he was telling me that I wanted to hear no more of it. But he went on after a minute.

"I didn't have no sense," he said. "I wasn't nothing but a kid." He waved his arm at a cluster of children standing on a street corner, quarrelling in loud voices. "No older than the biggest of them. And so, I reckon the baby, she was sick two, three days, probably, without me knowing it. She probably had a fever or something. Anyways, I remember she cried a lot, and I would put her in the bed and get in with her to try and quiet her down. I got *so* tired hearing her cry. And at night we would sleep together. One Saturday night we was laying together in the bed, me holding her and patting her. She'd been crying and crying most all day, until I was so mad and tired I didn't think I could listen to her no more. I was ready to go off and leave her. And all of a sudden she quit. She just went to sleep. And I was glad. I was so tired I slept, too, after she quit crying, all that night and most of the next morning. When I finally got up, I tippied out in the kitchen to fix us some breakfast without bothering her. But it was ready and still she didn't wake. I ate and I didn't even go back in to her. Lord, I needed a little peace. She slept and she slept. But I didn't think nothing of it one way or the other. Least I can't remember I did. I reckon I was still glad she was sleeping and not crying. So I let her be all that day. And that evening, long about dusk-dark, my uncle, the one lived down the road, come along and I was out in the yard playing. I remember it all like it was yesterday. He was a little bit of a man, not much taller than you, Miss. You wouldn't think he could of had all them children, much less taken care of them. But he was *strong*. He could chop *wood*.

I never seen a man could handle a ax no better than him. And he could pick three hundred pounds of cotton every day. I wished sometimes it would of been so he could take me and my sister in that year. We wouldn't of been no trouble to him, not if I could help it. Anyway, he come along the road there by the house and stopped, and I was sitting under a big old chinaberry tree in the front yard, just sitting, playing some game or other to myself, I reckon, but I don't remember what.

" 'How you all getting along, Jess?' he says.

" 'Fine,' I say. 'We getting along just fine.'

" 'You need me to cut you some wood this week?' he says.

" 'No, sir,' I say. 'We got plenty, Uncle Will.'

"He squats down there in the dust by me under the chinaberry tree, like he does 'most every week when he comes by, to talk awhile.

" 'What you been doing all day long, son?' he says.

" 'Just playing,' I say.

" 'How your garden coming along?'

" 'Greens is up. We ought to get a good mess by the end of the week.'

"He looks all around the yard. 'Where the baby?' he says.

" 'She in the house,' I say. 'She 'sleep.'

" 'Taking a nap, huh?' he says.

" 'Yes, sir, she been taking a nap all day.'

" 'What you say, Boy?'

" 'She been 'sleep all day,' I say, 'and all last night, too. She ain't cried once.'

"Course by that, he knew something was wrong. 'Come on,' he says. 'We better go wake her up.'

"So we went in the house and she was laying up in the bed all under the covers as quiet, and I watched him, and he turned back the covers and felt her and she was cold. Dead." Jesse nodded his head. "I reckon she been dead all day," he said, "and all the night before, ever since she stopped crying. But I never knew it. We took and buried her that afternoon, my uncle and me."

I was so sick I couldn't say anything except, "Oh, *Jesse.*"

We had reached Jesse's neat little house on Pearl Street now, and I drew up to the curb and stopped. But he did not get out of the car. Instead he went on with his story matter-of-factly.

"My mama was third wife to my step," he said. "My own daddy died when I was no more than two or three. I can't remember him. Like I said, I was eighth child to him. And he was a settled man when my mama married him. She didn't marry again for a long time after he died. She went back and stayed with her own daddy until *he* died. And then she married my step. She was sorry afterwards; she left him two, three times, took me and what other kids was with her and tried to make it on her own, but she couldn't. You know, Miss, nobody going to give no lone woman with children no crop to make. How could she do it? And so she would have to go back to him."

He paused and looked at me as if waiting for my comment, but I could not speak. I gripped the steering wheel with both hands and stared at him, concentrating on keeping the tears from coming to my eyes. He went on quietly.

"She always done the best she could for us," he said. "Hard times or good, she seen we went to school. All but two of us, my uncle told me, finished the sixth grade. And me, of course, because she died when I was in the fifth. But I could already write a good hand. It come easy to me. And she could cook, too, and sew, better than most. It never seemed right to me how bad my step done her, and she a good woman. I heard when I was grown that he beat the first two wives he had to death. And my mama, you wouldn't know it from looking at a great, skinny old man like me, but she was a little bitty mite of a thing, like a bird, a little brown pecky bird. He killed her, too. Might not of struck the blow that did it, but he *killed* her. Wore her and beat her to death. I seen him more than once take her by the heels and throw her through the door."

"Oh, Jesse," I said. "Where were the police and the sheriff? Couldn't somebody do something about him?"

"Miss, nobody cared about things like that in them days," Jesse said.

"I don't see how a little boy could live through such times and not be crazy," I said.

"I run off from there when I was thirteen," he said. "For a while after my little sister died, I stayed with a old man down the road didn't have no children and needed somebody to help him around his place. Then that winter my step come back. Lost the crop he'd had in the next county and they wouldn't keep him on. He didn't have nobody to help him and couldn't make it on his own, so he came back and got me. He kept me two years and I had no place to turn. He beat me some, but I was getting a big boy. Not big enough to beat *him*, but big enough to outrun him if I got a start, and big enough to know I would be big enough to beat him soon. So one day when I was thirteen, he caught me. He like to kilt me before I got loose from him, whaling me with the buckle end of his belt. I tore my shirt half off and run out in the road by our house and stood there in the dirt crying and screaming like a baby. 'I'll kill you,' I screamed. 'I'll kill you. I'll kill you.' And he stood on the porch sweating and catching his breath, and laughed at me. But I would have. I left that day, and I never went looking for him, but if I'd ever of seen him again, I would of killed him. I still would. But he's dead now, bound to be."

Jesse put on his hat, opened the car door, and got out. He opened the back door and, reaching in, pulled out his battered guitar case. "Man, it's hot today," he said again. When he had closed the back door he bent down to the front window and took off his hat. "You see, Miss," he said, gesturing behind him toward the washtub by his front steps, "them petunias and merrygolds bloomed out, but my wife got chrysanthemums coming on now in the back. I'm going to bring you a bunch when they begin to bloom."

"That'll be nice," I said. "Thank you."

"Well," he said, "I'll be seeing you Monday. I thank you for the ride." He straightened up and put on his hat again. "May you and the cap'n have a pleasant week-end," he said.

Jesse only worked for us about a month after that day. He came to the next two lessons drunk, and Richard and I made up our minds that we had to find someone else to teach Ralph. We didn't tell Jesse why. I just said that I thought Ralph was too young, that he had learned as much as he could at his age and we thought he should drop the lessons until he was older. Jesse agreed.

"He ain't made much progress lately," he said. "He ain't got his mind on it."

I haven't seen the old man since, except at a distance. I heard that he had bought an old car, and then shortly afterwards that he had been arrested for drunk driving. He didn't call on us to bail him out.

But a strange thing happened recently. I woke up one night from a nightmare about Jesse. I couldn't remember anything about it except that it had been long and confused, with a great many people in it, and Jesse wandering in and out, a child no older than Ralph, but skinny instead of stocky as Ralph is, and having not a child's head on his shoulders but the long seamed face and high, domed forehead of his old age. I was choking with anxiety when I woke up, and two sentences kept repeating themselves over and over in my mind until to exorcise them and sleep again, I turned on the light and wrote them in the margin of a magazine on my night table. When I got up the next morning, I could not remember what I had written or why, in the night, it had seemed so important. I picked up the magazine and read, "There are those of us who are willing to say, 'I am guilty,' but who is to absolve us? And do we expect by our confession miraculously to relieve the suffering of the innocent?" I had written first, "Do we expect to *escape* the suffering of the innocent?" but I had scratched through *escape* and written, *relieve*. I read the sentences over several times, but they did not dispel the anxiety I still felt. I remembered then the reason I had written them. I had thought in the night that if I could remember those words, I would understand everything. But the words were only questions. It wouldn't have mattered if I had forgotten them.

1961

Norman Podhoretz
My Negro Problem—
And Ours

If we—and . . . I mean the relatively conscious whites and the relatively conscious blacks, who must, like lovers, insist on, or create, the consciousness of the others—do not falter in our duty now, we may be able, handful that we are, to end the racial nightmare, and achieve our country, and change the history of the world.

—James Baldwin

TWO IDEAS puzzled me deeply as a child growing up in Brooklyn during the 1930's in what today would be called an integrated neighborhood. One of them was that all Jews were rich; the other was that all Negroes were persecuted. These ideas had appeared in print; therefore they must be true. My own experience and the evidence of my senses told me they were not true, but that only confirmed what a day-dreaming boy in the provinces—for the lower-class neighborhoods of New York belong as surely to the provinces as any rural town in North

Dakota—discovers very early: *his* experience is unreal and the evidence of his senses is not to be trusted. Yet even a boy with a head full of fantasies incongruously synthesized out of Hollywood movies and English novels cannot altogether deny the reality of his own experience —especially when there is so much deprivation in that experience. Nor can he altogether gainsay the evidence of his own senses—especially such evidence of the senses as comes from being repeatedly beaten up, robbed, and in general hated, terrorized, and humiliated.

And so for a long time I was puzzled to think that Jews were supposed to be rich when the only Jews I knew were poor, and that Negroes were supposed to be persecuted when it was the Negroes who were doing the only persecuting I knew about—and doing it, moreover, to *me*. During the early years of the war, when my older sister joined a left-wing youth organization, I remember my astonishment at hearing her passionately denounce my father for thinking that Jews were worse off than Negroes. To me, at the age of twelve, it seemed very clear that Negroes were better off than Jews—indeed, than *all* whites. A city boy's world is contained within three or four square blocks, and in my world it was the whites, the Italians and Jews, who feared the Negroes, not the other way around. The Negroes were tougher than we were, more ruthless, and on the whole they were better athletes. What could it mean, then, to say that they were badly off and that we were more fortunate? Yet my sister's opinions, like print, were sacred, and when she told me about exploitation and economic forces I believed her. I believed her, but I was still afraid of Negroes. And I still hated them with all my heart.

It had not always been so—that much I can recall from early childhood. When did it start, this fear and this hatred? There was a kindergarten in the local public school, and given the character of the neighborhood, at least half of the children in my class must have been Negroes. Yet I have no memory of being aware of color differences at that age, and I know from observing my own children that they attribute no significance to such differences even when they begin noticing them. I think there was a day—first grade? second grade— when my best friend Carl hit me on the way home from school and announced that he wouldn't play with me any more because I had killed Jesus. When I ran home to my mother crying for an explanation, she told me not to pay any attention to such foolishness, and then in Yiddish she cursed the *goyim* and the *schwartzes*, the *schwartzes* and the *goyim*. Carl, it turned out, was a *schwartze*, and so was added a third to the categories into which people were mysteriously divided.

Sometimes I wonder whether this is a true memory at all. It is blazingly vivid, but perhaps it never happened: can anyone really remember back to the age of six? There is no uncertainty in my mind, however, about the years that followed. Carl and I hardly ever spoke, though we met in school every day up through the eighth or ninth grade. There would be embarrassed moments of catching his eye or of his catching mine—for whatever it was that had attracted us to one another as very small children remained alive in spite of the fantastic barrier of hostility that had grown up between us, suddenly and out of nowhere. Nevertheless, friendship would have been impossible, and even if it had been possible, it would have been unthinkable. About that, there was nothing anyone could do by the time we were eight years old.

Item: The orphanage across the street is torn down, a city housing project begins to rise in its place, and on the marvelous vacant lot next to the old orphanage they are building a playground. Much excitement and anticipation as Opening Day draws near. Mayor LaGuardia himself comes to dedicate this great gesture of public benevolence. He speaks of neighborliness and borrowing cups of sugar, and of the playground he says that children of all races, colors, and creeds will learn to live together in harmony. A week later, some of us are swatting flies on the playground's inadequate little ball field. A gang of Negro kids, pretty much our own age, enter from the other side and order us out of the park. We refuse, proudly and indignantly, with superb masculine fervor. There is a fight, they win, and we retreat, half whimpering, half with bravado. My first nauseating experience of cowardice. And my first appalled realization that there are people in the world who do not seem to be afraid of anything, who act as though they have nothing to lose. Thereafter the playground becomes a battleground, sometimes quiet, sometimes the scene of athletic competition between Them and Us. But rocks are thrown as often as baseballs. Gradually we abandon the place and use the streets instead. The streets are safer, though we do not admit this to ourselves. We are not, after all, sissies—that most dreaded epithet of an American boyhood.

Item: I am standing alone in front of the building in which I live. It is late afternoon and getting dark. That day in school the teacher had asked a surly Negro boy named Quentin a question he was unable to answer. As usual I had waved my arm eagerly ("Be a good boy, get good marks, be smart, go to college, become a doctor") and, the right answer bursting from my lips, I was held up lovingly by the teacher as an example to the class. I had seen Quentin's face—a very dark, very cruel, very Oriental-looking face—harden, and there had been enough threat in his eyes to make me run all the way home for fear that he might catch me outside.

Now, standing idly in front of my own house, I see him approaching from the project accompanied by his little brother who is carrying a baseball bat and wearing a grin of malicious anticipation. As in a nightmare, I am trapped. The surroundings are secure and familiar, but terror is suddenly present and there is no one around to help. I am locked to the spot. I will not cry out or run away like a sissy, and I stand there, my heart wild, my throat clogged. He walks up, hurls the familiar epithet ("Hey, mo'f—r"), and to my surprise only pushes me. It was a violent push, but not a punch. A push is not as serious as a punch. Maybe I can still back out without entirely losing my dignity. Maybe I can still say, "Hey, c'mon Quentin, whaddya wanna do *that* for? I dint do nothin' to *you*," and walk away, not too rapidly. Instead, before I can stop myself, I push him back—a token gesture—and I say, "Cut that out, I don't wanna fight, I an't got nothin' to fight about." As I turn to walk back into the building, the corner of my eye catches the motion of the bat his little brother has handed him. I try to duck, but the bat crashes colored lights into my head.

The next thing I know, my mother and sister are standing over me, both of them hysterical. My sister—she who was later to join the "progressive" youth organization—is shouting for the police and screaming imprecations at those dirty little black bastards. They take me upstairs, the doctor comes, the police come. I tell them that the boy who did it was a stranger, that he had been trying to get money from me. They do not believe me, but I am too scared to give them Quentin's name. When I return to school a few days later, Quentin avoids my eyes. He knows that I have not squealed, and he is ashamed. I try to feel proud, but in my heart I know that it was fear of what his friends might do to me that had kept me silent, and not the code of the street.

Item: There is an athletic meet in which the whole of our junior high school is participating. I am in one of the seventh-grade rapid-advance classes, and "segregation" has now set in with a vengeance. In the last three or four years of the elementary school from which we have just graduated, each grade had been divided into three classes, according to "intelligence." (In the earlier grades the divisions had either been arbitrary or else unrecognized by us as having anything to do with brains.) These divisions by IQ, or however it was arranged, had resulted in a preponderance of Jews in the "1" classes and a corresponding preponderance of Negroes in the "3's," with the Italians split unevenly along the spectrum. At least a few Negroes had always made the "1's," just as there had always been a few Jewish kids among the "3's," and more among the "2's" (where Italians dominated). But the junior high's rapid-advance class of which I am now a member is overwhelmingly Jewish and entirely white—except for a shy lonely Negro girl with light skin and reddish hair.

The athletic meet takes place in a city-owned stadium far from the school. It is an important event to which a whole day is given over. The winners are to get those precious little medallions stamped with the New York City emblem that can be screwed into a belt and that prove the wearer to be a distinguished personage. I am a fast runner, and so I am assigned the position of anchor man on my class's team in the relay race. There are three other seventh-grade teams in the race, two of them all Negro, as ours is all white. One of the all-Negro teams is very tall—their anchor man waiting silently next to me on the line looks older than I am, and I do not recognize him. He is the first to get the baton and crosses the finishing line in a walk. Our team comes in second, but a few minutes later we are declared the winners, for it has been discovered that the anchor man on the first-place team is not a member of the class. We are awarded the medallions, and the following day our home-room teacher makes a speech about how proud she is of us for being superior athletes as well as superior students. We want to believe that we deserve the praise, but we know that we could not have won even if the other class had not cheated.

That afternoon, walking home, I am waylaid and surrounded by five Negroes, among whom is the anchor man of the disqualified team. "Gimme my medal, mo'f—r," he grunts. I do not have it with me and I tell him so. "Anyway, it ain't yours," I say foolishly. He calls me a liar on both counts and pushes me up against the wall on which we sometimes play handball. "Gimme my mo'f—n' medal," he says again. I repeat that I have left it home. "Le's search the li'l mo'f—r," one of them suggests, "he prolly got it *hid* in his mo'f—n' *pants*." My panic is now unmanageable. (How many times had I been surrounded like this and asked in soft tones, "Len' me a nickel, boy." How many times had I been called a liar for pleading poverty and pushed around, or searched, or beaten up, unless there happened to be someone in the marauding gang like Carl who liked me across that enormous divide of hatred and who would therefore say, "Aaah, c'mon, le's git someone else, *this* boy ain't got no money on 'im.") I scream at them through tears of rage and self-contempt, "Keep your f—n' filthy lousy black hands offa me! I swear I'll get the cops." This is all they need to hear, and the five of them set upon me. They bang me around, mostly in the stomach and on the arms and shoulders, and when several adults loitering near the candy store down the block notice what is going on and begin to shout, they run off and away.

I do not tell my parents about the incident. My team-mates, who have also been waylaid, each by a gang led by his opposite number from the disqualified team, have had their medallions taken from them, and they never squeal either. For days, I walk home in terror, expecting to be caught again, but nothing happens. The medallion is put away into a drawer, never to be worn by anyone.

Obviously experiences like these have always been a common feature of childhood life in working-class and immigrant neighborhoods, and Negroes do not necessarily figure in them. Wherever, and in whatever combination, they have lived together in the cities, kids of different groups have been at war, beating up and being beaten up: micks against kikes against wops against spicks against polacks. And even relatively homogeneous areas have not been spared the warring of the young: one block against another, one gang (called in my day, in a pathetic effort at gentility, an "S.A.C.," or social-athletic club) against another. But the Negro-white conflict had—and no doubt still has—a special intensity and was conducted with a ferocity unmatched by intramural white battling.

In my own neighborhood, a good deal of animosity existed between the Italian kids (most of whose parents were immigrants from Sicily) and the Jewish kids (who came largely from East European immigrant families). Yet everyone had friends, sometimes close friends, in the other "camp," and we often visited one another's strange-smelling houses, if not for meals, then for glasses of milk, and occasionally for some special event like a wedding or a wake. If it happened that we divided into warring factions and did battle, it would invariably be half-hearted and soon patched up. Our parents, to be sure, had nothing to do with one another and were mutually suspicious and hostile. But we, the kids, who all spoke Yiddish or Italian at home, were Americans, or New Yorkers, or Brooklyn boys: we shared a culture, the culture of the street, and at least for a while this culture proved to be more powerful than the opposing cultures of the home.

Why, *why* should it have been so different as between the Negroes and us? How was it borne in upon us so early, white and black alike, that we were enemies beyond any possibility of reconciliation? Why did we hate one another so?

I suppose if I tried, I could answer those questions more or less adequately from the perspective of what I have since learned. I could draw upon James Baldwin—what better witness is there?—to describe the sense of entrapment that poisons the soul of the Negro with hatred for the white man whom he knows to be his jailer. On the other side, if I wanted to understand how the white man comes to hate the Negro, I could call upon the psychologists who have spoken of the guilt that white Americans feel toward Negroes and that turns into hatred for lack of acknowledging itself as guilt. These are plausible answers and certainly there is truth in them. Yet when I think back upon my own experience of the Negro and his of me, I find myself troubled and puzzled, much as I was as a child when I heard that all Jews were rich and all Negroes persecuted. How could the Negroes in my neighborhood have regarded the whites across the street and around the corner as jailers? On the whole, the whites were not so poor as the Negroes, but they were quite poor enough, and the years were years of Depression. As for white hatred of the Negro, how could guilt have had anything to do with it? What share had these Italian and Jewish immigrants in the enslavement of the Negro? What share had they—downtrodden people themselves breaking their own necks to eke out a living—in the exploitation of the Negro?

No, I cannot believe that we hated each other back there in Brooklyn because they thought of us as jailers and we felt guilty toward them. But does it matter, given the fact that we all went through an unrepresentative confrontation? I think it matters profoundly, for if we managed the job of hating each other so well without benefit of the aids to hatred that are supposedly at the root of this madness everywhere else, it must mean that the madness is not yet properly understood. I am far from pretending that I understand it, but I would insist that no view of the problem will begin to approach the truth unless it can account for a case like the one I have been trying to describe. Are the elements of any such view available to us?

At least two, I would say, are. One of them is a point we frequently come upon in the work of James Baldwin, and the other is a related point always stressed by psychologists who have studied the mechanisms of prejudice. Baldwin tells us that one of the reasons Negroes hate the white man is that the white man refuses to *look* at him: the Negro knows that in white eyes all Negroes are alike; they are faceless and therefore not altogether human. The psychologists, in their turn, tell us that the white man hates the Negro because he tends to project those wild impulses that he fears in himself onto an alien group which he then punishes with his contempt. What Baldwin does *not* tell us, however, is that the principle of facelessness is a two-way street and can operate in both directions with no difficulty at all. Thus, in my neighborhood in Brooklyn, *I* was as faceless to the Negroes as they were to me, and if they hated me because I never looked at them, I must also have hated them for never looking at *me*. To the Negroes, my white skin was enough to define me as the enemy, and in a war it is only the uniform that counts and not the person.

So with the mechanism of projection that the psychologists talk about: it too works in both directions at once. There is no question that the psychologists are right about what the Negro represents symbolically to the white man. For me as a child the life lived on the other side of the playground and down the block on Ralph Avenue seemed the very embodiment of the values of the street—free, independent, reckless, brave, masculine, erotic. I put the word "erotic" last, though it is usually stressed above all others, because in fact it came last, in consciousness as in importance. What mainly counted for me about Negro kids of my own age was that they were "bad boys." There were plenty of bad boys among the whites—this was, after all, a neighborhood with a long tradition of crime as a career open to aspiring talents —but the Negroes were *really* bad, bad in a way that beckoned to one, and made one feel inadequate. *We* all went home every day for a lunch of spinach-and-potatoes; *they* roamed around during lunch hour, munching on candy bars. In winter *we* had to wear itchy woolen hats and mittens and cumbersome galoshes; *they* were bare-headed and loose as they pleased. *We* rarely played hookey, or got into serious trouble in school, for all our street-corner bravado; *they* were defiant, forever staying out (to do what delicious things?), forever making disturbances in class and in the halls, forever being sent to the principal and returning uncowed. But most important of all, they were *tough*; beautifully, enviably tough, not giving a damn for anyone or anything. To hell with the teacher, the truant officer, the cop; to hell with the whole of the adult world that held *us* in its grip and that we never had the courage to rebel against except sporadically and in petty ways.

This is what I saw and envied and feared in the Negro: this is what finally made him faceless to me, though some of it, of course, was actually there. (The psychologists also tell us that the alien group which becomes the object of a projection will tend to respond by trying to live up to what is expected of them.) But what, on his side, did the Negro see in me that made me faceless to *him*? Did he envy me my lunches of spinach-and-potatoes and my itchy woolen caps and my prudent behavior in the face of authority, as I envied him his noon-time candy bars and his bare head in winter and his magnificent rebelliousness? Did those lunches and caps spell for him the prospect of power and riches in the future? Did they mean that there were possibilities open to me that were denied to him? Very likely they did. But if so, one also supposes that he feared the impulses within himself toward submission to authority no less powerfully than I feared the impulses in myself toward defiance. If I represented the jailer to him, it was not because I was oppressing him or keeping him down: it was because I symbolized for him the dangerous and probably pointless temptation toward greater repression, just as he symbolized for me the equally perilous tug toward greater freedom. I personally was to be rewarded for this repression with a new and better life in the future, but how many of my friends paid an even higher price and were given only gall in return.

We have it on the authority of James Baldwin that all Negroes hate whites. I am trying to suggest that on their side all whites—all American whites, that is—are sick in their feelings about Negroes. There are Negroes, no doubt, who would say that Baldwin is wrong, but I suspect them of being less honest than he is, just as I suspect whites of self-deception who tell me they have no special feeling toward Negroes. Special feelings about color are a contagion to which white Americans seem susceptible even when there is nothing in their background to account for the suceptibility. Thus everywhere we look today in the North, we find the curious phenomenon of white middle-class liberals with no previous personal experience of Negroes—people to whom Negroes have always been faceless in virtue rather than faceless in vice—discovering that their abstract commitment to the cause of Negro rights will not stand the test of a direct confrontation. We find such people fleeing in droves to the suburbs as the Negro population in the inner city grows; and when they stay in the city we find them sending their children to private school rather than to the "integrated" public school in the neighborhood. We find them resisting the demand that gerrymandered school districts be rezoned for the purpose of overcoming de facto segregation; we find them judiciously considering whether the Negroes (for their own good, of course) are not perhaps pushing too hard; we find them clucking their tongues over Negro militancy; we find them speculating on the question of whether there may not, after all, be something in the theory that the races are biologically different; we find them saying that it will take a very long time for Negroes to achieve full equality, no matter what anyone does; we find them deploring the rise of black nationalism and expressing the solemn hope that the leaders of the Negro community will discover ways of containing the impatience and incipient violence within the Negro ghettos.

But that is by no means the whole story; there is also the phenomenon of what Kenneth Rexroth once called "crow-jimism." There are the broken-down white boys like Vivaldo Moore in Baldwin's *Another Country* who go to Harlem in search of sex or simply to brush up against something that looks like primitive vitality, and who are so often punished by the Negroes they meet for crimes that they would have been the last ever to commit and of which they themselves have been as sorry victims as any of the Negroes who take it out on them. There are the writers and intellectuals and artists who romanticize Negroes and pander to them, assuming a guilt that is not properly theirs. And there are all the white liberals who permit Negroes to black-mail them into adopting a double standard of moral judgment, and who lend themselves—again assuming the responsibility for crimes they never committed—to cunning and contemptuous exploitation by Negroes they employ or try to befriend.

And what about me? What kind of feelings do I have about Negroes today? What happened to me, from Brooklyn, who grew up fearing and envying and hating Negroes? Now that Brooklyn is behind me, do I fear them and envy them and hate them still? The answer is yes, but not in the same proportions and certainly not in the same way. I now live on the upper west side of Manhattan, where there are many Negroes and many Puerto Ricans, and there are nights when I experience the old apprehensiveness again, and there are streets that I avoid when I am walking in the dark, as there were streets that I avoided when I was a child. I find that I am not afraid of Puerto Ricans, but I cannot restrain my nervousness whenever I pass a group of Negroes standing in front of a bar or sauntering down the street. I know now, as I did not know when I was a child, that power is on my side, that the police are working for me and not for them. And knowing this I feel ashamed and guilty, like the good liberal I have grown up to be. Yet the twinges of fear and the resentment they bring and the self-contempt they arouse are not to be gainsaid.

But envy? Why envy? And hatred? Why hatred? Here again the intensities have lessened and everything has been complicated and qualified by the guilts and the resulting over-compensations that are the heritage of the enlightened middle-class world of which I am now a member. Yet just as in childhood I envied Negroes for what seemed to me their superior masculinity, so I envy them today for what seems to me their superior physical grace and beauty. I have come to value physical grace very highly, and I am now capable of aching with all my being when I watch a Negro couple on the dance floor, or a Negro playing baseball or basketball. They are on the kind of terms with their own bodies that I should like to be on with mine, and for that precious quality they seem blessed to me.

The hatred I still feel for Negroes is the hardest of all the old feelings to face or admit, and it is the most hidden and the most over-larded by the conscious attitudes into which I have succeeded in willing myself. It no longer has, as for me it once did, any cause or justification (except, perhaps, that I am constantly being denied my right to an honest expression of the things I earned the right as a child to feel). How, then, do I know that this hatred has never entirely disappeared? I know it from the insane rage that can stir in me at the thought of Negro anti-Semitism; I know it from the disgusting prurience that can stir in me at the sight of a mixed couple; and I know it from the violence that can stir in me whenever I encounter that special brand of paranoid touchiness to which many Negroes are prone.

This, then, is where I am; it is not exactly where I think all other white liberals are, but it cannot be so very far away either. And it is because I am convinced that we white Americans are—for whatever reason, it no longer matters—so twisted and sick in our feelings about Negroes that I despair of the present push toward integration. If the pace of progress were not a factor here, there would perhaps be no cause for despair: time and the law and even the international political situation are on the side of the Negroes, and ultimately, therefore, victory—of a sort, anyway—must come. But from everything we have learned from observers who ought to know, pace has become as important to the Negroes as substance. They want equality and they want it *now*, and the white world is yielding to their demand only as much and as fast as it is absolutely being compelled to do. The Negroes know this in the most concrete terms imaginable, and it is thus becoming increasingly difficult to buy them off with rhetoric and promises and pious assurances of support. And so within the Negro community we find more and more people declaring that they want *out*: people who say that integration will never come, or that it will take a hundred or a thousand years to come, or that it will come at too high a price in suffering and struggle for the pallid and sodden life of the American middle class that at the very best it may bring.

The most numerous, influential, and dangerous movement that has grown out of Negro despair with the goal of integration is, of course, the Black Muslims. This movement, whatever else we may say about it, must be credited with one enduring achievement: it inspired James Baldwin to write an essay* which deserves to be placed among the classics of our language. Everything Baldwin has ever been trying to tell us is distilled here into a statement of overwhelming persuasiveness and prophetic magnificence. Baldwin's message is and always has been simple. It is this: "Color is not a human or personal reality; it is a political reality." And Baldwin's demand is correspondingly simple: color must be forgotten, lest we all be smited with a vengeance "that does not really depend on, and cannot really be executed by, any person or organization, and that cannot be prevented by any police force or army: historical vengeance, a cosmic vengeance based on the law that we recognize when we say, 'Whatever goes up must come down.'" The Black Muslims Baldwin portrays as a sign and a warning to the intransigent white world. They come to proclaim how deep is the Negro's disaffection with the white world and all its works, and Baldwin implies that no American Negro can fail to respond somewhere in his being to their message: that the white man is the devil, that Allah has doomed him to destruction, and that the black man is about to inherit the earth. Baldwin of course knows that his nightmare inversion of the racism from which the black man has suffered can neither win nor even point to the neighborhood in which victory might be located. For in his view the neighborhood of victory lies in exactly the opposite direction: the transcendence of color through love.

Yet the tragic fact is that love is not the answer to hate—not in the world of politics, at any rate. Color is indeed a political rather than a human or a personal reality and if politics (which is to say power) has made it into a human and a personal reality, then only politics (which is to say power) can unmake it once again. But the way of politics is slow and bitter, and as impatience on the one side is matched by a setting of the jaw on the other, we move closer and closer to an explosion and blood may yet run in the streets.

* Originally published in the *New Yorker* under the title "Letter from a Region in My Mind," it has been reprinted (along with a new introduction) by Dial Press under the title *The Fire Next Time*.

Will this madness in which we are all caught never find a resting-place? Is there never to be an end to it? In thinking about the Jews I have often wondered whether their survival as a distinct group was worth one hair on the head of a single infant. Did the Jews have to survive so that six million innocent people should one day be burned in the ovens of Auschwitz? It is a terrible question and no one, not God himself, could ever answer it to my satisfaction. And when I think about the Negroes in America and about the image of integration as a state in which the Negroes would take their rightful place as another of the protected minorities in a pluralistic society, I wonder whether they really believe in their hearts that such a state can actually be attained, and if so *why* they should wish to survive as a distinct group. I think I know why the Jews once wished to survive (though I am less certain as to why we still do): they not only believed that God had given them no choice, but they were tied to a memory of past glory and a dream of imminent redemption. What does the American Negro have that might correspond to this? His past is a stigma, his color is a stigma, and his vision of the future is the hope of erasing the stigma by making color irrelevant, by making it disappear as a fact of consciousness.

I share this hope, but I cannot see how it will ever be realized unless color does *in fact* disappear: and that means not integration, it means assimilation, it means—let the brutal word come out—miscegenation. The Black Muslims, like their racist counterparts in the white world, accuse the "so-called Negro leaders" of secretly pursuing miscegenation as a goal. The racists are wrong, but I wish they were right, for I believe that the wholesale merging of the two races is the most desirable alternative for everyone concerned. I am not claiming that this alter-can be pursued programmatically or that it is immediately feasible as a solution; obviously there are even greater barriers to its achievement than to the achievement of integration. What I am saying, however, is that in my opinion the Negro problem can be solved in this country in no other way.

I have told the story of my own twisted feelings about Negroes here, and of how they conflict with the moral convictions I have since developed, in order to assert that such feelings must be acknowledged as honestly as possible so that they can be controlled and ultimately disregarded in favor of the convictions. It is *wrong* for a man to suffer because of the color of his skin. Beside that clichéd proposition of liberal thought, what argument can stand and be respected? If the arguments are the arguments of feeling, they must be made to yield;

and one's own soul is not the worst place to begin working a huge social transformation. Not so long ago, it used to be asked of white liberals, "Would you like your sister to marry one?" When I was a boy and my sister was still unmarried, I would certainly have said no to that question. But now I am a man, my sister is already married, and I have daughters. If I were to be asked today whether I would like a daughter of mine "to marry one," I would have to answer: "No, I wouldn't *like* it at all. I would rail and rave and rant and tear my hair. And then I hope I would have the courage to curse myself for raving and ranting, and to give her my blessing. How dare I withhold it at the behest of the child I once was and against the man I now have a duty to be?"

1963

William Melvin Kelley
The Only Man On
Liberty Street

She was squatting in the front yard, digging with an old brass spoon
in the dirt, which was an ocean to the islands of short yellow grass. She
wore a red and white checkered dress, which hung loosely from her
shoulders and obscured her legs. It was early spring and she was barefoot. Her toes stuck from under the skirt. She could not see the man
yet, riding down Liberty Street, his shoulders square, the duster he wore
spread back over the horse's rump, a carpetbag tied with a leather
strap to his saddle horn and knocking against his leg. She could not see
him until he had dismounted and tied his horse to a small, black, iron
Negro jockey and unstrapped the bag. She watched now as he opened
the wooden gate, came into the yard, and stood looking down at her,
his face stern, almost gray beneath the brim of his wide hat.

She knew him. Her mother called him Mister Herder and had told
Jennie that he was Jennie's father. He was one of the men who came

riding down Liberty Street in their fine black suits and starched shirts and large, dark ties. Each of these men had a house to go to, into which, in the evening usually, he would disappear. Only women and children lived on Liberty Street. All of them were Negroes. Some of the women were quite dark, but most were coffee-color. They were all very beautiful. Her mother was light. She was tall, had black eyes, and black hair so long she could sit on it.

The man standing over her was the one who came to her house once or twice a week. He was never there in the morning when Jennie got up. He was tall, and thin, and blond. He had a short beard that looked as coarse as the grass beneath her feet. His eyes were blue, like Jennie's. He did not speak English very well. Jennie's mother had told her he come from across the sea and Jennie often wondered if he went there between visits to their house.

"Jennie? Your mother tells me that you ask why I do not stay at night. Is so?"

She looked up at him. "Yes, Mister Herder." The hair under his jaw was darker than the hair on his cheeks.

He nodded. "I stay now. Go bring your mother."

She left the spoon in the dirt, and ran into the house, down the long hall, dark now because she had been sitting in the sun. She found her mother standing over the stove, a great black lid in her left hand, a wooden spoon in her right. There were beads of sweat on her forehead. She wore a full black skirt and a white blouse. Her one waist-length braid hung straight between her shoulder blades. She turned to Jennie's running steps.

"Mama? That man? My father? He in the yard. He brung a carpet-bag."

First her mother smiled, then frowned, then looked puzzled. "A carpetbag, darling?"

"Yes, Mama."

She followed her mother through the house, pausing with her at the hall mirror, where the woman ran her hand up the back of her neck to smooth stray black hair. Then they went onto the porch, where the man was now seated, surveying the tiny yard and the dark green hedge that enclosed it. The carpetbag rested beside his chair.

Her mother stood with her hands beneath her apron, staring at the bag. "Mister Herder?"

He turned to them. "I will not go back this time. No matter what. Why should I live in that house when I must come here to know what home is?" He nodded sharply as if in answer to a question. "So! I stay. I give her that house. I will send her money, but I stay here."

Her mother stood silently for an instant, then turned to the door. "Dinner'll be on the table in a half hour." She opened the screen door. The spring whined and cracked. "Oh." She let go the door, and picked up the carpetbag. "I'll take this on up." She went inside. As she passed, Jennie could see she was smiling again.

After that, Jennie's mother became a celebrity on Liberty Street. The other women would stop her to ask about the man. "And he staying for good, Josie?"

"Yes."

"You have any trouble yet?"

"Not yet."

"Well, child, you make him put that there house in your name. You don't want to be no Sissie Markham. That white woman come down the same day he died and moved Sissie and her children right into the gutter. You get that house put in your name. You hear?"

"Yes."

"How is it? It different?"

Her mother would look dazed. "Yes, it different. He told me to call him Maynard."

The other women were always very surprised.

At first, Jennie too was surprised. The man was always there in the morning and sometimes even woke her up. Her mother no longer called him Mister Herder, and at odd times, though still quite seldom, said no. She had never before heard her mother say no to anything the man ever said. It was not long before Jennie was convinced that he actually was her father. She began to call him Papa.

Daily now a white woman had been driving by their house. Jennie did not know who she was or what she wanted but, playing in the yard, would see the white woman's gray buggy turn the corner and come slowly down the block, pulled by a speckled horse that trudged in the dry dust. A Negro driver sat erect in his black uniform, a whip in his fist. The white woman would peer at the house as if looking for an address or something special. She would look at the curtained windows, looking for someone, and sometimes even at Jennie. The look was not kind or tender, but hard and angry as if she knew something bad about the child.

Then one day the buggy stopped, the Negro pulling gently on the reins. The white woman leaned forward, spoke to the driver and handed him a small pink envelope. He jumped down, opened the gate, and without looking at Jennie, his face dark and shining, advanced on the porch, up the three steps, which knocked hollow beneath his boots, opened the screen door, and twisted the polished brass bell key in the center of the open winter door.

Her mother came, drying her hands. The Negro reached out the envelope and her mother took it, looking beyond him for an instant at the buggy and the white woman, who returned her look coldly. As the Negro turned, her mother opened the letter, and read it, moving her lips slightly. Then Jennie could see the twinkling at the corners of her eyes. Her mother stood framed in the black square of the doorway, tall, fair, the black hair swept to hide her ears, her eyes glistening.

Jennie turned back to the white woman now and saw her lean deeper into her seat. Then she pulled forward, shouting shrilly, and spoke like Jennie's father. "You tell him he has got one wife! You are something different!" She leaned back again, waved her gloved hand, and the buggy lurched down the street, gained speed, and jangled out of sight around the corner.

Jennie was on her feet and pounding up the stairs. "Mama?"

"Go play, Jennie. Go on now, *play!*" Still her mother stared straight ahead, as if the buggy and the white woman remained in front of the house. She still held the letter as if to read it. The corners of her eyes were wet. Then she turned and went into the house. The screen door clacked behind her.

At nights now Jennie waited by the gate in the yard for her father to turn the corner, walking. In the beginning she had been waiting too for the one day he would not turn the corner. But each night he came, that day seemed less likely to come. Even so, she was always surprised to see him. When she did, she would wave, timidly, raising her hand only to her shoulder, wiggling only her fingers, as if to wave too wildly would somehow cause the entire picture of his advancing to collapse, as only a slight wind would be enough to disarrange a design of feathers.

That night too she waved and saw him raise his hand high over his head, greeting her. She backed away when he reached the gate so he might open it, her head thrown way back, looking up at him.

"Well, my Jennie, what kind of day did you have?"

She only smiled, then remembered the white woman. "A woman come to visit Mama. She come in a buggy and give her a letter too. She made Mama cry."

His smile fled. He sucked his tongue, angry now. "We go see what is wrong. Come." He reached for her hand.

Her mother was in the kitchen. She looked as if she did not really care what she was doing or how, walking from pump to stove, stove to cupboard in a deep trance. The pink envelope was on the table.

She turned to them. Her eyes were red. Several strands of hair stuck to her temples. She cleared her nose and pointed to the letter. "She came today."

Her father let go Jennie's hand, picked up the letter and read it. When he was finished he took it to the stove and dropped it into the flame. There was a puff of smoke before he replaced the lid. He shook his head. "She cannot make me go back, Josephine."

Her mother fell heavily into a wooden chair, beginning to cry again. "But she's white, Maynard."

He raised his eyebrows like a priest or a displeased schoolteacher. "Your skin is whiter."

"My mother was a slave."

He threw up his hands, making fists. "Your mother did not ask to be a slave!" Then he went to her, crouched on his haunches before her, speaking quietly. "No one can make me go back."

"But she can get them to do what she say." She turned her gaze on Jennie, but looked away quickly. "You wasn't here after the war. But I seen things. I seen things happen to field niggers that . . . I was up in the house; they didn't bother me. My own father, General Dewey Wilson, he stood on a platform in the center of town and promised to keep the niggers down. I was close by." She took his face in her hands. "Maynard, maybe you better go back, leastways—"

"I go back—dead! You hear? Dead. These children, these cowardly children in their masks will not move me! I go back dead. That is all. We do not discuss it." And he was gone. Jennie heard him thundering down the hall, knocking against the table near the stairs, going up to the second floor.

Her mother was looking at her now, her eyes even more red than before, her lips trembling, her hands active in her lap. "Jennie?"

"Yes, Mama." She took a step toward her, staring into the woman's eyes.

"Jennie, I want you to promise me something and not forget it."

"Yes, Mama." She was between her mother's knees, felt the woman's hands clutching her shoulders.

"Jennie, you'll be right pretty when you get grown. Did you know that? Promise me you'll go up North. Promise me if I'm not here when you get eighteen, you'll go North and get married. You understand?"

Jennie was not sure she did. She could not picture the North, except that she had heard once it was cold and white things fell from the sky. She could not picture being eighteen and her mother not being there. But she knew her mother wanted her to understand and she lied. "Yes, Mama."

"Repeat what I just said."

She did. Her mother kissed her mouth, the first time ever.

From the kitchen below, came their voices. Her father's voice sounded hard, cut short; Jennie knew he had made a decision and was sticking to it. Her mother was pleading, trying to change his mind. It was July the Fourth, the day of the shooting match.

She dressed in her Sunday clothes and coming downstairs heard her mother: "Maynard, please don't take her." She was frantic now. "I'm begging you. Don't take that child with you today."

"I take her. We do not discuss it. I take her. Those sneaking cowards in their masks . . ." Jennie knew now what they were talking about. Her father had promised to take her to the shooting match. For some reason, her mother feared there would be trouble if Jennie went downtown. She did not know why her mother felt that way, except that it might have something to do with the white woman, who continued to ride by their house each morning after her father had left for the day. Perhaps her mother did not want to be alone in the house when the white woman drove by in her gray buggy, even though she had not stopped the buggy since the day two months ago when the Negro had given her mother the pink evenlope.

But other strange things had happened after that. In the beginning she and her mother, as always before, had gone downtown to the market to shop amid the bright stalls brimming with green and yellow vegetables and brick-red meats, tended by dark country Negroes in shabby clothes and large straw hats. It would get very quiet when they passed, and Jennie would see the Negroes look away, fear in their eyes, and knots of white men watching, sometimes giggling. But the white women in fine clothes were the most frightening; sitting on the verandas or passing in carriages, some even coming to their windows, they would stare angrily as if her mother had done something terrible to each one personally, as if all these white women could be the one who drove by each morning. Her mother would walk through it all, her back straight, very like her father's, the bun into which she wove her waistlength braid on market days gleaming dark.

In the beginning they had gone to the suddenly quiet market. But now her mother hardly set foot from the house, and the food was brought to them in a carton by a crippled Negro boy, who was coming just as Jennie and her father left the house that morning.

Balancing the carton on his left arm, he removed his ragged hat and smiled. "Morning, Mister Herder. Good luck at the shooting match, sir." His left leg was short and he seemed to tilt.

Her father nodded, "Thank you, Felix. I do my best."

"Then you a sure thing, Mister Herder." He replaced his hat and went on around the house.

Walking, her hand in her father's, Jennie could see some of the women of Liberty Street peering out at them through their curtains.

Downtown was not the same. Flags and banners draped the verandas; people wore their best clothes. The Square had been roped off, a platform set up to one side, and New Marsails Avenue, which ran into the Square, had been cleared for two blocks. Far away down the Avenue stood a row of cotton bales onto which had been pinned oilcloth targets. From where they stood, the bull's-eyes looked no bigger than red jawbreakers.

Many men slapped her father on the back and, furtively, looked at her with a kind of clinical interest. But mostly they ignored her. The celebrity of the day was her father, and unlike her mother he was very popular. Everyone felt sure he would win the match; he was the best shot in the state.

After everyone shot, the judge came running down from the targets, waving his arms. "Maynard Herder. Six shots, and you can cover them all with a good gob of spit!" He grabbed her father's elbow and pulled him toward the platform, where an old man with white hair and beard, wearing a gray uniform trimmed with yellow, waited. She followed them to the platform steps, but was afraid to go any farther because now some women had begun to look at her as they had at her mother.

The old man made a short speech, his voice deep but coarse, grainy-sounding, and gave her father a silver medal in a blue velvet box. Her father turned and smiled at her. She started up the steps toward him, but just then the old man put his hand on her father's shoulder.

People had begun to walk away down the streets leading out of the Square. There was less noise now but she could not hear the first words the old man said to her father.

Her father's face tightened into the same look she had seen the day the letter came, the same as this morning in the kitchen. She went halfway up the stairs, stopped.

The old man went on: "You know I'm no meddler. Everybody

knows about Liberty Street. I had a woman down there myself . . . before the war."

"I know that." The words came out of her father's face, though his lips did not move.

The old man nodded. "But, Maynard, what you're doing is different."

"She's your own daughter."

"Maybe that's why . . ." The old man looked down the street, toward the cotton bales and the targets. "But she's a nigger. And now the talking is taking an ugly turn and the folks talking are the ones I can't hold."

Her father spoke in an angry whisper. "You see what I do to that target? You tell those children in their masks I do that to the forehead of any man . . . or woman that comes near her or my house. You tell them."

"Maynard, that wouldn't do any real good *after* they'd done something to her." He stopped, looked at Jennie, and smiled. "That's my only granddaughter, you know." His eyes clicked off her. "You're a man who knows firearms. You're a gunsmith. I knew firearms too. Pistols and rifles can do lots of things, but they don't make very good doctors. Nobody's asking you to give her up. Just go back home. That's all. Go back to your wife."

Her father turned away, walking fast, came down the stairs and grabbed her hand. His face was red as blood between the white of his collar and the straw yellow of his hair.

They slowed after a block, paused in a small park with green trees shading several benches and a statue of a stern-faced young man in uniform carrying pack and rifle. "We will sit."

She squirmed up onto the bench beside him. The warm wind smelled of salt from the Gulf of Mexico. The leaves were a dull, low tambourine. Her father was quiet for a long while.

Jennie watched birds bobbing for worms in the grass near them, then looked at the young stone soldier. Far off, but from where she viewed it, just over the soldier's hat, a gliding sea gull dived suddenly behind the rooftops. That was when she saw the white man, standing across the street from the park, smiling at her. There were other white men with him, some looking at her, others at the man, all laughing. He waved to her. She smiled at him though he was the kind of man her mother told her always to stay away from. He was dressed as poorly as any Negro. From behind his back, he produced a brown rag doll, looked at her again, then grabbed the doll by its legs, and tore it partway up the middle. Then he jammed his finger into the rip between the doll's legs. The other men laughed uproariously.

Jennie pulled her father's sleeve. "Papa? What he doing?"

"Who?" Her father turned. The man repeated the show and her father bolted to his feet, yelling: "I will kill you! You hear? I will kill you for that!"

The men only snickered and ambled away.

Her father was red again. He had clenched his fists; now his hands were white like the bottoms of fishes. He sighed, shook his head and sat down. "I cannot kill everybody." He shook his head again, then leaned forward to get up. But first he thrust the blue velvet medal box into her hand. It was warm from his hand, wet and prickly. "When you grow up, you go to the North like you mother tell you. And you take this with you. It is yours. Always remember I gave it to you." He stood. "Now you must go home alone. Tell your mother I come later."

That night Jennie tried to stay awake until he came home, until he was there to kiss her good night, his whiskers scratching her cheek. But all at once there was sun at her window and the sound of carts and wagons grating outside in the dirt street. Her mother was quiet while the two of them ate. After breakfast, Jennie went into the yard to wait for the gray buggy to turn the corner, but for the first morning in many months the white woman did not jounce by, peering at the house, searching for someone or something special.

1963